The State and
the Labor Market

PLENUM STUDIES IN WORK AND INDUSTRY

Series Editors:
Ivar Berg, *University of Pennsylvania, Philadelphia, Pennsylvania*
and Arne L. Kalleberg, *University of North Carolina, Chapel Hill, North Carolina*

WORK AND INDUSTRY
Structures, Markets, and Processes
Arne L. Kalleberg and Ivar Berg

THE BUREAUCRATIC LABOR MARKET
The Case of the Federal Civil Service
Thomas A. DiPrete

ENSURING MINORITY SUCCESS IN CORPORATE MANAGEMENT
Edited by Donna E. Thompson and Nancy DiTomaso

INDUSTRIES, FIRMS, AND JOBS
Sociological and Economic Approaches
Edited by George Farkas and Paula England

MATERNAL EMPLOYMENT AND CHILDREN'S DEVELOPMENT
Longitudinal Research
Edited by Adele Eskeles Gottfried and Allan W. Gottfried

THE STATE AND THE LABOR MARKET
Edited by Samuel Rosenberg

WORKERS, MANAGERS, AND TECHNOLOGICAL CHANGE
Emerging Patterns of Labor Relations
Edited by Daniel B. Cornfield

A Continuation Order Plan is available for this series. A continuation order will bring delivery of each new volume immediately upon publication. Volumes are billed only upon actual shipment. For further information please contact the publisher.

The State and the Labor Market

Edited by

Samuel Rosenberg

Roosevelt University
Chicago, Illinois

With a Foreword by
Lloyd Ulman
University of California, Berkeley
Berkeley, California

Plenum Press • New York and London

Library of Congress Cataloging in Publication Data

The state and the labor market / edited by Samuel Rosenberg.
    p.   cm. — (Plenum studies in work and industry)
    Includes bibliographical references and index.
    ISBN 0-306-43170-X
    1. Labor policy—Europe—Congresses. 2. Labor policy—United States—Congresses. 3.
Europe—Full employment policies—Congresses. 4. United States—Full employment
policies—Congresses. I. Rosenberg, Samuel. II. Series.
HD8376.5.S76   1989
331.12′042′094—dc20

89-33437
CIP

© 1989 Plenum Press, New York
A Division of Plenum Publishing Corporation
233 Spring Street, New York, N.Y. 10013

Printed in the United States of America

Contributors

Anne Marie Berg, Work Research Institute, Oslo, Norway

Gerhard Bosch, WSI, Hans-Böchler Strasse 39, Düsseldorf, West Germany

Sebastiano Brusco, Department of Political Economy, University of Modena, Modena, Italy

Lluis Fina, Department of Applied Economics, Autonomous University of Barcelona, Belleterra, Spain

Peter Galasi, Department of Labor Economics, Karl Marx University of Economics, Budapest, Hungary

Annie Gauvin, Labor Economics Research Institute, University of Paris 1, Paris, France

Alberto Meixide, Department of Economics, University of Santiago de Compostela, Santiago de Compostela, Spain

François Michon, Labor Economics Research Institute, University of Paris 1, Paris, France

Michael J. Piore, Department of Economics, Massachusetts Institute of Technology, Cambridge, Massachusetts

Marilyn Power, Department of Economics, California State University-Sacramento, Sacramento, California

Samuel Rosenberg, Department of Economics, Roosevelt University, Chicago, Illinois

Jill Rubery, Department of Applied Economics, University of Cambridge, Cambridge, Great Britain

Paul Ryan, King's College, University of Cambridge, Cambridge, Great Britain

Werner Sengenberger, International Institute for Labor Studies, Geneva, Switzerland

György Sziráczki, Department of Labor Economics, Karl Marx University of Economics, Budapest, Hungary

Roger Tarling, PA Cambridge Economic Consultants Limited, Cambridge, Great Britain

Luis Toharia, Department of Basic and Historical Economics, University of Alcalá de Henares, Alcalá de Henares, Spain

Paola Villa, Department of Economics, Catholic University, Milan, Italy

Frank Wilkinson, Department of Applied Economics, University of Cambridge, Cambridge, Great Britain

Foreword

In the two decades before the mid-1970s, macroeconomic policies in Western Europe were frequently accompanied by policies of direct wage restraint in the pursuit of acceptable levels of employment, inflation, and international competitiveness. The same period witnessed a proliferation of social welfare programs, elements of which were sometimes commingled with demand management and pay policies in trilateral bargaining processes involving governments, unions, and employers. In the wake of such subsequent developments as the oil price shocks, sharply intensified international competition, and slowing of growth rates in productivity, however, governments resorted more frequently to deflationist macroeconomic policies and also to policies aimed directly at increasing "flexibility" in wage determination and the deployment of labor by the firm.

It is a major theme of this very interesting book that these labor market policies have not been demonstrably (or at least sufficiently) effective in combating the high rates of unemployment which have been prevalent in most of the countries of Western Europe since the late 1970s. This theme emerges from the chapters on labor market developments and policies in six countries of Western Europe, the United States, and Hungary (a welcome addition to this type of scholarship), as well as another set of chapters devoted to specific policy areas. In effect, Samuel Rosenberg and his colleagues—an international team of nineteen economists and sociologists—are repeating in concrete terms a sermon preached by Keynes over a half century ago. Keynes' critics may have been quite correct in maintaining that wage and price flexibility could ensure full employment (without accelerating inflation) as a condition of long-run equilibrium under static conditions in a perfectly competitive economy; but this of course represents a considerable departure from the real-world conditions that confront the policymaker—and which provided the grist for Keynes' own intellectual mill. The real-world conditions which inspired conservative European policymakers in the 1980s were found by them in the U.S.A., a place in which they saw whole economic sectors being deregulated, major labor markets becoming dis-organized, and real wages falling— while employment was increasing strongly. But they staged Hamlet without the prince, for this scenario ignores the role played by the heroic Keynesian budget deficits that were being racked up by a conservative administration as it cut taxes while increasing defense spending. Lacking the faith of the true believer in Reaganomics, they retained an old-fashioned reluctance to incur the risk of domestic deficits and inflation, and of external deficits and indebtedness—although, in the case of West Germany, the bellwether economy of the area, these risks might indeed have been smaller than those rashly assumed by the Reagan Administration in the U.S. Thus, they had to rely only on "structural" policies, although these have sometimes included youth training programs and incentives to encourage early retirement (which are discussed in this book), as well as policies designed to weaken collective bargaining structures and protection of workers against dismissal.

Nevertheless, conservative governments have not been heavily penalized by the failure of their pro-competition policies to make progress in reducing unemployment in the 1980s; in the U.K. and West Germany, conservative governments won reelection against an overhang of high unemployment. One reason for this might have been the failure of alternative structural initiatives, notably a shorter workweek (which is discussed in several chapters), to elicit great expectations of success. In its weak form, without compensatory increases in wage rates,the reduced workweek would leave employed workers with reduced incomes. With compensatory wage increases on the other hand, the shorter workweek has aroused fear (even within some union movements) that it could raise unit costs and thus reduce the demand for labor.

A more important reason why the high levels of unemployment in Europe have failed to elicit greater popular and political reaction (as had been widely feared in the 1960s and early 1970s) has been the buffering influence of the welfare state. It has of course been argued that high levels of unemployment have been *caused* by high levels of social transfer payments and are thus "voluntary" in nature; but it is a more plausible proposition that the "safety nets" provided by modern systems of social welfare have rendered "involuntary" unemployment sufficiently bearable to make deflationary macroeconomic policies viable options for policymakers and politicians. In these pages and elsewhere, moreover, it is pointed out that double-digit unemployment has persisted despite serious erosion in relative benefit levels and coverage of unemployment and other social insurances. Such erosion has been associated with budgetary stringency and the persistence of unemployment itself, but it may also entail erosion of popular patience and poltical acceptability of high-level unemployment. There has been much discussion among economists about processes of "hysteresis," whereby states of unemployment tend to perpetuate themselves, but there may be processes whereby the prolongation of unemployment tends to undermine the social and political base on which it rests.

Even if such processes do unfold, it remains a fact that, as Professor Rosenberg writes in one of the chapters on the U.S. experience, "To some degree a sociopolitical regulation of the labor market and employment relations is being replaced by market forces" (p. 63). The same conclusion can be applied to the experience of all the other countries reviewed in this volume. In identifying and documenting an important turning point in the making of labor market policies in the decade of the 1980s, and also in emphasizing the redistributional aspects of policies designed to make wages and labor markets more responsive to adverse changes in demand and supply, this book makes a most valuable and timely contribution to scholarship in labor economics and industrial relations.

Lloyd Ulman
Department of Economics
University of California, Berkeley
Berkeley, California

Preface

Dramatic changes have occurred in North American and European labor markets since the late 1960s. Relatively low levels of unemployment were the rule rather than the exception. Full employment characterized some economies, and labor shortages even emerged.

The prosperity of the late 1960s was replaced by the serious economic recessions of the 1970s and 1980s. The low levels of unemployment were temporary. Labor surpluses replaced labor shortages.

Although government policies were not the only factors lying behind the emergence of substantial unemployment, they did play a role. And although government policies cannot guarantee a return to the low levels of unemployment of the 1960s, they can serve to expand employment opportunities. Given the importance of state policies to labor market developments, the International Working Party on Labor Market Segmentation devoted three of its meetings to questions concerning the state and the labor market. The chapters in this volume, focusing on current directions in governmental labor-market policies in the United States and Europe, are based on presentations made to this group.

The Working Party is indebted to Jean-Jacques Silvestre and Jean-Paul de Gaudemar for organizing the Aix-en-Provence conference, to György Sziráczki, Janos Timar, and Gabor Révész for planning the Budapest session, and to Jill Rubery and Frank Wilkinson for arranging the Cambridge meeting. The Centre National de la Recherche funded the Aix-en-Provence conference. The Karl Marx University and the Hungarian Academy of Sciences sponsored the Budapest meeting. The *Cambridge Journal of Economics* and the Department of Applied Economics of the University of Cambridge funded the Cambridge session.

Arne Kalleberg made helpful comments on the entire manuscript. Kendy Kloepfer helped with the typing of the manuscript.

Samuel Rosenberg

Chicago, Illinois

Contents

Chapter 3

Fissure and Discontinuity in U.S. Labor Management Relations 47
Michael J. Piore

Chapter 4

The Restructuring of the Labor Market, the Labor Force, and the
   Nature of Employment Relations in the United States in the 1980s   63
Samuel Rosenberg

Chapter 5

Employment Policy, the State and the Unions in the Federal Republic
   of Germany 87
Gerhard Bosch and Werner Sengenberger

Chapter 6

Reregulating the Labor Market amid an Economic and Political Crisis:
Spain, 1975–1986 107

Lluis Fina, Alberto Meixide, and Luis Toharia

Chapter 7

The State, the Unions, and the Labor Market: The Italian Case, 1969–
1985 127

Sebastiano Brusco and Paola Villa

Chapter 8

State Regulation, Enterprise Behavior and the Labor Market in
Hungary, 1968–1983 151

Peter Galasi and György Sziráczki

PART III. YOUTH, ANTIDISCRIMINATION, AND WORKING-TIME POLICIES

Chapter 9

Youth Interventions, Job Substitution, and Trade Union Policy in Great
Britain, 1976–1986

Paul Ryan

Chapter 10

The Reagan Administration and the Regulation of Labor: The Curious
Case of Affirmative Action

Marilyn Power

PART IV. CONCLUSION

I
Introduction

1

Labor Market Restructuring in Europe and the United States

The Search for Flexibility

Samuel Rosenberg

Over the past two decades, labor market conditions in many advanced industrial societies have dramatically changed. The relatively low levels of unemployment of the 1960s have been replaced by the high and, for the most part, persistent levels of unemployment of the 1980s.

The year 1973, the time of the first "oil crisis," marked the turning point for many European countries. Unemployment began rising. For the United States, the timing was somewhat different. Growing unemployment began appearing in 1970, at the close of the Vietnam War-induced expansion of the 1960s.

The labor market changes have not been uniform across countries, and some countries have not experienced the rise of mass unemployment. For example, unemployment rates in Norway and Sweden have remained quite low, being 2.5% and 2.8% in 1985, respectively (OECD, 1986a, p. 140).

Yet it is not to the Norwegian and Swedish experiences that many European policymakers are turning. Rather, many European policy initiatives have been framed either by actual developments in the United States or by misperceptions of the American experience. The American "jobs miracle" has been contrasted with the stagnating employment levels of many members of the Organization for Economic Development and Cooperation (OECD). From 1973 to 1983, the beginning of the recovery from the serious recession of the early 1980s, the real gross national product (GNP) of European members of the OECD grew by almost as much as in the United States—18% as compared with 22%. Yet net employment grew by nearly 16 million in the United States,

Samuel Rosenberg • Department of Economics, Roosevelt University, Chicago, Illinois 60605.

3

whereas there was no net increase in employment in OECD Europe (OECD, 1986a, pp. 7–8).

The economic recovery began earlier in the United States. It has also been stronger as has employment growth. Thus by 1986, the unemployment rate in the United States was 7.0%, whereas in OECD Europe it was 11%.

Unemployment rates in the United States have not always been lower than in Europe. During the 1960s and much of the 1970s, unemployment rates in the United States generally exceeded those in such European countries as the Federal Republic of Germany, France, Italy, and the United Kingdom.

Many European policymakers, often but not always of a conservative political persuasion, consider the secret behind the American "jobs miracle" to be flexibility—labor market flexibility. They view the American labor market, often simplistically, as "flexible" in contrast to the "rigidities" they see prevailing in European labor markets. Thus for them, a central goal of labor market policy is the restructuring of the labor market by removing "rigidities" so as to increase labor market "flexibility." In addition, although the United States labor market is viewed as relatively "flexible," the government has also wished to improve labor market "flexibility."

Governmental initiatives can affect the level of employment, the nature of employment, and the overall structure of the labor market. Given the importance of state policies to the evolution of labor markets, the International Working Party on Labor Market Segmentation devoted three of its meetings to issues concerning the state and the labor market. The chapters in this volume have their roots in presentations made to this body.[1] They analyze current directions in governmental labor market initiatives in the United States and Europe. They demonstrate that, although improving labor market flexibility has been a goal of many governments, the policies vary substantially across countries.

I. LABOR MARKET SEGMENTATION[2]

A more flexible labor market is a restructured labor market. This restructuring can occur in the internal labor market, involving work relations within the firm, or it can take place in the external labor market, outside of the firm. The current controversies concerning labor market flexibility can be situated within a general debate over the structure of the labor market that began toward the end of the 1960s.[3]

At that time, case studies of urban labor markets in the United States

[1]This is the third volume based on meetings of the International Working Party on Labor Market Segmentation. See Wilkinson (1981) and Tarling (1987) for earlier work of this body.
[2]This section is based on Rosenberg (1987).
[3]In fact, controversies over labor market structure predate the late 1960s. See Kerr (1954) for an earlier discussion of balkanized labor markets.

pointed to the existence of a dual labor market, with primary and secondary sectors. The primary sector is characterized by high wages, relatively good working conditions, employment stability, and opportunities for advancement; the secondary sector, by low wages, poor working conditions, high labor turnover, and little chance for advancement. The urban working poor were seen as being confined to the secondary labor market.

Initially, Piore (1970) argued that the behavioral characteristics of secondary labor market workers were important factors in explaining both the high turnover postulated to exist in the secondary sector and the barriers to upward mobility from that segment of the labor market. Though having the necessary work skills, these people were barred from primary jobs because they tended to work unreliably or intermittently. The instability of disadvantaged workers and of the jobs available to them were the primary causes of their relatively high unemployment rates.

Emphasizing the behavioral traits of secondary sector workers implicitly precludes the possibility of a large number of them serving as a reserve labor force to the primary market, at least until they acquire the necessary primary market characteristics. Thus, in terms of labor force flows, the two segments of the labor market are viewed as virtually distinct.[4] Much empirical work has been done to determine the extent of intersectoral mobility.[5]

Not only are the labor markets distinct, the wage-setting practices differ across sectors. The wage structures within primary market firms are relatively rigid, affected minimally if at all by competitive market forces. The wages in the secondary labor market are more strongly influenced by competitive market forces.[6]

The dual labor market theory focused on explaining a fairly stable structure of pay and job inequalities. It reflected the seemingly relatively stable, prosperous period of the late 1960s. But economic conditions changed in the 1970s. Prosperity gave way to recession and economic stability to economic uncertainty. The economic changes together with the findings of a host of empirical studies on intersectoral occupational mobility led to a reformulated, more dynamic theory of dualism.

The empirical investigations demonstrated more intersectoral mobility than dual labor market theorists had postulated. Piore (1979a,b,c, 1980) and Berger and Piore (1980) accept the thrust of these studies and, without always being explicit, attempt to integrate them into a new dualist analysis. The labor

---

[4]Although this version of the dual labor market hypothesis would become highly influential, a richer alternative version of the theory was developed virtually simultaneously. See Doeringer and Piore (1971) for a conceptualization that lay somewhere between a dichotomous and a continuous labor market. In fact, they are aware that the data available at the time "do not uniquely support either a continuous or a discontinuous theory of the labor market" (Doeringer & Piore, 1971, p. 183).

[5]See Rosenberg (1987) for a discussion of these investigations.

[6]However, Piore (1979b, p. xxv) argues that wage determination in the secondary sector "is no more clearly responsive to the competitive market forces of conventional theory than is the process in the primary sector."

markets of all advanced industrial societies are pictured as dualistic. This "macroeconomic dualism arises when there is a broad similarity throughout most of the economy in the pressures for a division between secure and insecure jobs, in the particular institutions through which the division is created and maintained, and in the groups employed in the insecure sector" (Piore, 1980, p. 382).

A primary factor causing this macroeconomic dualism is the variability and uncertainty that characterizes all modern industrial economies. Those working in primary labor market positions are able to insulate themselves to a large degree, whereas those in the secondary sector bear the brunt of the uncertainty.

Individual behavioral traits are no longer pointed to in explaining who is working in each labor market segment. Rather, those working in unstable jobs in the secondary sector—mainly foreign migrants, youth, housewives, and peasant workers—view employment as a temporary adjunct to their primary social roles.[7] But many members of these groups are quite capable of working in the primary sector, if needed. This upward mobility is quite compatible with segmentation "as long as behavioral patterns of mobile workers changed as they crossed the relevant boundaries" (Piore, 1979b, p. xiii).

The secondary sector is viewed as complementing the primary sector by absorbing demand that cannot be sustained there. Thus, to a point, the secondary sector serves to protect wages, working conditions, and job security in the primary sector. But the secondary labor market has the potential of undermining the security arrangements in the primary sector if costs of production become too low there relative to those in the primary sector (Piore, 1979a, p. 42). It would then become profitable for a primary sector owner to subcontract additional work to secondary sector businesses. In sum, Piore is now proposing a more direct linking between the primary and secondary sectors than was postulated earlier.

Sengenberger (1981), too, sees the primary and secondary labor market being dynamically interconnected. Yet, rather than grounding his analysis of dualism in systemic tendencies common to all advanced industrial societies, as does Piore, Sengenberger gives primary importance to employer strategies, both in creating primary and secondary-type labor arrangements and in shifting the boundaries of labor market segmentation in response to changing economic conditions. His case study is the Federal Republic of Germany, but his theoretical analysis is applicable to other advanced industrial societies.

During the period of full employment of the 1960s, internal labor markets within firms grew in importance. Labor was scarce, especially skilled labor, and employers were interested in creating a loyal, firmly attached, and internally mobile work force. In general, the indigenous labor force worked under primary market conditions. Foreigners held secondary jobs.

The boundaries of labor market segmentation changed during the reces-

---

[7]But this argument does not hold for blacks who are also concentrated in secondary sector positions (Piore, 1979c, p. 12).

sion of 1974–1975. No longer were foreigners the only participants in the secondary labor market. Now, members of the domestic labor force—mainly women, unskilled workers, youth, and older workers nearing retirement age—found themselves working under secondary labor market conditions. Employers were more selective in providing primary-type employment and more interested in exposing their workers to the competition represented by surplus labor in the external labor market. Fixed short-term contracts and leasing personnel from agencies became more prevalent.

The preceding analyses of labor market segmentation all took place within a dualist framework. Yet a labor market can be segmented but not along dualist lines. More recent investigations of labor market structures, although incorporating some insights of dualism, take a much broader approach to segmented labor markets.[8] Based on evidence from the United Kingdom, Rubery (1987) argues that there is a much greater diversity in employment practices between firms than is theorized in dualist models. The primary determinants of the structure of jobs and employment opportunities, and thus of the nature of labor market segmentation, are industrial structure and employer strategy. Labor supply conditions are just one of the many factors influencing employer strategy. Thus there is no mechanism guaranteeing that labor will be paid according to its actual or potential productivity. Institutional, collective, legal, and social forms of organizations are central to the structure and functioning of labor markets and to the nature of employment within firms and industries.

Within this framework, the identifying features of segmented labor markets are that differences in the pecuniary and nonpecuniary aspects of employment are no guide to the relative skills and capabilities of employees. Workers of equal skills and capabilities may be employed at widely differing terms and conditions of employment.

Case studies have been utilized demonstrating the usefulness of this framework and distinguishing it from other labor market segmentation analyses. Craig, Garnsey, and Rubery (1984) study women's employment in secondary sector firms in the United Kingdom. Wages are low, and there are only minor differentials for job content, experience, or merit, just as the various versions of dual labor market theory would predict. But contrary to the theory, the jobs are skilled, and workers only perform at acceptable levels of productivity after significant periods of experience. A differentiated or segmented labor supply—labor whose cost is low relative to its productivity—is required for there to be workers willing to do skilled tasks at low pay and, at the same time, display a strong orientation to work. The employment system and the system of social reproduction interact to make many women willing to hold such positions. The existence of disadvantaged groups plays a role in creating and helping to legitimize secondary employment.[9]

---

[8]See Tarling (1987) for examples of such analyses.
[9]This argument differs from the dualism of Piore (1980) wherein segmented labor markets evolve independently of the characteristics of the labor supply. But it bears some similarity to Piore

Labor markets are fragmented, but they are not inflexible. Among those people already in the labor market, flexibility is achieved by those in the lower tiers serving as labor reserves to upper-tier jobs. Such upgrading is achieved relatively easily during an economic expansion because workers are generally underemployed, and all that is required is a change in hiring rules rather than any radical retraining program (Wilkinson, 1987, p. 169). And during contractions, the lower tier positions serve as a safety net for workers displaced downward. Flexibility in the size of the labor force can be achieved by factors such as changes in labor force participation rates and interregional and international migration. Thus segmented labor markets are not necessarily antithetical to flexible labor markets.

II. WHAT IS LABOR MARKET FLEXIBILITY?

Although Wilkinson (1987) finds segmented labor markets to be flexible labor markets, many of those calling for more labor market flexibility do not. They view increasing labor market flexibility and decreasing labor market segmentation as synonymous. According to Guy Standing, the new orthodoxy of economic theory, claiming that unemployment can be lowered by a great increase in labor market flexibility, merely amounts to calling for the labor market to operate more like a commodity market responsive to the laws of supply and demand (Standing, 1986a, p. 5).

These differing views on labor market flexibility point to a prior question. What is labor market "flexibility," and what are labor market "rigidities"? These words are used rather loosely in policy debates and policy proclamations. And there does not seem to be any accepted definitions for them. Some construe the notion of flexibility rather broadly as the "capacity to adapt to change" (Boyer, 1987; Michon, 1987). Yet, which aspects of the economy need to adapt, how is that adaptation to occur, and who will bear the costs of adaptation? Needless to say, such a definition of flexibility does not provide answers to these questions.

And it is just the vagueness that leads some to conclude that discussions of flexibility are a veil behind which other matters are being debated. Behind *flexibility*—a word with extremely positive connotations—lies the more serious question of the relative balance of power between different groups in society. Those critical of the whole notion of flexibility argue that calls for increased flexibility are really calls for increasing the autonomy and freedom of action of the most powerful groups in society, weakening the welfare state, and "placing the burden of adjustment on the shoulders of the weakest" (Meulders & Wilkin, 1987, p. 4).

(1970), wherein the behavioral traits of secondary workers are said to be important in generating the unstable jobs of the secondary labor market. But for Craig, Garnsey, and Rubery (1984), it is not unstable behavior but women's role in social reproduction that makes them willing to hold secondary jobs and employers willing to create positions with secondary labor market qualities.

Although that may in fact be the case, it still is useful to attempt to define flexibility more narrowly, to develop a typology of flexibility. Discussions of flexibility focus on the use of labor. Four types of flexibility are often analyzed: wage flexibility, numerical (or employment) flexibility, functional flexibility, and flexibility of working time.

Wage flexibility refers to the extent to which wage levels or differentials can be adjusted to prevailing labor market conditions. With increasing wage flexibility at the microlevel, wages become more enterprise and worker specific. Questions of intrafirm, interfirm, and interindustry parity are relegated to the background. At the macrolevel, wages more quickly adjust to trends in unemployment, productivity, and terms of trade. Various institutional factors, or rigidities, such as rules and regulations concerning minimum wages or automatic wage-indexing provisions are eliminated or decline in importance.

Increasing numerical flexibility means expanding the freedom of employers to vary the amount of hours of work and the size of the work force in response to cyclical or structural variations in demand and/or technological change. As restrictions, or rigidities, on dismissals, fixed-term contracts, temporary work, and part-time work are weakened, numerical flexibility is enhanced.

Functional flexibility concerns the ability of a firm to effectively utilize its relatively permanent full-time work force by varying the work performed to the changing requirements of production. This type of flexibility is related to the mobility of workers within the enterprise. Such mobility is enhanced if workers are able to perform a variety of tasks and contractually established work rules are not out of step with the changing requirements of production.

Working time flexibility concerns the adaptability of work schedules and the organization of working time. It covers a variety of elements including laws and collective agreements fixing hours of work and duration of paid vacation and paid leave, overtime, work outside of authorized hours such as weekend work, and entry into or retirement from the labor force. This form of flexibility is often related to the reduction and restructuring of working time.

III. THE RATIONALES FOR LABOR MARKET FLEXIBILITY

Proponents of increased labor market flexibility argue that it will, among other things, lead to increased net employment growth and a lowering of unemployment. The reasons provided vary, depending upon the particular type of flexibility being addressed.

Wage flexibility and numerical flexibility are often discussed together. Many neoclassical economists and policymakers influenced by this perspective argue that the relatively high levels of unemployment and stagnating levels of employment in many European countries are due to high and inflexible real wages and the inability of employers to adjust their work forces in response to changing product demand because of institutional rigidities in the labor market. This is in contrast to the United States where real wages are more flexible, especially in a downward direction, and there are virtually no legal restrictions on an employer's freedom to adjust employment levels.[10]

Both microlevel and macrolevel explanations have been advanced in support of the beneficial effects of wage flexibility. At the microlevel, the downward flexibility of wages where required by the economic conditions of the enterprise will lead to employment growth. As the cost of labor falls relative to the cost of other factors of production, employers will utilize more labor to produce any given level of output. The scale of production will likely expand, as well, causing profits to grow. Increased investment resulting in more jobs will follow the growth in profits.

Also, at the microlevel, downward wage flexibility is discussed in relation to the worker's individual performance, age, and skills. To the extent that wages more accurately reflect individual productivity, employment opportunities will increase for those priced out of the labor market by high, rigid wages. This line of argument is often applied to unemployed youth whose labor market options are limited by rules and regulations setting excessively high minimum wages.

The microlevel analysis ignores the impact of wages on aggregate demand and thus on aggregate unemployment. At the macrolevel, the question of downward wage flexibility is posed in relation to trends in the share of wages and profits in national income. The battle over income shares in the late 1960s in several European countries led to excessively high wage levels. During the 1970s, the rate of productivity growth slowed, and the terms of trade shifted against many European economies, given the oil price increases of 1973–1974 and 1979–1980. Yet real wages did not adjust accordingly, and wages grew at the expense of profits. Investment slumped, and what investment did occur was designed to be labor saving rather than to expand capacity (Lawrence & Schultze, 1987, p. 9). Thus, for employment to grow, the wage share must fall and the profit share must rise.

This analysis of share imbalance has, at least, one major flaw with it.[11] What should be the ideal share of wages and profits in national income? This is virtually impossible to determine. Merely to show that the wage share is rising and the profit share is falling is inadequate unless one is to assume that

---

[10]In August 1988, a law was passed in the United States requiring employers to provide workers with 60 days notice of plant closings and layoffs. Although there are minimal legal restrictions on an employer's ability to adjust employment levels in the United States, Piore (1986) shows that layoffs based on seniority together with "bumping" rights—a usual arrangement under collective bargaining contracts in the United States—substantially increase the costs to American employers of downsizing the work force during an economic downturn. Comparative measures of wage flexibility must be interpreted with care. For example, whereas cross-industry measures of wage dispersion show the United States to have more wage dispersion than the United Kingdom, within the United Kingdom, local wage rates are more responsive to local unemployment rates than they are within the United States (Freeman, 1988, p. 68).

[11]See Boyer (1987) for an excellent analysis of the problems with this approach to unemployment conditions in Europe. See Bowles and Boyer (1988) for an interesting theoretical investigation of wage-led and profit-led employment regimes.

the initial share levels are the optimal levels. And there is no basis in fact for making that assumption.[12]

As in the case of wage flexibility, numerical flexibility is seen as a way to lower labor costs and thus foster employment growth. Employment protection rules increase the cost of dismissals by making them more difficult and/or requiring compensation for dismissals. Thus, it is argued, they encourage a capital for labor substitution in the production process. For example, the difficulties and costs of dismissals prevent employers from hiring additional workers as needed because they know they will not be able to fire them easily if conditions change.

Eliminating or weakening such rules, for example those requiring dismissal pay, would lower overall labor costs. This should encourage the substitution of labor for capital leading to additional employment. Similarly, easing the process for dismissals should make employers more willing to add to their labor forces, at least during periods of economic growth.

Yet, whether these policies would increase employment, at least in the short run, is open to question. Limited or no employment protection rules are likely to result in greater cyclical swings in layoffs, dismissals, and hires compared to situations where job terminations are regulated. However, if those dismissed are to find jobs, there must be an adequate number of vacancies. But as unemployment has grown in Europe, job offers have fallen (Boyer, 1987, p. 119).

Although in the short run, these rules governing employment protection may have minimal impact on overall employment, they may affect the nature of employment. Employment security for some may entail the lack of employment security for others. This is so because employment protection legislation "typically covers only a part of the work force and excludes, for example, many part-time workers and people on short-term contracts" (OECD, 1986b, p. 110). Thus, to the extent allowed, employment growth may be more likely to occur through part-time or temporary work.

And a further means of fostering numerical flexibility is to allow a greater use of part-time and temporary workers. Such a policy may foster employment growth or may serve to replace full-time jobs by part-time jobs and normal unlimited work contracts by fixed-time contracts. In addition, it may facilitate a more complex segmentation of the labor force along with a smaller protected core of the labor force.

Furthermore, there is likely to be a trade-off between numerical flexibility and functional flexibility. Workers are likely to be more responsive to employer demands for functional flexibility if they feel they have job security. Functional flexibility may lead to improvements in labor productivity. Improvements in labor productivity may lead to fewer workers being utilized to

---

[12]Wilkinson (1983, p. 428) very aptly speaks to this issue. "What constitutes economic progress and an 'efficient' distribution of income is essentially a political question because the objectives are political and social in character and not purely economic in the usual, narrow sense of the term."

produce the requisite output. Because workers do not wish to work themselves out of a job, they are more likely to be willing to undertake the required training, cooperate in efficient teamwork, and accept the introduction of new technology and the changing of contractually established work rules if their jobs are protected. And employers are more likely to provide an extensive range of in-house training if they anticipate retaining their workers for a long period of time.

Thus one rationale for functional flexibility is that it results in higher labor productivity. In a more general sense, functional flexibility is advanced as a means for handling an increasingly uncertain business environment. As product demand changes, resources must be able to be shifted to new uses. If this does not occur, companies are more likely to close plants or attempt to drastically lower wages. Functional flexibility is the more socially beneficial approach to the new economic environment.

Yet there may be another side to the way functional flexibility is actually being applied in practice. Rather than being in the interests of workers, the introduction of new technologies and the reorganization of the shop floor, at least in the United States, may serve to intensify work and increase managerial control over the production process (Shaiken, Herzenberg, & Kuhn, 1986).[13] In addition, functional flexibility may entail the creation of a "functionally flexible" core of skilled workers and a "quantitatively flexible" periphery of less protected workers (OECD, 1986b, p. 114).

As with functional flexibility, working time flexibility has the potential to increase productivity. This especially holds for changes in working time arrangements, for example, allowing weekend work or more flexible work scheduling, which enable enterprises to make fuller use of their equipment. Yet the rationale for working time flexibility as a means for reducing unemployment goes beyond the issue of productivity and varies, depending on the nature of working time flexibility being discussed. For example, the shortening of the workweek may create jobs, or at least maintain jobs that would otherwise have disappeared, by sharing the available work among more people. Reducing the retirement age substitutes younger workers for older ones and may lower unemployment by shrinking the labor force, not by creating jobs.

Emphasizing early retirement is akin to accepting stagnant employment levels and taking labor demand as given, rather than attempting to improve the functioning of the economy, thereby increasing employment opportunities. In theory, reducing weekly working hours can increase employment. But the reality is more complex. The crucial issues concern whether weekly wages remain the same, whether there is a simultaneous restructuring of working time, and whether unit labor costs change. If higher unit labor costs emerge, will they negatively affect employment?

[13]The disputes over functional flexibility in the United States demonstrate that, at least on this measure of flexibility, the labor market in the United States is less flexible than in some European countries. Lorenz (1988) argues that compared with German and Italian manufacturing, British, French, and American manufacturing have encountered considerable obstacles to achieving flexible work organization.

IV. THE STATE AND LABOR MARKET FLEXIBILITY

Just as there are different notions of labor market flexibility, there are different paths to attaining flexibility. Government policies can be utilized to improve labor market flexibility, however defined. But, here too, there are various policy options. The particular policies chosen will be heavily influenced by the relative balance of power between labor and business. That relative balance of power will help to determine the overall political-economic perspective underlying the policy formulation process and the particular forms of labor flexibility emphasized.

It is not that all actions of government should be viewed as either in the interests of labor or, if not, then in the interests of business. Some state policies, such as expenditures on education and health, can be interpreted as furthering the common interest. Other activities can be regarded as serving the particular interests of either business or labor. For example, restrictive macroeconomic policies causing high levels of unemployment undermine labor's bargaining strength and thus increase the relative bargaining power of employers. On the other hand, providing generous unemployment benefits and mandating high minimum wages advance labor's interests by lessening the economic pain of unemployment and raising the floor of the wage structure.

The general tenor of the debate over labor market flexibility policies has been more in line with the interests of business than of labor. "Rights" that labor had come to expect under the post–World War II welfare state have now come to be defined by some as "rigidities." According to Standing (1986b, p. 112), these rights included the following: (a) labor market security through unemployment insurance and state-provided "full employment"; (b) income security through legitimized trade unionism and minimum wage legislation; (c) employment security through the imposition of rules preventing dismissals and the imposing of costs on employers for laying off workers; and (d) job security through work rules incorporated in collective bargaining agreements or in custom and practice.

These rights have not been present to the same degree in all advanced industrial societies. However, workers in all advanced industrial societies had come to expect some of these rights to some degree.

Policymakers of a neoclassical economics persuasion blame these rights that workers gained during an era of high employment for the large-scale unemployment present today. They assume the existence of a "natural rate of unemployment." In their eyes, this is equivalent to the frictional rate of unemployment, the rate to which an economy tends due to normal job changing behavior. However, trade union power and misguided government policies have served to impede the functioning of the forces of supply and demand. Thus they have served to raise the "natural rate of unemployment."

This is one of the primary factors lying behind the increased unemployment of the 1980s. More specifically, the economies of Europe and the United States were buffeted by exogenous "shocks," for example, the oil price "shocks" of the 1970s. These "shocks" necessitated a downward adjustment in real wages. But given wage rigidity, this did not occur. Rather, aggregate output stagnated, and unemployment rose.

The role for the state is clear—deregulate the labor market in order to eliminate the "rigidities" and approach a purely competitive labor market. This will directly increase wage and numerical flexibility. It will indirectly lead to more functional flexibility by weakening unions, thus increasing the freedom of employers to reorganize the work process in order to increase efficiency.

In theory, the deregulatory approach to labor flexibility may improve the overall productive efficiency of an economy. In practice, however, this is unlikely to be the case. Rather, as real wages fall, employers will feel less labor cost pressure and thus will be less inclined to invest in new plant and equipment. Any advantage a society following this path may achieve vis-à-vis its competitors on the world market may be due more to a general worsening of conditions faced by many members of its population than to an improved, more dynamic economy.

The deregulatory approach induces flexibility by increasing worker insecurity. An improved regulatory approach would foster flexibility, particularly functional flexibility at the level of the economy as a whole, by increasing worker security. Expansionary macroeconomic policy would be relied upon to increase employment opportunities. Lowering the rate of unemployment, improving trade union rights and extending collective bargaining to previously excluded groups, and raising the minimum wage would help to generate a high wage economy. Employers, especially those in the secondary labor market, would be less able to compete on the basis of offering lower wages. Rather, they would be pushed to invest in the most modern, technologically advanced plant and equipment to remain internationally competitive. At the macroeconomic level, a virtuous circle would be created "in which productivity growth, competitive success, and demand expansion interact to produce continuous increases in prosperity" (Wilkinson, 1983, p. 425).

At the level of the firm, functional flexibility would be enhanced by legal restrictions on dismissals, forcing firms to retain workers or requiring substantial severance payments. Rather than shrinking the size of the labor force, when product demand declined, workers would be reassigned to produce other products. Restrictive work rules limiting the crossing of job lines might be more easily eliminated in an environment of stable continuous employment.[14]

Public sector employment would be provided if an inadequate number of jobs were generated by the private sector. On balance, wage dispersion would diminish and the conditions facing many members of the population would improve.[15]

---

[14]See Sengenberger (1988) for a discussion of this phenomenon in the Federal Republic of Germany.

[15]See Standing (1986b, Chapter 8) for an alternate set of policies designed to mesh labor flexibility with increased economic security.

V. THE PLAN OF THE BOOK

Countries differ in their customary and legal mechanisms for regulating the labor market and in industrial relations systems. As a result, the nature of labor market flexibility or rigidity, however defined, varies across societies as do the specifics of state policies designed to improve labor market flexibility. Though the specifics may differ, many of the current governmental campaigns to improve labor market flexibility do share common elements.

The chapters in this volume demonstrate that, in some instances, calls for increased labor market flexibility are intertwined with a deregulatory politics. Such a politics emphasizes market solutions to socioeconomic problems, employer unilateralism, and the undermining of unions. However, this policy thrust also breeds resistance so that the policies do not always have their intended effects. In other instances, bargaining between labor organizations and employers' associations, or trilateral bargaining including the government, is the means for attaining greater flexibility.

The chapters are organized in three parts. The first group of seven papers are country studies discussing the recent evolution of government industrial relations and employment policies in the United Kingdom, the United States, the Federal Republic of Germany, Spain, Italy, and Hungary. The chapters on the United Kingdom, the United States, and the Federal Republic of Germany document the deregulatory approach to labor market flexibility being taken by the governments in those countries. Although the state policies are similar, the responses of unions have varied. British and American unions have been put on the defensive, whereas the German labor movement has fought back against the government's policy and has advanced an employment policy of its own—work time reduction. The chapters on Spain and Italy demonstrate how questions of labor market flexibility have been handled through centralized bargaining between employers and unions in Spain, and employers, unions, and the state in Italy. The chapter on Hungary is included to demonstrate that questions of labor market flexibility do not occupy governments just in capitalist societies. They are also at issue in socialist societies.

The second group of four studies are detailed evaluations of specific policies. They include youth policy in Great Britain, affirmative action in the United States, and working-time policies in France and Norway. These chapters further develop several of the themes raised by the country studies.

The last part consists of a concluding chapter that draws some lessons to be learned from the search for labor market flexibility.

VI. REFERENCES

Berger, S., & Piore, M. J. (1980). *Dualism and discontinuity in industrial societies.* Cambridge: Cambridge University Press.

Bowles, S., & Boyer, R. (1988). Labor discipline and aggregate demand: A macroeconomic model. *American Economic Review, 78* (2, May), 395–400.

Boyer, R. (1987). Labor flexibilities: Many forms, uncertain effects. *Labor and Society, 12* (1, January), 107–129.

Craig, C., Garnsey, E., & Rubery, J. (1984). Payment structures and smaller firms: Women's employment in segmented labor markets. Research Paper No. 48. London: Department of Employment.

Doeringer, P., & Piore, M. J. (1971). *Internal labor markets and manpower analysis*. Lexington, MA: D. C. Heath.

Freeman, R. B. (1988). Labor markets. *Economic Policy*, No. 6, April, 63–80.

Kerr, C. (1954). The balkanization of labor markets. In E. W. Bakke (Ed.), *Labor mobility and economic opportunity* (pp. 92–110). Cambridge, MA: MIT Press.

Lawrence, R. Z., & Schultze, C. L. (1987). Overview. In R. Z. Lawrence & C. L. Schultze (Eds.), *Barriers to European growth: A transatlantic view* (pp. 1–47). Washington, D.C.: The Brookings Institution.

Lorenz, N. (1988, December). *Trust and flexibility: International comparisons*. Paper presented at the Allied Social Science Associations Meetings, New York City.

Meulders, D., & Wilkin, L. (1987). Labor market flexibility: Critical introduction to an analysis of a concept. *Labor and Society*, 12 (1, January), 3–17.

Miçhon, F. (1987). Time and flexibility: Working time in the debate on flexibility. *Labor and Society*, 12 (1, January), 153–174.

OECD. (1986a). *OECD employment outlook*. Paris: OECD.

OECD. (1986b). *Flexibility in the labor market: The current debate*. Paris: OECD.

Piore, M. J. (1970). Jobs and training. In S. Beer & R. Barringer (Eds.), *The state and the poor* (pp. 53–83). Cambridge, MA: Winthrop.

Piore, M. J. (1979a). *Birds of passage: Migrant labor and industrial societies*. Cambridge: Cambridge University Press.

Piore, M. J. (1979b). Introduction. In M. J. Piore (Ed.), *Unemployment and inflation: Institutionalist and structuralist views* (pp. xi–xxx). White Plains, NY: M. E. Sharpe.

Piore, M. J. (1979c). Unemployment and inflation: An alternative view. In M. J. Piore (Ed.), *Unemployment and inflation: Institutionalist and structuralist views* (pp. 5–16). White Plains, NY: M. E. Sharpe.

Piore, M. J. (1980). Economic fluctuations, job security and labor market duality in Italy, France, and the United States. *Politics and Society*, 9 (4), 379–407.

Piore, M. J. (1986). Perspectives on labor market flexibility. *Industrial Relations*, 25 (2, Spring), 146–166.

Rosenberg, S. (1987). From segmentation to flexibility. Discussion Paper No. 5. Geneva: International Institute for Labor Studies.

Rubery, J. (1987). *Labor market segmentation in Britain*, ms.

Sengenberger, W. (1981). Labor market segmentation and the business cycle. In F. Wilkinson (Ed.), *The dynamics of labor market segmentation* (pp. 243–259). London: Academic Press.

Sengenberger, W. (1988). *Economic development and segmentation: The case of the Federal Republic of Germany*. Paper presented at the Conference on Economic Development and Segmentation: An International Comparison, Notre Dame University, Notre Dame, IN, April 18–21.

Shaiken, H., Herzenberg, S., & Kuhn, S. (1986). The work process under more flexible production. *Industrial Relations*, 25 (2, Spring), 167–183.

Standing, G. (1986a). Labor flexibility: Cause or cure for unemployment. Public Lecture No. 25. Geneva: International Institute for Labor Studies.

Standing, G. (1986b). *Unemployment and labor market flexibility: The United Kingdom*. Geneva: International Labor Office.

Tarling, R. (Ed.). (1987). *Flexibility in labor markets*. London: Academic Press.

Wilkinson, F. (Ed.). (1981). *The dynamics of labor market segmentation*. London: Academic Press.

Wilkinson, F. (1983). Productive systems. *Cambridge Journal of Economics*, 7 (3/4, September/December), 413–429.

Wilkinson, F. (1987). Deregulation, structured labor markets and unemployment. In P. J. Pedersen & R. Lund (Eds.), *Unemployment: Theory, policy and structure* (pp. 167–185). Berlin: Walter de Gruyter.

II
Government Policy and the Labor Market
Country Studies

The country studies document two thrusts of state labor market policy in which calls for increased flexibility are intertwined with a deregulatory politics. The first is to increase competition in the labor market, at a given level of unemployment, by reducing the social wage, lowering the effective minimum wage, diminishing legal controls on hiring and firing, and fostering labor mobility. Such increased labor market competition may lead to increased downward wage flexibility. The second is to reduce union power through higher aggregate levels of unemployment, increased labor market competition, and the passage of new laws and the reinterpretation of existing legislation. Weakening unions, in and of itself, may lead to unionists becoming more exposed to the competitive forces of the labor market and may increase downward wage flexibility. In short, these two thrusts of government policy amount to increasing the size of the labor reserve and its impact on employed workers.

Where centralized bargaining over flexibility occurs, the situation may be different. The end result may be a partial deregulation of the labor market. However, workers may gain some quid pro quos for agreeing to such a labor market policy. If that occurs, workers may be less exposed to the brute force of the labor reserve than would otherwise be the case.

Jill Rubery, Frank Wilkinson, and Roger Tarling describe the attempts of the Thatcher government in the United Kingdom to "free-up" the labor market. Against a background of rising unemployment, a consequence of a monetarist deflationary policy, the government made it more difficult to qualify for unemployment benefits, strengthened the availability-for-work criteria, and lowered the benefits.

It viewed overly generous unemployment compensation as one of the factors causing labor market rigidity. To an extent, such nonwage income provides workers with the freedom to refuse to relocate, or accept lower pay and less skilled jobs than they have been accustomed to. Workers taking a lax

17

attitude to job search are not functioning as an effective labor reserve. In addition, the level and availability of unemployment compensation may affect the bargaining power of unions. A generous unemployment scheme may make workers less willing to give in to employer demands and more willing to risk unemployment. To the extent that labor mobility is reduced or the bargaining power of labor increased, the downward wage flexibility desired by the government is less likely to occur.

The level and scope of minimum pay legislation has also been reduced. The government actions in this area include the following: ceasing to require government contractors to observe the customary—usually union—negotiated minimum terms and conditions for their industry or locality, privatizing services in the public sector so that union wages need not be paid, and removing all people under the age of 21 from the scope of the Wages Councils, bodies that set minimum wages in selected industries.

The unfair dismissal protection of employees has been eroded. Eligibility under the unfair dismissal laws now requires 2 years employment with the same employer instead of 6 months.

Legislation has been enacted designed to reduce union power. The right not to belong to a union has been strengthened, whereas the right to belong to a union has been weakened. Employers can now fire strikers without notice. Legal immunities have been withdrawn for strikes deemed to be sympathy, interunion, or political. Picketing has been severely curtailed. The closed shop has been made more difficult to attain.

Rubery, Wilkinson, and Tarling conclude that the government's policies have not improved the operation of the labor market but have merely concentrated the costs of adjustment on those least able to bear them, especially the unemployed and the low paid. Given the circumstances, unions have been relatively unscathed as union membership has remained strong. There have been relatively few instances of wage cutting or rollback agreements.

Unions in the United States have not fared as well. Michael Piore provides a broad overview of the evolution of the post–World War II system of industrial relations in the United States. Although this system has not collapsed, he finds that it has come under severe stress in recent years. The concession bargaining of the 1980s is a reflection of this strain.

Three factors have caused the pressure for union concessions. The first factor is the declining political influence of the labor movement and the resultant deterioration in the legal protection of the right to organize and bargain collectively. The second is the worsening economic climate including the recession of 1980–1982, the deterioration of the United States' position in world markets, and deregulation in the trucking and airline industries. Government policy has played a central role in creating such conditions. The third, and perhaps most important, factor is the decline in mass production.

The postwar system of industrial relations was oriented toward mass production industries. With their relative decline, for the labor movement to survive it must develop new trade union institutions consistent with the emerging new economic order of flexible specialization and create a place for these new labor institutions within this new environment. Piore believes there is a definite place for trade unions in a system of flexible production.

Piore's broad overview provides a useful context for Samuel Rosenberg's more detailed analysis of the Reagan administration's employment, welfare, and industrial relations initiatives. The Reagan policies are similar to some of those of the Thatcher regime. Rising unemployment was a consequence of a monetarist deflationary program. Taxes were increased on unemployment compensation, and unemployment benefits beyond the standard 26 weeks were made more difficult to attain.

The effective minimum wage has declined. The federal minimum wage has remained unchanged since 1981.

Government industrial relations policy has set an antiunion tone. The rulings of the National Labor Relations Board have made it more difficult for union organizing drives to succeed and for unionized workers to achieve their goals. Employers are now more able to engage in unfair labor practices to stop a union victory in a representation election without suffering negative consequences. It is now easier for employers to move union jobs to nonunion locations. Unions are no longer able to fine workers who resign their union membership during a strike and return to work in violation of union rules. Employers can more easily lock out their workers in a labor dispute.

Concession bargaining has prevailed with minimal wage improvements, at best, the erosion of previous wage bargaining patterns, and work rule changes more to the liking of employers. As a quid pro quo, some workers may have been able to gain enhanced job security. At the same time, the growth of contingent forms of employment points to increased insecurity for other workers.

Overall, the labor market in the United States has become more competitive. Wage inequality appears to be increasing. The floor of the wage structure has fallen.

The aim of government employment policy in the Federal Republic of Germany, as is the case for the United States and the United Kingdom, is to let more market forces rule the labor market. Yet unlike in the United States and the United Kingdom, the German labor movement has organized a centralized campaign against the government's policy and has advanced an employment policy of its own—work time reduction. Gerhard Bosch and Werner Sengenberger view developments in the German labor market as reflecting mutually reinforcing relationships between flexibilization policies, a reactivated labor reserve, heightened structural divisions in the labor market, and power relations changed in favor of employers at the expense of workers.

The two thrusts of flexibilization policy are rolling back the social wage and deregulating and destandardizing the terms of employment. Unemployment benefits have been reduced, suitable work has been redefined, and the minimum contribution period that would entitle a person to unemployment compensation has been lengthened. The Employment Promotion Act of 1985 allows for the greater use of fixed-term contracts and personnel leasing, makes part-time work more attractive, grants special relief for small firms from existing employment protection legislation, and increases the freedom of employers to lay off workers without consulting the works council. These measures serve to activate the labor reserve mechanism by first increasing the need of the jobless to sell their labor in the market and, secondly, increasing the freedom of employers to hire and fire at will.

Many German unions argue the Employment Promotion Act is a misnomer. Rather than promoting employment, it has served to replace full-time jobs by part-time jobs and normal unlimited work contracts by fixed-term contracts. To combat unemployment, the German labor movement favors shortening the workweek for full-time employees. It has had some success in achieving this goal through labor–management negotiations and strikes.

As a result of these successes, the government has attempted to weaken union strength. In this regard, the government has ended the eligibility of workers indirectly affected by strikes or lockouts for unemployment compensation.

The labor market policies of all governments are influenced by past social, political, and economic conditions. Spain, in contrast to the more politically stable societies such as the United Kingdom, the United States, and the Federal Republic of Germany, has undergone a major political transformation since 1975, the year when Franco died. Lluis Fina, Alberto Meixide, and Luis Toharia argue that Spanish policies have been aimed at establishing a new kind of wage and employment flexibility consistent with the ongoing political transition.

In the United Kingdom, the United States, and the Federal Republic of Germany, increasing labor market competition has been the means for increasing wage flexibility. But in Spain, centralized agreements between employers and unions have played the same role. The pattern for these agreements was set by the Moncloa Pacts of 1977, which covered economic, social, and political issues and problems. These pacts were agreed to by all the parliamentary parties and de facto accepted by employers and unions.

In the negotiations leading up to these agreements, union leaders have been relatively restrained in their demands. This reflects the rising unemployment and the labor movement's desire to achieve a stronger institutional position in Spanish society as well as gain a variety of welfare provisions, especially unemployment compensation.

To combat unemployment, the government created new grounds for the use of part-time, temporary, and fixed-term labor contracts, and provided incentives for hiring young people on a temporary basis. Hiring increased sharply after these measures were introduced. In addition, the legal grounds for dismissals were enlarged, and their costs were reduced and made more predictable. Overall, they argue the balance of power has shifted in favor of the employers as the post-Franco industrial relations system has evolved.

In Italy, as in Spain, questions of wage flexibility and employment flexibility have been handled through centralized bargaining. But in Italy, the government has intervened more directly in the bargaining process. Sebastiano Brusco and Paola Villa provide a broad overview of Italian industrial relations from the "hot autumn" of 1968 to 1985. They identify three main themes emerging at different times: "pansyndicalism" from 1968–1975, "national solidarity government" from 1975–1980, and "trilateral bargaining" from 1980–1985.

During the time of pansyndicalism, there was strong economic growth, and the rate of inflation remained low. Decentralized, strong, and unified unions made the shopfloor the focal point of industrial conflict and bargaining activity. Wages rose, wage differentials fell, and workers gained some control over the organization of work. Toward the end of the period, the union confederations and the employers' associations signed two agreements creating a more egalitarian wage indexation system and increasing the availability of payments in the event of layoffs. Though the workers benefited from these agreements, they also represented the employers' attempts to move the locus of bargaining from the shopfloor to the level of union confederations and employers' associations.

This shift in the main location of bargaining occurred during the government of national solidarity, a government that included the cooperation of the Italian communist party. During this period the economy stagnated, large firms were in crisis, and the rate of inflation accelerated. The government actively, but not formally, negotiated with the union confederations. In order to deal with the economic crisis, the unions pursued a policy of wage moderation and did not strongly object to laws restricting the wage indexation program. The wage indexation system still functioned to reduce wage differentials as inflation remained high. The unions gained an expansion of the right to strike and better layoff payments.

The national solidarity government eventually fell. To handle the economic crisis and lower the rate of inflation, the various coalition governments conducted formal negotiations with the union confederations and the employers' associations. A trilateral agreement was signed in 1983 restraining wage increases, reducing the cost of living allowance, and shortening annual working hours by 40. The government agreed to reduce the tax burden for workers and introduce legislation concerning employment, pensions, layoff payments, and the national health system. The legal changes in the wage indexation system together with the lowering of the rate of inflation led to a widening of the wage structure.

A weakened union movement was unable to block the partial deregulation of the labor market. To increase employment and foster industrial restructuring, laws were passed making it easier to implement temporary and part-time contracts. In addition, a special type of temporary contract aimed at reducing youth unemployment was introduced.

The previous country studies have treated capitalist societies. The last country study, that of Hungary, focuses on a socialist society. The economic and political institutions of capitalist societies differ from those of socialist societies. Thus, it is interesting that Hungarian economic policy has also centered on improving the flexibility of the economy. Peter Galasi and György Sziráczki provide a broad overview of state regulation, enterprise behavior, and the operation of the labor market from the economic reforms of 1968 to the antistagnation program of the early 1980s.

The 1968 reforms liberalized the system of economic planning and provided more independence to enterprises. The labor market was deregulated as legal provisions restricting job changes were abolished and the central determination of enterprise employment levels was ended. The "second" economy—small enterprises lying outside the state-controlled system of production—expanded. Although there was economic growth and living standards improved, the economy did not function sufficiently well to meet the expectations of the political leaders.

Thus, beginning in 1972, the state intervened more directly in the economy. To meet the labor shortage, the authorities tightened control over the labor market by influencing labor allocation among enterprises and limiting wage competition. Although the economy grew until the end of the 1970s, the rate of inflation increased, and the rise in living standards slowed. The recentralization of the economy did not work as well as expected.

The economy stagnated in the late 1970s and early 1980s. Policies were designed to improve labor market flexibility. The compulsory allocation of labor ceased. What is most important is that steps were taken furthering the development of the "second" economy. The "second" economy would make stagnation in the state sector more bearable by absorbing any unemployment occurring there and cushioning any fall in state sector real wages by widening earnings opportunities. If conditions were to improve in the state sector, workers would then concentrate more of their activity in that sector. In effect, the ebbs and flows of the "second" economy would provide the needed flexibility for the state sector.

The seven chapters demonstrate that many governments in Europe and the United States have implemented policies designed to increase labor market flexibility, ostensibly to increase job growth and lower unemployment. The paths for achieving such flexibility vary across countries. The extent to which a more flexible labor market has actually emerged likely varies across countries as well.

2

Government Policy and the Labor Market

The Case of the United Kingdom

Jill Rubery, Frank Wilkinson, and Roger Tarling

I. INTRODUCTION

Government policy under Thatcher has been based on two main elements. The first element, deflation through control of the public sector deficit, became operative in the early stages of the first Thatcher administration and was continued throughout most of the first two periods of office. However, even within the first period of office, the scope for further major reductions in public spending was seen by the cabinet as highly constrained and partly self-defeating because it causes a shrinking of the tax base (Ward & Nield, 1978). In 1987, there was a reversal of the policy, funded by selling off nationalized industries. Meanwhile, the second element in the government's policy has come to the fore, that of "freeing-up" the labor market. This policy has taken longer to come to fruition because of the extent of institutional and legislative changes required to stimulate low-paid employment. Deregulation involved reducing trade union rights, legal controls over employment, and privatizing public sector services. In the first part of the chapter, we describe and assess the Thatcher government's policy toward specific aspects of the labor market against a background of previous governments' policies and changing economic, political, and social conditions. Four areas of policy with specific relevance to the labor market are identified: macroeconomic, industrial and labor market, industrial relations, and social security and family. In the second part

Jill Rubery and Frank Wilkinson • Department of Applied Economics, University of Cambridge, Cambridge CB3 9DE, Great Britain.   Roger Tarling • PA Cambridge Economic Consultants Limited, Cambridge CB2 1RQ, Great Britain.

of the chapter, we consider the political and industrial response to these policies, and we conclude by considering their impact on labor market organization in the United Kingdom (UK).

II. GOVERNMENT POLICY AND THE LABOR MARKET

A. Macroeconomic Policy: Unemployment, Inflation, and Income Distribution

Until the middle of the 1974–1979 Labor government, all UK governments had espoused a broadly Keynesian full-employment policy, although inflation had been increasingly regarded as the main economic problem. As inflation accelerated and the balance of payments deteriorated in the 1960s and 1970s, macroeconomic policy became more consistently deflationary. The Labour government was elected in 1974 on a policy program that included a commitment to full employment but in 1976, under pressure from the International Monetary Fund (IMF), implemented a monetarist deflationary policy based on controlling the money supply and the size of the public sector borrowing requirement by public expenditure cuts. The Conservative government elected in 1979 completed the transition to monetarism and portrayed it as the only rational policy program.

Unemployment rose steeply under the 1974–1979 Labor government (rising between 1973 and 1980 from .6 to 1.6 million) followed by an even more rapid increase to 2.5 million between 1980 and 1981. Unemployment continued to rise up until 1986 to a peak of 3.29 million.[1] Although unemployment rose throughout the late 1970s, the main impact on the number of jobs came in the 1980s when the dramatic rise in unemployment was accompanied by a major collapse of employment, particularly in manufacturing. Thus, although in the 1970s the rise in unemployment took place against a rising labor supply (mainly female), from 1979 the growth in the labor force slowed, and so the increase in unemployment meant a declining employment base.

One justification for the pursuit of monetarist policies has been the search for a "leaner, fitter" industrial structure, and evidence of an increase in productivity per person employed in 1982/1983 provided a major element in the Conservative government's reelection campaign. However, there has been no dramatic increase in productivity growth since 1979. Investment has remained low,[2] so that much of the recorded productivity growth is statistical—the effect on the average of scrapping old plants. Moreover, much of the investment behavior reveals "short termism," aimed at cost cutting through minor adjustments and not radical change aimed at increasing capacity and output. Thus the macroeconomic deflationary policies have not provided a sound microbasis for further growth, even among those firms that have survived.

---

[1]See section D for changes in the definition of unemployment introduced in the 1980s.
[2]Investment in real terms in manufacturing was 35% down on its 1979 level in 1983 and was still below 1979 levels in 1987.

High unemployment has been the central plank of the government's antiinflation policy. The post-1979 Conservative government has consistently rejected income policies to control private sector pay that had provided the main tool of antiinflation policy for Labour and Conservative governments from the mid-1960s to 1979. High unemployment and antitrade union legislation have been used in preference as a means of restoring "market forces." The government also purports not to be operating an income policy in the public sector, but the use of strict cash limits on public spending, including specific limits on the wage content, effectively serves the same purpose. This non-income-policy position has nevertheless, allowed the government more flexibility: to avoid clashes over their general pay policy by raising the cash limits in parts of the public sector where the unions were less prepared to accept low increases (for example, initially the miners, electricity supply workers, and professional groups such as doctors and, even at times, teachers and nurses). However, as in income policy periods in overall terms, public sector pay has fallen relative to that in the private sector.

The Thatcher government's strategy to bring down the rate of money wage settlements proved relatively successful. The rate of money wage increases declined sharply both absolutely and relative to price increases in 1980/1981; however, from the end of 1982 money wage increases have been almost consistently higher than the rate of retail price increase. Manufacturing led the decline in money wage settlements followed by private non-manufacturing and then the public sector. Settlements were kept up in the public sector by comparability pay awards stemming from the previous Labour government but implemented largely after the 1979 election. Public sector pay subsequently became subject to the "cash limits" policy, and it is these settlements that have been falling behind the private sector since the early 1980s.

Average net real wages only fell between 1981 and 1983, and even then these falls were the result of increases in direct taxation (Table 1). The maintenance of real wage levels in the 1979–1981 period was achieved through the high exchange rate policy of the government that kept down import price rises aided by the decline in commodity prices with the world recession. Real aftertax wages rose again in 1983 and have continued their upward progress as increases in average money wages have been maintained despite the decline in the rate of inflation and reduction in direct taxation. However, individual groups have suffered real wage losses, particularly male manual workers in the 1979 to 1981 periods, whereas for nonmanual workers, average real wages have continued to rise throughout the Thatcher administration (Table 2). Within these groups, there is also considerable diversity of experience, with low-paid workers (see Table 3) and, after 1981, public sector employees in particular falling behind.

Taxation policy has been a prime determinant of both real wage growth and of changes in income distribution from the 1960s. Table 1 indicates the contribution of tax changes to aftertax average real earnings: Fiscal drag reduced real take home pay from 1974 to 1977 and again between 1980 and 1982, but in other years direct tax made a positive contribution to net pay.

Table 1. Changes in Average Earnings, Direct Taxes and Retail Prices in the UK, 1974–1982[a]

| | Percentage increase over previous year | | Reductions to the value of increase in earnings resulting from changes in | |
	Gross earnings	After tax real earnings	Direct taxes	Retail prices
1975	26.4	−2.30	−4.20	−24.50
1976	15.6	−2.56	−1.68	−16.48
1977	9.0	−4.83	+1.11	−14.94
1978	13.0	+9.60	+5.07	− 8.47
1979	15.5	+3.12	+1.51	−13.89
1980	20.8	+2.93	+0.55	−18.42
1981	12.9	−1.71	−2.58	−12.03
1982	9.4	−0.39	−0.97	− 8.82
1983	8.4	+4.23	+0.57	− 4.80
1984	6.1	+3.93	+1.12	− 5.05
1985	8.5	+5.41	+0.83	− 6.24
Second quarter 1985 to second quarter 1986	8.1	+3.80	+1.21	− 5.01

[a]Economic Trends Tables 5, 40, 42.
Source: Central Statistical Office. Economic trends. London: HMSO.

The redistributive effects of the Thatcher government's tax changes are suggested by Table 4. After 1979, the effective average increased despite the government's stated objective of increasing incentives to work through reducing direct taxes. In practice, by 1985 only the very highest income groups had had a net reduction in tax, and the tendency has been for tax increases to be

Table 2. Changes in Real Earnings for Manual and Nonmanual Workers, 1975–1984 (1975 = 100)[a]

| | Full-time manual workers | | Full-time nonmanual workers | |
	Hourly earnings	Weekly earnings	Hourly earnings	Weekly earnings
Men (April)				
1975	100	100	100	100
1979	99.9	100.7	99.9	99.6
1981	99.8	96.7	106.2	105.4
1983	103.9	100.1	111.8	110.6
1984	104.6	102.8	115.4	115.4
Women (April)				
1975	100	100	100	100
1979	103.1	103.7	100.5	100.5
1981	102.6	102.6	108.2	107.9
1983	106.3	106.3	113.3	112.8
1984	107.4	108.8	115.5	115.6

[a]Average weekly earnings excluding those affected by absence; average hourly earnings excluding overtime hours and overtime pay April 1975 = 100
Source: Department of Employment *Employment Gazette*: New Earnings Survey data.

Table 3. Changes in the Earnings Distribution, 1970–1983

	1970	1975	1979	1981	1983	1985[a]
Lowest decile—median (ratio of all full-time employees)						
Men: hourly earnings	68.6	69.8	69.3	67.5	65.9	64.4
weekly earnings	66.8	67.0	66.0	65.6	64.1	62.2
Women: hourly earnings	68.0	68.5	71.2	68.5	66.9	66.8
weekly earnings	67.7	67.4	69.4	68.0	66.4	65.6
Manual—nonmanual (ratio of medians for full-time employees)						
Men: hourly earnings	68.8	74.6	72.6	68.3	67.7	66.6
weekly earnings	81.5	86.0	85.1	76.7	76.5	75.7
Women: hourly earnings	76.1	83.6	83.9	78.7	76.9	75.9
weekly earnings	80.5	86.4	87.7	82.0	80.3	78.6
Female earnings—male earnings (ratio of medians for full-time employees)						
Manual: hourly earnings	58.8	67.5	69.8	69.7	69.5	68.8
weekly earnings	50.0	58.3	60.4	62.5	62.4	61.3
Nonmanual: hourly earnings	53.1	60.2	60.4	60.4	61.2	60.2
weekly earnings	50.6	58.1	58.6	58.4	59.4	58.9
<18/18+ (ratio of average weekly earnings by age group of full-time employees)						
Men: manual	36.3	46.0	45.1	46.1	44.0	43.2
nonmanual	26.2	34.6	34.3	33.1	30.9	30.5
Women: manual	60.4	74.8	70.3	66.0	65.3	65.2
nonmanual	47.2	54.8	53.9	52.8	47.7	48.4

[a]1985 data adjusted on basis of 1983 data to take account of change in definitions. Up to 1983 data refer to men 21 and over and women 18 and over. 1985 data are for employees on adult rates.
Source: New Earnings Survey.

higher the lower the level of taxable income. Table 3 shows that, whereas the increase of the average tax rate was marginal on earnings of twice the national average, on wages half the average the share of earned income taken in tax in 1982/1983 compared to 1978/1979 was 5.5 percentage points higher for a married man with two children and almost 7 percentage points higher if there were four young children in the family. Even after the 1983 and 1984 budgets, when the government claimed to be reducing the tax burden, compared to 1978/1979, tax rates on these households had still increased by 4.1 and 5.5 percentage points, respectively.

B. Labor Market and Industrial Policies

High levels of unemployment are now considered a permanent feature of the economy. Unemployment has fallen since 1986, under the impact of reflation and further adjustments to the unemployment count, but no prospect of

Table 4. Average Tax Rates on Married Men with Children
at Different Levels of Income

	Half average earnings	Three-quarters average earnings	Average earnings	One and a half times average earnings	Twice average earnings
		Two children under 11			
1974/1975	7.4	17.5	22.6	26.7	28.3
1978/1979	10.5	18.8	23.6	28.3	29.4
1979/1980	12.4	19.7	23.5	27.0	27.7
1980/1981	13.7	20.7	24.5	27.9	28.5
1981/1982	16.1	22.6	26.2	29.9	30.1
1982/1983	16.0	22.8	26.5	29.4	30.7
1983/1984	15.4	22.3	26.1	29.1	30.4
1984/1985	14.6	21.9	25.8	28.2	29.7
		Four children two under 11, two under 16			
1974/1975	5.9	11.2	19.3	23.2	25.6
1978/1979	7.3	15.5	20.9	26.2	27.9
1979/1980	10.9	18.0	21.9	25.7	26.7
1980/1981	12.1	19.1	22.9	26.8	27.5
1981/1982	14.2	20.7	24.4	28.4	29.0
1982/1983	14.0	20.8	24.7	28.9	29.5
1983/1984	13.0	19.9	23.9	28.3	29.4
1984/1985	12.8	19.0	23.8	27.6	28.9

Source: Hansard, 1974/1978–1982/1983, estimates, 1983/1984–1984/1985.

a return to full employment is offered. This contrasts with the mid-1970s when job creation and job protection policies were enacted by the Labour government to provide temporary alternatives to unemployment during what was regarded as a severe cyclical depression. One of the main elements in the Labour government's program was the Temporary Employment Subsidies (TES) policy that paid subsidies to employers if they agreed not to go ahead with planned redundancies and was designed to prevent long-term loss of existing jobs and skills. The Conservative government converted this scheme into the Temporary Short-Time Working Compensation paid to encourage "work sharing" and again to maintain jobs in readiness for the expected upturn in demand. But the decision was taken to phase the program out when the economic upturn failed to materialize. Employers and workers had become disillusioned with solutions based on temporary subsidies, but more important, this program did not fit easily with a Conservative government's policy of encouraging industrial restructuring in the private sector and the elimination of "overmanning."

Job protection has therefore been abandoned as a policy in the current recession and privatizing public services makes explicit this aspect of government policy; the replacement of public by private service provision carries no guarantees of rehiring for the redundant public sector workers. Job protection for the individual has also been reduced through the weakening of individual employment rights (see Section C). Moreover, policies that, it is claimed, are designed to help the young or long-term unemployed have a dual purpose of "freeing-up" the labor market and reducing job protection.

The Labour government also initiated employment programs for young people, culminating in the Youth Opportunities Program (YOP) under which young people were paid a low-income allowance by the state during 6 months of work experience in companies. This initiated strong criticism by trade unions for its potential use in the substitution of low-paid youth labor for higher paid regular employees, despite safeguards to prevent this abuse. The Conservative government extended the YOP's schemes and then converted it into the Youth Training Scheme (YTS) and introduced the Young Workers Scheme (YWS). This apparent continuation of policy obscures the change from a short-term expedient to a permanent youth employment strategy that is closely linked to a broader strategy of reducing labor's power in the labor market. Thus the Youth Training Scheme was established as a permanent institution and has now been extended from 1 year to 2 years. Young people on YTS are given a low allowance by the state and are guaranteed at least 13 weeks off-the-job training during each year of work experience in a firm. This scheme forms part of the wider New Training Initiative, designed to change the nature of control and funding of skill acquisition and training in the UK (Goldstein, 1984). Most industrial training boards have now been abolished, and firms have been freed to develop firm-specific instead of general training. The YTS challenges trade union control over apprenticeship schemes and apprenticeship wages by providing an alternative and lower paid form of training. Despite the emphasis on training and built-in safeguards, there is little doubt that YTS forms a cheap source of labor for employers, particularly in the lower skilled areas. The take-up rate for YTS has been lower than originally anticipated, but around 300,000 young people have usually been in training at any one time, although the number entering the scheme over the year is much greater.

The Young Workers Scheme was linked directly to government policies to lower wages, especially for the young and the unskilled. Firms were given a subsidy for employing young workers, provided they did not pay them more than a given amount (in 1984 a £15 subsidy if workers were paid less than £50). However, the evidence showed that the majority of subsidized jobs would have been available without the scheme, so that the main effect of the policy, which was phased out in 1985, was to lower wages rather than to create jobs (Incomes Data Services, 1983).

The Conservative government reduced the scale of the job creation program of the Labour government on coming into office but has expanded them again in the 1980s. Current policies in this area are almost entirely concentrated on the long-term unemployed and are based again on low wage employment. One recent scheme involves providing a subsidy for 6 months to long-term unemployed who are willing to take a low paid job. In 1984, the combined effect of employment measures for young and long-term unemployed placed 670,000 people in jobs with an estimated effect on total measured unemployment of −415,000 (September 1984, Department of Employment).

Apart from these specific employment measures, the main policy of the government to encourage job creation is to foster the growth of small firms. This policy has a strong ideological base: Small firms fit with the model of a free market economy and reduced trade union control. Moreover entrepreneurship can be presented as an alternative to unemployment, and one scheme explicitly aids the unemployed to set up in business by paying them a flat rate subsidy and no deductions for earned income for 1 year (this scheme concerned 37,000 people in July 1984). Local enterprise zones have also been established throughout the UK, which are exempt from rates, regulations on development, and other controls. Early research suggests that far from heralding the birth of free market competition, these zones have distorted markets by the advantage given to firms inside relative to those outside, have diverted rather than created jobs, and have absorbed large sums of public funding for infrastructure development (Shutt 1984). There is little evidence of any *net* job creation, but the effect of the switch of employment to enterprise zones is potentially to increase the share of nonunion, low-paid employment.

The second strand of government industrial policy has been to privatize public sector enterprises and services. This policy is again only indirectly linked to job creation, through the hypothesis that it is only under private sector ownership and subjected to competition that enterprise can flourish. However, the government has also been concerned to raise as much revenue as possible from the sale of public assets, and, for this purpose, there has been a strong emphasis on increasing the profitability and maintaining the monopoly position of the corporations to be privatized before they are sold off. The process of preparing public sector enterprises for privatization has, in almost all cases, resulted in substantial and often dramatic job losses. These have been brought about not only through closures and work intensification but also through major investment programs. This rationalization has extended to industries that are not immediate candidates for privatization such as steel and coal and has been implemented on a scale that would not have been possible in a privatized and fragmented industry (Burns, Newby, & Winterton, 1985). In practice, the government's industrial policy for its nationalized industries has been to use long-term strategic planning for its investment programs but to reject any criteria other than short-run profit and loss considerations in determining a redundancy program, thereby maximizing the rate of employment reduction and capacity closure.

Privatization has also been part of the government's policy to free-up the labor market and reduce job protection. Unable to destroy easily its long-established tradition as a good employer offering a high level of job security, the government sought instead to transfer public sector employment to the private sector by either splitting off whole industries or by subcontracting out services. Competition from these subcontracting services has been used in turn as a justification for increases in work intensity within the public sector.

It is in the subcontract service areas that the most blatant policy of lowering wages and conditions for workers employed on the provision of public services has been pursued, involving cuts in earnings, holiday and sick pay entitlement, hours of work, and in staffing levels.

An alternative to providing employment for the unemployed is to reduce the level of unemployment through decreasing activity rates. This type of policy has only been taken up by the government from a particularly narrow perspective, that of reducing the number of people recognized as unemployed (documented in Section D). These policies include the YTS and other job-creation schemes as well as policies to reduce eligibility for benefit. There has been no government support either for working time reductions[3] (which, it is argued, would raise labor costs) or indeed for general early retirement policies. It has been left primarily to employers to offer early retirement as an alternative to general redundancies, although the existence of these schemes is indicated by the drop in participation rates for older workers. The only state-funded scheme is the Job Release Scheme, involving 92,000 workers in July 1984; workers approaching retirement can receive a pension if they are replaced by workers on the unemployment register.

C. Industrial Relations Policy

1. Collective Bargaining and Wage Determination

Voluntary collective bargaining has been the accepted and preferred means of wage determination for all governments in the postwar period up until the election of the Thatcher government that espouses the determination of wages by "market" forces. However, this has not led to a policy-induced dismantling of the main institutions of voluntary collective bargaining. Instead, the government's policy has concentrated on reducing the influence of trade unions and collective bargaining where trade union organization is weak. This has reversed the postwar trends toward increased regulation of terms and conditions of employment outside of unionized sectors through direct state regulation or by the encouragement of trade union organization and regulation. Nevertheless, in contrast to many European countries, the UK still had not, by 1979, established national minimum terms and conditions of employment; the only legal minimum wages and conditions are set by wage councils, specific to certain industries and sectors. Extension of employment regulation to nonunion areas usually requires legal or state intervention, and it is in these areas that the current government has taken direct steps to weaken the regulation of the market. These include the abolition of legislation that provided the possibility for industrywide agreements setting minimum terms and conditions to be applied to nonunion firms; the abolition of the Fair Wages Resolution that required government contractors to observe the customary,

---

[3] Its job splitting scheme attracted only minimal interest with only 883 people covered in July 1984.

usually union-negotiated minimum terms and conditions for their industry or locality, declaring union-labor-only requirements for subcontractors to be illegal, privatization of services in the public sector so that nonunion wages can be paid, lodging objections to wage councils' orders, and in 1986 enacting a bill to reduce wage councils' power and to remove under-21-year-olds from the scope of the legislation.

The outcome of the government policies of deregulation in the weakest segments of the labor market is illustrated in Table 3 (see p. 27), which shows a general widening of the earnings distribution after 1979 in contrast to the general narrowing throughout the 1970s. Young people, low-paid men and women, and manual workers have all suffered relative declines. Only women have largely retained the significant improvement in their pay achieved as a result of equal pay legislation and flat rate incomes policies in the early 1970s.

Although the government has not generally directly challenged the existence of the institutions of voluntary collective bargaining in either the public or the private sector, it has sought to change the nature of the wage determination process within these institutions and reduce their influence. The public sector has been subjected to strict cash limits that have formed the basis for pay determination in place of the time-honored principles of fair comparison. The government has also endeavored to end the use of arbitration in the public sector, both because of the likelihood that arbitrators will reintroduce fair comparison and not accept the principle that cash limits are equivalent to ability to pay in the private sector and because it runs counter to the strategy favored by the government in both the public and private sectors of presenting a final offer to workers without negotiations.

2. Trade Union Rights

Potentially the most damaging part of the Conservative government's labor market policy for the long-term strength of the labor movement is its so-called employment legislation, enacted so far in three stages, 1980, 1982, and 1984, and designed to reduce trade union immunities on a wide front. The significance of this legislation must be understood first against the context of the voluntarist tradition in UK industrial relations and second, against the background of previous legislative changes in the 1970s.

The voluntarist tradition in the UK meant that up until 1971 no legal rights to belong or not belong to trade unions existed, nor was there any legal right to strike. The employment contract was controlled by common law as interpreted by the judiciary. Apart from legal restriction on the employment of women and children and health and safety rules incorporated in the Factory Acts (implemented from the early nineteenth century), the contract was regarded as a voluntary individual contract between the employer and employed enforceable at law. Parliament intervened in the legal process by establishing immunity for trade unions first in criminal courts and later in civil courts against actions brought because of damages caused to employers by organized workers "in pursuit of trades disputes." Thus British industrial relations law was based on "negative" immunities against certain forms of legal action rather than "positive" rights to belong to a trade union, establish collective bargaining procedures with employers, or to strike.

The slow rate of growth coupled with relatively high inflation led to growing criticism of the industrial relations system in the 1960s, but there remained a broad consensus in favor of voluntarism, and the major problem was seen as the lack of control of the rank and file by the trade union leadership. The growing number of unofficial strikes during the 1964–1969 Labour government led to legislative proposals designed to strengthen the position of trade union leaders relative to their members, but faced with opposition from within the labor movement, the government abandoned its plans.

The first major attempt to reform British industrial relations came in the 1971 Industrial Relations Act that marked a significant departure from the voluntarist tradition. This act aimed to establish a legal framework for the control of the industrial relations system using a special Industrial Relations Court. Trade unions were obliged to register with the newly created Registrar of Trade Unions and Employers Association, and "approved" rules and procedures were conditions of registration. Legal immunity was confined to disputes initiated by registered trade unions and withdrawn from certain types of industrial actions including interunion disputes, sympathy and political strikes, and secondary boycotts. Emphasis was given to secrecy in balloting before recognition and bargaining rights were established, and the government was given the right to establish a "cooling-off" period of up to 60 days in the event of strike action. The act also gave positive rights to belong to trade unions by requiring employers to recognize unions once a majority had voted in favor.[4] Positive rights *not* to belong to a union were implemented by the prohibition of preentry closed shops and the conditions that in postentry closed shops workers could either pay the fee to the unions without being a member or pay the fee to a charity on the grounds of conscience. Under the provision of the act, the Department of Employment drew up a list of unfair industrial relations practice to guide the deliberation of the Industrial Relations Court.

The most important feature of the 1979 act is that its provisions were for the most part not implemented due to a mass refusal by trade unions to register under the act. With few registered trade unions, so that few had any legal immunities, distinctions between fair industrial practices (i.e., subject to immunities) and unfair practices became inoperative. The Industrial Relations Court, rather than dealing with small groups of militants taking unofficial action, found itself passing judgment on the largest unions, and when the payment of fines was refused, sequestrating union property. When the government enforced strike ballots, union members voted overwhelmingly for strike action, and when trade unionists were imprisoned for refusing to observe the court ruling to cease picketing, widespread strike action obliged the

[4]But unions were not allowed to seek recognition for 2 years after a recognition claim had failed.

government to intervene and release the prisoners. By 1973, the regulation of collective bargaining through the act had effectively been abandoned.

The Labour government elected in 1974 was committed through the social contract with the unions to repeal the 1971 Industrial Relations Act, to abolish the Industrial Relations Court, to introduce new legislation to restore legal immunities removed by the 1971 legislation, establish immunity for secondary boycotting and for sympathy strikes, and to remove liabilities established by the courts under conspiracy laws. Some reforms introduced by the 1971 act were retained, notably unfair dismissal legislation and the right to join a trade union, but the right not to join a trade union was abolished, thereby "legalizing" the closed shop. The thrust of the Labour government's legislation was to extend and consolidate some collective and individual rights in the workplace, while maintaining the tradition of trade union and employer control over collective bargaining. For example, unions were also required to register under this new legislation, but the purpose was to establish that they were independent of employers, not to vet the rule book. New arbitration and conciliation machinery was established that was independent of government and that could be used as a framework for unions to obtain recognition from reluctant employers.

In contrast, the impact of the new Conservative legislation is to severely limit the degree of legal immunity offered to trade union action and to re-establish and strengthen the right not to belong to a trade union and weaken the right to belong to trade unions. Legal immunities have been withdrawn for strikes deemed to be sympathy strikes, interunion strikes, or political. Secondary picketing, the blacklisting of nonunion firms, and the insertion of union-labor-only clauses in subcontracts have been prohibited. Damages caused by such action are now recoverable in civil courts, and both union members and unions are liable for damages. In this latter respect, the recent legislation has restored the position that existed before 1906. The responsibility for deciding the status of a dispute is left with the judge, and therefore a great area of uncertainty exists as to what is and what is not immune from court action. The only action that is clearly immune is that between workers and their immediate employer over wages and conditions of work; even industry-based disputes may be outside current immunities. Picketing has also been severely curtailed and peaceful picketing—that is, that not requiring the police to take action—is defined to involve not more than six people.

The ability of trade unions to recruit new members has also been affected by the abolition of procedures to establish trade union recognition and those for enforcing recognized terms and conditions of employment on low-paying employers. And, although the closed shop has not been abolished, its implementation now requires the support of 80% of all workers covered (or 85% of those voting), and its maintenance requires a similar majority in a ballot at least every 5 years. The government has also placed great emphasis on secret ballots, first insisting on them for establishing closed shops and offering government financial support for secret ballots for strike action or electing trade union officials. The 1984 legislation has withdrawn legal immunity for strikes for which no secret ballot has been held and requires unions to hold secret ballots for union elections and for the holding and distribution of political funds.

Because this legislation is based on the traditional system of removal of immunities in the civil courts, its application depends on individual initiatives by employers. This indirect system in fact increases the potential power of the legislation as it can be used selectively and therefore does not present an immediate "full-frontal" assault on the trade union movement. Its existence still serves to create uncertainty over the consequences of industrial action in almost all instances. Trade unions will be held responsible for all actions by their members unless these actions are immediately repudiated. The more fearful the main leadership becomes of financial losses in the courts, the more likely they are to disassociate themselves from rank and file action, thereby causing divisions within the unions themselves.[5]

The 1984 legislation has provided the framework for the most direct attack on the centers of trade union power, determining the procedures for internal organization (secret ballots for elections to be compulsory), the procedures for taking action (secret ballots for all strikes to be compulsory), and by restricting the political freedom of the trade union movement (by tightening up the conditions under which a union can hold political funds). The government has therefore moved from an initial policy program that would have most effect in increasing "competition" in the nonunion sector, to a policy of challenging union power in both its main industrial and political contexts. The impact of these legislative changes on the practice of industrial relations in Britain is, as we discuss in Section B, still uncertain but is undoubtedly significant. Thus from the vantage point of the mid-1980s, the optimism of the labor movement after the defeat of the 1971 act that it could never be effectively subjected to the law appears misplaced.

3. Individual Rights at the Place of Work

From the 1960s onward, there has been a departure from the pure voluntarist tradition evidenced not only by government's efforts to control both wage bargaining and trade union rights but also by the establishment of some legal rights to the individual in employment in areas where previously workers had had to rely for protection primarily on trade unions and collective bargaining. This development stopped far short of establishing minimum pay, standard hours, or minimum holiday entitlement, such as is common in other countries. Nevertheless, significant rights with respect to employment protection, equal opportunities, and trade union rights have been introduced. The thrust of the Thatcher government's legislation has been to weaken some

---

[5]Fear of financial loss was indeed a major factor in the Trades Union Congress's decision not to back the National Graphical Association (NGA) in the first major confrontation over the new legislation when the NGA was fined for picketing firms using nonunion labor to print a free local newspaper.

of these rights, except those that strengthen the individual vis a vis the trade union.

(a) Unemployment Protection. In the 1960s, for the first time statutory rights were established for periods of notice prior to dismissal and for redundancy payments, both of which varied with years of employment. In the 1970s, the right to a contract of employment was established, and in the 1971 act, protection was afforded against "unfair dismissal"; this protection was subsequently strengthened in the 1974/1975 legislation that extended it to small firms. The Labour government also brought in rights to maternity leave, to time-off work for trade union activities and for holding public office, and guaranteed layoff pay for 5 days in 3 months was introduced.

The Thatcher government has eroded both the unfair dismissal protection and the right to maternity leave. Eligibility under the unfair dismissal laws now require 2 years' employment with the same employer instead of 6 months. There is now no statutory right to maternity leave in very small firms, and the right to return to the same job has been weakened. Part-timers, working for less than 16 hours, have always been excluded from employment protection, but there are current proposals to extend the minimum to 20 hours. These restrictions are significant in Britain where almost half the female labor force is part-time.

(b) Equal Opportunities. In 1968, legislation was introduced against racial discrimination, including discrimination in employment. This legislation and its system of enforcement were changed again under the 1974–1979 Labour government: The post-1979 Conservative government has kept the legislation intact but has cut the budget for its administration, thereby severely curtailing its effectiveness.

In 1970 an Equal Pay Act was introduced to be made fully enforceable by 1975. This act only provided for equal pay for women doing the same work as men in the same establishment, not for work of equal value so provided for in the Treaty of Rome: Nevertheless, under its impact, combined with the effect of flat-rate income policies in the 1970s, women's wages underwent their first major relative improvement in the postwar period, from around 60% to around 70% of men's. In 1975, a Sex Discrimination Bill was also introduced, making discrimination in hiring or training illegal. In 1983 the Conservative government, under pressure from the European Economic Community (EEC) and following a ruling by the European Court, extended legal rights to equal pay to include equal pay for work of equal value. The amendments were such as to provide only a narrow basis for lodging equal value claims, but even so, the potential exists for challenging wide wage differentials between men and women. This is particularly so in the public sector where the scope for comparison is much greater because claims against pay discrimination on sexual grounds can only be made against differentials on the wages paid by a single employing organization.

(c) Trade Union Rights. The 1971 act for the first time established the right to belong and the right not to belong to a trade union. The 1974/1975 Labour government legislation abolished the latter right, legalizing the "closed shop," and strengthened the former right by establishing higher levels of compensation for dismissals on grounds of union membership and by providing facilities and funds by which workers in nonunion firms could seek to get management to recognize trade unions.

The right not to belong to a trade union has been restored and opting out of trade union membership in closed shops is now allowed on the grounds of "deeply held personal convictions." The damages for unfair dismissal on the grounds of refusing to belong to a trade union are set at a higher level than for other causes, and trade unions can be "joined" with the employer in the action and can be judged to be liable to pay damages. This legislation— against all precedents—has been made retrospective so that workers dismissed between 1974 and 1979 for refusing to join a trade union can now claim damages, despite the fact that dismissal had been fair according to the law ruling at the time. The Conservative legislation has also weakened workers' rights to belong to trade unions by changing the law on the contract of employment by making it no longer "unfair" and hence actionable for an employer to sack strikers without notice and to selectively dismiss strikers. The right *not* to belong to a trade union has become the main focus of action on individual rights with the policy presented as one of protecting the individual against the power of the trade unions. At the same time, legal assistance to nonunionists seeking union recognition has been abolished.

D. Social Security and Family Policy

Soon after coming into power, the Thatcher government embarked on reforming the social security system, initially in a piecemeal fashion but culminating in the 1986 Social Security Act in a major restructuring. Four main themes can be detected in these developments: the reduction of the categories of people eligible to claim benefits, the reduction in the level of benefits, the reintroduction or reinforcing of the distinction between the "deserving" and the "undeserving" poor, and the limitation of the role of the social security system to that of a minimum floor of last resort. Each of these elements has direct labor market implications; for example by reducing the *measured* rate of unemployment, increasing incentives to work at low wages, minimizing the tax burden of unemployment on the employed, and increasing social divisions between the employed and unemployed, with obvious implications for labor market segmentation, by identifying the jobless with the "undeserving" poor and the "work shy."

The main categories of people to have their rights to unemployment benefit curtailed are the young, the old, married women, those who quit employment voluntarily, and those apparently unwilling or unable to travel in search of work or to provide evidence that they are immediately available for work. The young have been taken out of the unemployment count mainly through YTS and by removing their rights to claim benefits for 2 months after leaving school. Older workers who become unemployed are now automatically put onto long-term social security benefit, thereby reducing the unemployment count by 161,800 people between April and August 1983. The basis for measuring unemployment was changed from those seeking work to those claiming benefits in 1984, reducing unemployment by around 112,000. Women are less likely to be eligible to claim benefit and are thus less likely now to be counted as unemployed. Women also have to demonstrate their immediate availability for work by proving they have access to alternative child care arrangements, even though they neither need nor can afford alternative child care while unemployed. Availability for work tests has recently been strengthened for all, with certain types of people, for example, those seeking managerial jobs, having to be willing to travel outside their own town before being deemed available for work. Those who leave jobs voluntarily have in the past not been able to claim benefits for 6 weeks, but this was extended to 13 weeks in October 1986.

Cuts in the categories of people eligible to claim benefits also cut the cost of benefits, but further economies have been made, by abolishing the earnings-related supplements to unemployment and sick pay, by taxing benefits, by abolishing the higher rate of unemployment pay for householders under 25 and establishing a rate some £7 less than the adult rate for all under 25, by abolishing rights to extra need payments and establishing these on a discretionary basis linked to a fixed budget and by ending benefits in kind such as school meals and free milk. Some benefits have been increased, for example, the income support benefit that replaces the family income supplement, both of which provide for families with a low-paid breadwinner. These extra costs are incurred because the higher level benefits provided by income support have been seen as a necessary part of the policy to encourage the unemployed to take low-paid jobs.

An integral part of this last policy, to increase the incentives to take low-paid jobs in preference to being unemployed, has been to establish that the unemployed are part of the "undeserving" poor. The new Social Security Act abolishes all supplements for long-term claimants but reestablishes these in different forms for almost all groups other than the unemployed (Lynes 1986). Those who go "voluntarily" into unemployment are being excluded from benefit for longer periods, young people who "unreasonably" refuse or leave a YTS place suffer cuts in benefits, and the young and married women are seen to be properly dependent on their families and not on the state for income support when unemployed. Possibly the most serious way in which the status of the benefit recipient is being undermined is by the replacement of what were payments as of right by discretionary payments, for example, in the case of claims for extra expenses such as furniture, bedding, school clothes, house repairs, fuel bills, and the like. Appeals against discretionary awards by claimants will only be heard internally, and there will be no right of appeal to an independent tribunal.

Table 5. The Development of Replacement Rates over Time:
13 Weeks Unemployment Spell[a]

	Average replacement rate	Percentage with replacement rate greater than .9	Percentage with replacement rate less than .5
1978	.79	21.0	2.3
1980	.73	12.0	8.0
1982/1983	.60	3.2	28.0
1984	.59	3.1	30.2

[a]Replacement rates are the ratio of income received when unemployed to income received when in employment.
Source: Institute of Fiscal Studies data.

The impact of the cuts in benefit and the restriction of benefits paid as of right reduces the role of social security to that of a minimum provider of last resort. The earnings-related supplements and payments of mortgage interest[6] were both intended to cushion people in their first few months of unemployment as they adjusted to reductions in their living standards and to enable people to move between jobs without suffering major disruptions to their income levels or living conditions. Now there is a minimum floor, with even housing payments increasingly standardized, and increasingly no one is spared from pressure to take low-paying jobs, even if they would then require considerable subsidy from the state in the form of income support benefits. The effects of the changes in the social security system are reflected in the much smaller percentage of claimants where the benefits received represent even 50% of their previous income levels (see Table 5). This change to a minimum support system is also evident in the major reform of the state occupational pension scheme, which reduces the proportion of earnings paid as pensions from 25% to 20% and reduces entitlement particularly for widows and those who have spent periods in part-time or low-paid employment.

The government's family policy oscillates between the reestablishment of the nuclear family and the dependent wife, to the encouragement of the participation by women in the labor market as this increases the supply of labor for low-paid jobs and reduces the welfare costs of dependents. Thus the government has not been slow to cut entitlement to widow's benefits on the grounds that most women now work and to reduce widow's pension entitlement from 100% to 50% of her husband's pension, but in calculating entitlements to pensions in their own right, women who spend whole years out of the labor force are in some circumstances better protected than women who participate at low wages (Lynes 1986). Similarly the government would ideally have liked to have transformed the tax system to benefit those couples where the woman is not in employment (Knight, 1983). But the actual scheme

[6]From January 1987, only half the mortgage interest will be paid during the first 4 months of unemployment.

decided on for separate taxation, to be implemented in 1990, will not benefit nonworking wives or affect most women's marginal tax rates. Fear of political opposition from two earner families who now constitute the majority of families and the possibility that such a tax policy would reduce the labor supply for low-paid part-time jobs may explain this decision. The government is also increasing the level and period of family responsibility for children by reducing real values of child benefits, providing low allowances to young people on YTS, and reducing the unemployment benefits for the young. However, it had to backtrack on its plans to extend this to the middle classes by cutting student grants because of opposition from its supporters. Substitution of loans for grants is once more under active consideration.

III. LIMITS TO GOVERNMENT POLICY: POLITICAL AND INDUSTRIAL RESPONSES

A. Political Responses

Economic and labor market policy under the Thatcher administration has been primarily determined by Mrs. Thatcher and a small group of close supporters. Indeed, debate over policy options within the Conservative party has been severely constrained and almost eliminated within the cabinet: The practical use of the discipline of the sack within the Conservative government itself has proved extremely effective in restoring "managerial prerogative" to the Prime Minister, helped by the massive majority in Parliament. Outside the Conservative party, the effectiveness of a political response to these policies by other interests has been constrained in a number of ways: the Labour party was split during the Thatcher government's first period of office and distracted by the rise of the Alliance parties as a potential alternative opposition. Although Labour has to some extent regained control over the position of "official opposition" in the second and third parliaments, that position has itself been weakened by the large Conservative majority. The direct role of trade unions in national politics in Britain has been traditionally weak, with their main political influence coming indirectly through their links with the Labour party. It is a widely held view that trade unions should not be involved in politics, and even trade disputes with a political purpose are not considered legitimate. The period when the trade unions were most actively involved in national politics was under the Social Contract between the Labour party and the trade unions in the 1974–1979 Labour government. The Thatcher government, elected in 1979, regarded this incipient "corporatism" as a threat to democracy and refused to negotiate directly with trade unions or even consult with them. This denial of any legitimate role for trade unions in the debate over national policy issues has forced the trade unions back into their traditional strongholds, that of workplace- and industry-based collective bargaining and left the Trades Union Congress floundering for a role, alternating between seeking any possible form of consultation, and making symbolic gestures of withdrawing in protest from tripartite bodies that, in any case, are largely ignored by the current government. The Confederation of British Industry (CBI) has hardly received any better treatment: Industry is expected loyally to support the Conservative government, and even mild suggestions, for example, the abolition of the employers' national insurance surcharge, have been treated as unwarranted interference.

The traditional channels for political response at the national level have proved ineffective and still appear unpromising. The most effective external political constraints on the government's policies have come from Labour-controlled local authorities, but this opposition has been weakened by the government's decision to abolish metropolitan authorities, thereby removing the institutions around which opposition was organized.

Internal constraints, that is, the government's own perception of the limits or constraints to the policy of "freeing-up" the market have probably been the main reason why in many respects it has stopped short of pursuing its policy to its logical conclusions. For example, it has not directly attacked the legitimacy of *voluntary* collective bargaining, and it has largely retained the institutions of collective bargaining in the public sector. One of the reasons for this "restraint" is that the industrial structure and social context in which this labor market policy is being implemented does not fit with the competitive industrial structure on which the model is based (Moore, 1982). What precisely does it mean to fix wages by free market forces in an economy where the public sector and large corporations together account for the majority of employment? Unless it can answer these questions, the government cannot carry this policy through. Attempts to substitute "cash limits" for "market forces" have not been fully successful: Cash limits are generally seen as government-determined edicts and not as the workings of impersonal and unchangeable market forces.

The government has also recognized the need to meet the expectations of real living standards of its main political supporters. Real wages for those in employment and in particular those in middle-income, white-collar employment were protected by cheap imports resulting from high exchange rates in the early years of the administration and more recently by declining world prices. Plans to cut elements of the social wage, for example, by switching from student grants to loans, were postponed because of their effects on middle-income voters. The general difficulties experienced in reducing levels of current public expenditure because of its effects on established expectations constrained the government's program of public expenditure cuts, once all the cuts in capital expenditure had been made. Later, in the run up to the election of June 1987, the government recognized the need to meet increasing concern with the provision of health and education services by increasing public expenditures funded by the profits of privatization instead of higher taxes.

Finally, the government has tried to avoid direct confrontations with the most powerful sections of the labor movement, first, by using a "variable" cash limits policy and, second, by making selective use of its new legislation, for example, by not using it directly against the miners. This step-by-step approach may in the end prove to be a very powerful weapon; by attacking the weakest segments first, the ground may be better prepared for confronting the "core."

B. Industrial Responses

The outcome of the government's labor market policies is critically dependent on the responses by employers and workers. The attempt by the previous Conservative government to change labor market behavior through the 1971 Industrial Relations Act failed because of the solid opposition of the unions and the lack of enthusiasm by employers to take up the opportunities to use legal sanctions to regulate and control industrial relations. It is in contrast to that spectacular failure that the policies of the Thatcher government in industrial relations must be considered. There is emerging evidence that unions have changed their procedures and behavior, including using secret ballots and withholding support from secondary action, in the light of the new regulations, and even those unions that have come into direct conflict with the law and refused to observe injunctions have not maintained outright resistance to the law and have eventually "purged their contempt."[7] Employers also have been found to have used the law in their handling of industrial disputes to an extent thought unlikely after the failure of the 1971 act. For example, Evans (1985) found that a relatively large minority of employers used injunctions to control picketing after the 1980 legislation was passed, even if the object of the injunctions was to bring the disputes to some kind of resolution rather than to penalize the unions: Moreover, the majority of the major disputes have involved some recourse to the law, even if, as in the case of the miners' strike, it was individuals choosing to make use of legislation already on the statute book prior to 1979.[8] In short, there indeed appears to have been a major change in climate where use of the law by both sides and indeed by individuals has become a normal or expected part of the conduct of industrial disputes.

These changes in industrial relations behavior, even though significant, must, however, be considered in context. Fosh and Littler's analysis (1985) of the use of law in several major disputes suggests that the extent to which legal sanctions are pursued depends on the particular nature of the dispute. Where firms are engaged in radically transforming the system of competition and the form of industrial organization, then they are likely to use the law to the limit; for example, in the disputes over the privatization of British Telecom and in the newspaper industry. Where a company is not engaged in radical restructuring, it is less likely to involve the law and more likely to withdraw from its use without invoking full penalties.

---

[7] The two most notable examples were provided by the miners' union and the print workers SOGAT 82 in their dispute with Rupert Murdoch over firing print workers and opening a new plant manned by electricians.

[8] In the miners' strike, the main use of the law involved individual miners taking cases against their own union for not following the rule book.

Moreover, these changes in behavior with respect to the conduct of industrial disputes are not indicative of a widespread collapse of the labor movement or of the institutions of collective bargaining. One of the more surprising outcomes of the Conservative government's legislation on secret ballots, at least to the instigators of the legislation, was that when unions held ballots to establish whether or not to have a political fund (which are used in general to support the Labour party), the overwhelming majority voted in favor.

Levels of union membership have also remained remarkable intact, once adjustments are made to account for loss at membership through redundancy (Rubery, 1986, Table 3-6, p. 81). Surveys find no evidence of a widespread dismantling of collective bargaining at plant level (Batstone, 1984; Edwards, 1986). Moreover, although many wage settlements have declined, real wage levels for those in employment have been rising relatively fast, particularly in the private sector, and there have been very few instances of wage cutting or roll-back agreements such as were concluded in the United States. Evidence of a widening dispersion of company settlements (Brown 1986) can also be taken as an indicator of the continuation in general of relatively strong plant-level bargaining against the background of a wide dispersion of the ability of firms to pay.

The main problem for British trade unions has been that their traditional strength at the plant level does not provide a very suitable basis on which to develop a united and coherent defense against national government policy. The public sector has in fact provided the forum for the main opposition to Thatcher's policies for two reasons. It is public sector pay that has been directly controlled through cash limits, and it is in the public sector that the most radical restructuring has been implemented, through the rationalization of nationalized industries and through the privatization of services. The major fights against rationalization in steel, cars, and coal revealed the weakness of the traditional plant-based forms of worker organizations against the consolidated power of a public sector employer backed by an intransigent government. For example, the miners' strike failed not only because of the unyielding stance by the government and the National Coal Board (NCB) but because of the divisions between the safe and profitable pits and vulnerable pits.

However, the campaigns by the service workers in the public sector, in health and education, have both demonstrated the potential importance of the newer forms of unionization, among both low-grade and professional service and nonmanual workers and have played a major role in increasing public awareness of the declines in the health and education services. These concerns were directly responsible for the change in public expenditure policy in 1986, allowing for increases in spending on the services in the period leading up to the election. The political importance of these campaigns is probably greater than their actual economic achievements, even though fights against privatization have done much to slow down its spread through alerting local politicians and administrators to the inherent problems and dangers associated with a loss of direct control and reductions in resources made available for cleaning and other services. Even the central government has occasionally been apparently forced into a change of policy as a result of concerted industrial action. For example, the teachers' campaign for higher pay in 1985 led to an agreement to fund a much larger pay increase in 1986/1987, provided that the teachers agreed to changes in their contract conditions.

However, the government is also taking action to reduce the opportunities for public sector workers to utilize their collective strength in the future, by, for example, recommending local authorities to withdraw from national agreements and by imposing centralized control over teachers' pay so as to reduce solidarity between local authority employers and unions in their demands for higher funding for education. These strategies increase the likelihood that internal struggles between workers and employers over the sharing-out a given cake will overshadow the objective of increasing the size of the available cake, thereby reducing effective political opposition.

IV. CONCLUSION

Government policies to free-up the labor market have not resulted in the creation of a competitive labor market with the neoclassical hallmarks of competitive equalization of prices, increased flexibility and mobility and real wage levels responsive to overall conditions of demand and supply. Employees have become relatively more attached to their firms, with turnover rates falling even when involuntary quits are included and peoples' chances in the labor market have become more and more dependant on the circumstances of their employing organization. This dependency applies to pay as well as to job security, with differentials widening between public and private sectors and dispersions of wage settlements within the private sector also increasing. Moreover, this dispersion of wage settlements has taken place around a generally upward trend in real wages for those in work. Thus there has been no simple movement toward competitive wage determination, with all firms taking the opportunity to pay labor in "excess supply" at low wages. Firm-specific pay structures have remained intact, bolstered and maintained by their institutions of collective bargaining. Some widening of differentials has occurred within companies, but the most significant changes in the overall pay structure have probably come about through structural and sectoral change, on the one hand from the increasing importance of service sectors and of small firms in the private sector and, on the other hand, from the relative lowering of public service worker pay, both for those employed by the public sector and for those working for private contractors providing public services.

Deregulated labor markets are thus not synonymous with *competitive* labor markets; they increase the scope for inequality primarily by removing protection from the weak and not by exposing all groups to competition. Moreover deregulated labor markets have in practice required a more frequent recourse to the law in order to regulate the system of industrial relations. This greater involvement of the law is probably an irreversible development, for, if the Conservative government is defeated, opposition parties have recognized that a policy of simply sweeping away industrial relations legislation and returning to a voluntarist system is no longer either an acceptable nor a desirable option. The ease with which the protection afforded to the weaker segments by the voluntarist system has been dismantled indicates the need for a much more positive use of the law to establish minimum levels of protection (Deakin, 1986). The Labour party is proposing to adopt a bill of positive employment rights and to establish a legal minimum wage. Thus whatever the outcome of future elections, this period of active labor market policy by a Conservative government has brought about a permanent break with the voluntarist traditions, which had, however, already been substantially modified in the 1960s and 1970s by the rapid growth of labor legislation.

V. REFERENCES

Batstone, E. (1984). *Working order*. Oxford: Blackwell.
Brown, W. (1986). Facing up to incomes policy. In P. Nolan & S. Paine (Eds.), *Rethinking socialist economics* (pp. 341–355). Oxford: Polity Press.
Burns, A., Newby, M., & Winterton, J. (1985). The restructuring of the British coal industry. *Cambridge Journal of Economics, 9*, 93–110.
Central Statistical Office. *Economic trends*. London: HMSO.
Deakin, S. (1986). *Deregulation, social legislation, and positive rights*. Paper presented to the 8th Annual Conference of the International Working Party on Labor Market Segmentation, Cambridge.
Department of Employment. *Employment gazette*. London: HMSO.
Edwards, P. (1986). Myth of the macho manager. *Personnel Management*, April, 32–35.
Evans, S. (1985). Picketing under the Employment Acts. In P. Fosh and C. Littler (Eds.), *Industrial relations and law in the 1980s* (pp. 118–152). Aldershot: Gower.
Fosh, P., & Littler, C. (Eds.). (1985). *Industrial relations and labor law in the 1980s*. Aldershot: Gower.
Goldstein, N. (1984). The new training initiative: A great leap backwards. *Capital and Class*, No. 23, 83–106.
Hansard. House of Commons Parliamenting Debates. Official Reports. London: HMSO.
Incomes Data Services. (1983). *Young workers pay*. Study 291. London: Incomes Data Services.
Knight, E. (1983). Women and the UK tax system: The case for reform. *Cambridge Journal of Economics, 7*, 151–165.
Lynes, T. (1986). How Fowler's benefits work. *New Society*, August 1.
Moore, R. (1982). Free market economics, trade union law, and the labor market. *Cambridge Journal of Economics, 6*, 297–315.
New Earnings Survey. (1970–1985). London: HMSO.
Rubery, J. (1986). Trade unions in the 1980s: The case of the United Kingdom. In R. Edwards, P. Garonna, & F. Tödtling (Eds.), *Unions in crisis and beyond: Perspectives from six countries* (pp. 61–113). Dover, MA: Auburn House.
Shutt, J. (1984). Tory enterprise zones and the labor movement. *Capital and Class*, No. 23, 19–44.
Ward, T. S., & Nield, R. (1978). *The measurement and reform of budgetary policy*. London: Heinemann.

3

Fissure and Discontinuity in U.S. Labor Management Relations

Michael J. Piore

The industrial relations system of the United States has, in the last several years, come under significant pressure. The central role of unions and collective bargaining in the determination of wages and employment conditions is for the first time in the postwar period being called into question. There has been a rapid growth in the nonunion sector. Employers have become increasingly aggressive in their efforts to establish and maintain nonunion establishments. With the election of Ronald Reagan, the federal government turned hostile toward unions and to the social and economic programs of the trade union movement, and most of those programs have been cut back or eliminated. The union membership base was further eroded by the 1981–1982 recession that has been especially severe in the areas of greatest union strength, like autos, steel, and rubber, and the declining membership base has strained labor's financial resources and made it increasingly difficult to defend itself. Finally, a large number of unions have been forced to engage in concession bargaining and to relinquish contract provisions that had been won gradually over the postwar period.

The significance of these developments is the subject of a growing debate among industrial relations practitioners and academic observers of the U.S. industrial scene (Katz, 1985). One side in that debate sees recent developments as simply another shift in the perpetual oscillation of power between labor and management which the U.S. system is designed to accommodate (Dunlop, 1982; Mitchell, 1982). But some of us see these developments as the markers of fundamental change in the very structure of the system itself. This chapter develops that argument. The contention is not that the industrial

Michael J. Piore • Department of Economics, Massachusetts Institute of Technology, Cambridge, Massachusetts 02139.

relations system has actually collapsed. The strains that have been placed upon it have been accommodated in a way that preserves the outline of the original framework and would permit its restoration in a more favorable economic and political climate. The reemergence of a climate of this kind is, however, very problematic.

I. THE CHARACTERISTICS OF THE POSTWAR SYSTEM

To appreciate the strains that the system is now under, it is first necessary to identify what the system has been. A complete description is impossible in a chapter of this kind, but the essential elements may be summarized as follows: Prior to the Great Depression, union organization in the United States was confined to a small group of skilled craft workers. The mass production industries that had come to dominate the economic structure in the early twentieth century had successfully resisted union organizations. In the Depression, however, two events changed this pattern. First, national legislation was passed favoring union organization and collective bargaining and creating a framework through which workers could establish governmentally protected unions through a majority vote within the shop or enterprise. Second, the major mass production industries (among them, autos, steel, and rubber) were organized in a spontaneous wave of worker protests, and the newly formed unions were recognized by their respective employers who entered into collective bargaining agreements with them. This mass organization occurred outside the framework of the legislation, but the unions were then able to use the moral and financial support of the newly organized workers to consolidate their gains through government-supervised elections, and they proceeded to do so in World War II and the immediate postwar period. The acceptance by big business of union organization and collective bargaining set the tone for the business community as a whole. Union organization remained confined to a relatively small portion of the labor force compared to other countries. But collective bargained wages and working conditions set the pattern for the economy. The threat of nonunion competition was contained by social legislation mandating minimum wages and labor standards and by the capacity of the labor movements to organize nonunion shops that got too far out of line. Labor's political power forced legislated standards to pace bargaining gains, and other wages, pressed by legislation from below and pulled by union bargains from above, followed.

The procedures and practices of the newly organized unions in collective bargaining and in the shop were worked out, under governmental supervision, in the World War II period and consolidated through negotiations and experimentation in the immediate postwar years. By 1950, it was possible to speak of a national "accommodation" between labor and management that governed industrial relations in the United States from that time up until at least 1970. Some observers have spoken of a *compact* or *accord*, but in my view, what is at stake is much more a system of shared understandings, some elements of which were explicit, but many of which were defined by practices and procedures that were only partially articulated. Elsewhere, I have tried to summarize the nature of those understandings in three points (Piore, 1983). First, the understandings rested upon a particular diagnosis of the economic crisis of the 1930s. That diagnosis was legitimized by Keynesian economics, although it was not exactly Keynesian economics as taught by economists. Basically, it was an underconsumptionist view of the Great Depression. The view, in brief, held that at the heart of the economy was a series of mass production industries producing, or linked to industries that were producing, mass consumption goods. The Depression had been caused by the failure of purchasing power to keep pace with the productive capacity of these industries. It had been cured by the government demand for mass produced war material in World War II, and the resurgence of the Depression could be prevented by sustaining the purchasing power of the consumers whose spending replaced that of government when the latter declined at the war's end. This view was widely shared among Americans generally. It created a rationale for institutions like unions that sustained purchasing power by placing upward pressure on wages and for much of the substantive legislation that unions supported, like the minimum wage, social security, and unemployment insurance, for these also sustained mass consumption.

This understanding provided the background for a 1948 agreement between General Motors and the United Automobile Workers in which the parties established the principle that annual wage increases equal 3% plus the cost of living. The 3%, known as the annual improvement factor, represented the historic long-term rate of productivity increase. This formula became key to wage determination throughout the economy. It was spread from the automobile industry, through pattern bargaining in the unionized sector, social legislation and the threat of unionization in the unorganized private sector, and the administrative procedures of wage determination in the public sector. It insured that national purchasing power would expand at the same rate as national productive capacity.

The second component of the understandings that defined labor's place in the postwar period was a particular set of institutions and mechanisms regulating practices in the shop and controlling income, job security, and industrial democracy. The institutions revolve around a system of highly articulated and sharply delimited jobs assigned to a particular worker and surrounded by complexes of specific rules, customs, and precedents concerning how the work is to be done and the obligations of the worker to the employer. Thus current income is controlled by attaching to each of these specific jobs a particular wage rate. Unions control career income by rules governing the allocation of internal job vacancies among candidates for promotion. Job security is maintained by a set of rules that determine in case of economic layoff which workers are unemployed and how the remaining work is allocated among the labor force. Industrial democracy has been reduced to a particular form of industrial jurisprudence in which work and disciplinary standards are clearly defined and fairly administered and disputes over the application of rules and customs are impartially adjudicated. The workings of this system require that jobs are unambiguously defined and changes in job definitions and work assignments be sharply delimited; if this is not the case, it is meaningless to attach specific wages and employment rights to them, and the governing rules and customs become too ambiguous to be effectively administered through the grievance procedure.

This system is clearly not the only way in which income, job security, and industrial democracy are effectuated, even in the United States. In the craft unions that predate the Great Depression, there is much more of a tendency to define wages in terms of skill levels and to use work sharing rather than reallocation by seniority to effect job security. Craft contracts, particularly in construction, are frequently tailored to (or "renegotiated in the light of") the requirements of specific projects in a process that is not unlike worker participation, or at least union leadership participation, in management. These practices, however, have over the postwar period increasingly been revised and reoriented so that they conform more closely to the model sketched out here.

The precise origins of this system of shop regulation are obscure. It appears, however, that they are best understood as an adaptation of the newly formed industrial unions in the 1930s to the technology and managerial practice that American industry had developed for the mass production of standardized goods. The work had previously been broken down into a discrete set of clearly defined jobs by industrial engineers, following the practices codified by Frederick Taylor and his disciples; wage determination had already been linked to these specified jobs through time–motion studies and job evaluation; many of the work standards, disciplinary procedures, and grievance processes had already been codified and formalized in the attempt of high-level management to assert their central authority over the foreman at the point of production that was required to obtain coordination in mass production. The unions thus found a whole set of mechanisms already in place; they sought first to insure conformity with established principles in order to curtail favoritism and capriciousness in shop management and, in so doing, were drawn into a bargaining relationship about the substance of the work process that presupposed these basic managerial instruments and procedures and focused upon their content rather than upon the instruments and institutions themselves. Practices that grew up in this way in the mass production industry then became standards by which labor relations in other industries were judged and evaluated, and a set of national labor relations and labor market institutions developed that gradually shaped practice in all industries to conform to the mass production model. Labor legislation, for example, made a sharp distinction between workers and supervisors and defined a set of "managerial" prerogatives outside the scope of mandatory bargaining that made the craft mode of job control difficult to maintain. Similarly, the unemployment insurance system excluded involuntary part-time workers, thus favoring the industrial union practice of layoffs over the old craft model of work sharing.

The third important component of the understandings governing post-war American industrial relations was the labor movement's attempt to present itself to American society as the spearhead of a broad, progressive coalition, whose concerns extended to the whole structure and substance of American life. Labor was aided in this effort by Keynesian theory, which gave labor a special role in sustaining economic prosperity, but it also brought with it broad social commitments growing out of the Depression experience. This is not to deny labor's extensive activity on behalf of its immediate constituencies and the pursuit of narrow political goals designed to further the particular interests of those members at the workplace. It does emphasize, however, the very broad social program to which these particular goals were attached. As I have argued elsewhere, the kind of industrial unions that came to dominate American labor relations in the postwar period could not have survived without attaching their narrow program to a broad, political appeal (Piore, 1980). They had to do this first because their existence was predicated upon the protective legislative framework buttressed by supportive judicial and administrative rulings that could never have been justified to the American electorate, let alone the courts, on the narrow particularistic grounds of business unionism. But, it had to do this also because the economic gains of the unionized sector depended upon containing the nonunion establishments in a band whose lower floor was defined by the minimum wage provisions of the Fair Labor Standards Act as amended periodically to keep up with inflation and productivity. Labor's political program thus went well beyond anything understandable in terms of narrow particular interests to include social security benefits, what we now call equal employment opportunity, and national medical insurance.

II. THE PRESSURES OF THE LAST DECADE

The strains that the system is now under have cumulated over the last 15 years. The most significant of these would appear to be the fact that unions have lost control over the political process, and the legislative framework in which the postwar system was embedded has, as a result, progressively deteriorated. In retrospect, the most significant event in this process was the 1972 election in which the Democratic party, over the strong opposition of organized labor, nominated the antiwar candidate George McGovern and the AFL-CIO withdrew from the campaign in a way that favored the reelection of Richard Nixon. But this event symbolized the split between labor and other members of the progressive coalition that had begun in the middle 1960s over the war in Vietnam and various conflicts between collective bargaining and new legislation—legislation that ironically would not have been passed without labor's lobbying efforts on its behalf—favoring the rights of racial minorities and women and imposing governmentally defined standards protecting health and safety, the environment, consumers, and the like. As a result of this split, labor came increasingly to be perceived, and to perceive itself, as a special interest group, pursuing the narrow, particularistic claims of its own members, and lost its position as chief spokesman of a larger progressive coalition representing a broad set of humanitarian values.

Its political weakness was reflected in increasing difficulties in organizing new workers. After 1965, the number of National Labor Relations Board (NLRB) elections, that unions managed to generate and the number of workers whom they succeeded in organizing in this way began to decline, and after 1970, the decline was precipitous and dramatic. The decline appears to be clearly the result of changes in the interpretation of the basic labor legislation in ways that made it easier for employers to intimidate their workers (Freeman, 1985; Klein & Wanger, 1985). The shifting interpretations reflected the changing composition of the NLRB and the courts. There remained a substantial pool of unorganized workers favorably disposed to unions, and support for trade unions among unorganized workers was particularly high among women and blacks, and even in the traditionally hard-to-organize South, once other attributes are taken into account (Farber, 1985). In Canada, with a very similar institutional framework but a much more favorable political climate and a resolution in favor of unions of a series of legal issues that have been resolved against unions in the United States, the labor movement has managed to expand over the period of U.S. contraction (Meltz, 1985).

Within the legal climate, increasingly favorable to them, employers developed new strategies of what they euphemistically called "union avoidance." These included aggressive antiunion tactics in organizing campaigns and an attempt to locate new production facilities in areas where workers were believed to be least hospitable to union organization and the political authorities most tolerant of the new tactics of intimidation. But it also included managerial techniques designed to avoid the abuses of authority that had been conducive to organization in the past and to encourage worker identification with the enterprise and its goals (Verma & Kochan, 1985). As part of these efforts, nonunion plants began to move away from Tayloristic forms of work organization around which the union system of job control had developed and to replace them with more flexible job assignments and greater work participation in decisions that had previously been reserved for management. A gap thus began to emerge between work practices in the union and the nonunion sector, and to the extent that the system of job definitions and control has been critical to the postwar industrial relations system, this, too, began to crack.

These changes in managerial attitudes were formally signaled to the labor movement in the battle for labor law reform in 1977–1978. Organized labor saw the reform legislation as essentially designed to restore its capacity to maintain its base that had been weakening through progressive court interpretations. There is no indication that the business community saw it in different terms. The determined, and ultimately successful, campaign of opposition by the organized business community and the acquiescence in that campaign of the major corporate leaders thus spelled the end of the postwar understandings. Clearly, the business community was no longer committed to operate in an environment in which collective bargaining established the norms for the economy as a whole. And in retrospect, it seems only a matter of time after that before the threat of nonunion competition became so great that it was capable of setting the standards for the unionized sector.

The concession bargaining of the early 1980s, which is certainly the most dramatic if not the most significant sign of the defensive position in which labor now finds itself, must be understood in these terms. The major industrial unions have been forced to reopen their contracts early, and negotiate new agreements decidedly less favorable to their work force. The exact dimensions of this phenomenon are difficult to gauge. In a 1982 *Business Week* survey, 36% of the firms contacted suggested that they had engaged in concession bargaining. Most of these "concessions" have taken place in firms, which were actually experiencing serious competitive pressure and often in extreme financial distress, but the more general nature of the phenomenon is suggested by the fact that 11% of the enterprises surveyed by *Business Week* and involved in concession bargaining reported no particular problems of this kind (Capelli & McKersie, 1985).[1]

Concession bargaining is not itself something new. As several observers have pointed out, American unions have generally been willing to make accommodations when their industries were in economic distress and they thought such accommodations would forestall significant job loss (Mitchell, 1982). There have been other periods when the number of such accommodations were large enough to attract national attention, most notably the late 1950s. What has been called *concession bargaining,* moreover, has not all been a one-way street. Some unions have made potentially important gains in job security, profit sharing, and participation in management in return for what was given up in terms of wages and work rules. And the concessions have been limited to very specific industrial sectors.

What makes the recent round of concession bargaining significant is the strategic importance in the postwar industrial relations system of what is being conceded. In particular, the 3% plus cost-of-living formula has been compromised in autos and steel: The role of these industries as pattern setters for the wage level of the economy as a whole has been compromised. And although the pressure for concessions in these two industries seems to derive primarily from foreign competition and the 1981–1982 depression, other sectors have been under heavy pressure from nonunion competitors suggesting that the role of organized industry as a pattern setter has also been compromised. Finally, concessions in work rules have moved away from the basic job control model. To the extent that work rules concessions are moving toward an identifiable pattern, it appears also to be the system of shop organization pioneered in nonunion establishments.

One speaks here of *compromise* because the new contracts were carefully worded to preserve the principles involved and to define the particular circumstances in which they were no longer being applied as exceptional. Thus,

[1]See Capelli and McKersie (1985) for a detailed analysis of the concession bargaining of 1982.

for example, the wage increases under the 3% improvement factor in automobiles were "postponed," not eliminated. The cost of living allowance (COLA) in basic steel was "temporarily suspended." The most far-reaching changes in work rules and the system of job control were introduced through quality of work life programs that were classified as "experimental." The fact that the concessions were made in this way suggests just how fundamental the issues upon which they touched were to the basic nature of the system as perceived by the bargaining parties.

But although the phraseology would facilitate a return to the basic system, it will not alone insure that the return takes place. That will depend upon whether the environmental factors militating in favor of these concessions abate. And to know whether or not that is likely to happen, one must turn from the language of the concessions to examine the circumstances under which they have been made.

III. ENVIRONMENTAL PRESSURES

Three factors seem to have created the pressures for bargaining concessions. One of these is the declining influence of the trade union movement over the political climate in which they are operating and the resultant deterioration in the legal protection of the right to organize and collectively bargain mentioned before.

The second factor that has severely undermined union strength is the economic climate, the recession of 1981–1982, the deterioration of the United States' position on world markets, and deregulation in the trucking and airline industry. This economic climate, however, is also the product of American politics. The recession is the deliberate creation of the Federal Reserve Board and its policy of high interest rates. The high interest rates have in turn driven up the value of the dollar relative to other currencies. The gains in the dollar value and the resultant increase in the price of our goods relative to those of our competitors is thus more than equal to the value of the concessions in the steel and auto contracts under even the most extreme assumptions about what they are worth. The concessions are, in other words, merely compensating for the *cost* effects of domestic economic policy. The same effect would have been achieved at no expense to the union or the industrial relations system through Federal Reserve policy, either in the domestic market to bring down interest rates or in international currency markets, to stabilize the dollar at a different level. The other factor responsible for the deterioration of our competitive position has been the competition of the newly developing Third World countries directly and indirectly through the pressures they have created on our principal industrial competitors, particularly Japan. Here too, American politics has intensified this competition: Most of these Third World regimes have pursued a low-wage, low-consumption policy, not only through their monetary and fiscal policies but also through the direct suppression of worker organizations. The United States has encouraged them in these ends both by lending support to overtly suppressive political regimes and by support for the International Monetary Fund (IMF) policy that imposes as a condition for debt refinancing even more restrictive domestic economic policies. Finally, of course, governmental deregulation is itself a public policy. There have been variations in the intensity with which these various policies have been pursued over the last few years; they have been harsher under the Reagan administration than under the Carter administration, but there has been a basic continuity in the thrust of policy under both administrations.

The third factor responsible for the deterioration of the trade union position, however, is a long-run structural shift in the position of the industries in which unions have been strong in the world economy. Although a number of analysts subscribe to the notion that basic structural changes are in process and are responsible for the social and economic problems of the last decade, there is no consensus about what those structural shifts are. I would place primary emphasis upon a shift from a technological dynamic associated with mass production to one that favors economies in smaller scale operations and encourages flexibility in the product and process. Several factors are favoring this development. One of these is the fact that stable, growing mass markets for standardized products that will support mass production technologies were increasingly difficult to create and sustain in the last decade. In most industrial countries, the domestic markets for the kinds of consumer durables that had supported this type of expansion earlier in the postwar period became saturated. The established producers thus came into competition with each other for existing markets and those of the developing world. But there were no institutional mechanisms that insured the expansion of these world markets at a rate sufficient to absorb the output of all of these producers. Competition was further intensified by the entrance of a number of newly developing countries into industries like automobiles, steel, and electronics, with modern mass production technologies purchased in the industrialized countries but with repressive wage policies that added nothing to world demand for the kinds of products they were producing. Mass production technologies have also been penalized by the uncertainty and variability of the parameters of business decisions: the fluctuations in the price of basic raw materials, especially fuel; the fluctuation in relative currency values under the regime of flexible exchange rates introduced in 1971; the fluctuations in the rate and direction of national economic activity as individual countries tried to cope with the effects of the oil price shocks; and so on. This climate penalized the investment in specialized capital equipment dedicated to particular product designs entailed by mass production and favored technologies that were more flexible and enabled the firm to move rapidly around in the market as demand shifted and the prices of various kinds of materials changed. Finally, flexible technologies were encouraged by the rapid development of computers and computer-aided production processes that made some of the savings previously available only in mass production available in much smaller production runs. With computers, changes in production processes or the product that previously would have required the purchase of a whole new set of machines can now be made simply by reprogramming existing equipment.

Because we in the United States pioneered in mass production, our institutional structure was the most completely oriented toward and adapted to long runs of standardized products. We have therefore found it most difficult to compete in the new economic environment that was increasingly ill adapted to this form of production, and we have been slower than our competitors to adjust our institutions and modes of throught to the requirements of the new environment. In recent years, however, the major corporations have begun to experiment with forms of management, work organization, and new corporate structures that provide the kinds of flexibility that the new environment seems to require. And this has made them increasingly impatient with trade union structures and modes of work control that grew up in the age of mass production and were oriented toward its requirements. In climates in which unions were stronger politically and on the offensive in the shop, business might have been forced to develop these new organizational forms through collective bargaining in consultation with the work force. But given the general weakness of the trade union movement and the resistance from other elements of the corporate structure, these new developments tended to take place in new nonunion facilities outside the purview and control of the labor movement. And this in turn has aggravated the problems of the labor movement. Management has come to associate these new, more competitive forms with nonunion status. The labor movement has been discouraged by its isolation from these organizational innovations, and its lack of familiarity with them causes them to confuse the changes with the antiunion biases of the managements that generated them. These innovations are in fact more conducive to underlying trade union values and goals than older work forms associated with mass production.

IV. THE RESOLUTION OF THE CRISIS

The new climate has also eliminated the Keynesian rationale for unions because the national markets that they sustain are no longer sufficient to maintain American industry and necessitated new forms of macroeconomic organization as well. If we are correct in pinpointing the demise of mass production as the major structural factor, it is possible to envisage two distinct resolutions of the current economic crisis. One of these would be to reconstruct on an international scale a system of stable, expanding mass markets comparable to the systems that governed the expansion of the major industrial countries prior to 1971—a kind of international Keynesianism. Such a system would require the participation of some, but by no means all, of the underdeveloped countries, for these countries contain the latent demand for the mass produced goods upon which the expansion would have to rest. The threat of exclusion would probably be sufficient to bring enough of the underdeveloped world into the system to make it work. The necessity of renegotiating the debt of the Third World provides the industrial world, particularly the United States, with the leverage necessary to start the negotiating process and probably to force it through to a successful conclusion. But the policies implied by this resolution of the crisis are almost precisely the opposite of those which the Reagan administration is pursuing internationally. They are basically policies of expansion rather than restraint and policies of managed international markets rather than of competition. The world would have to return to a system of fixed exchange rates and enough international liquidity to permit the adjustment through long-term structural policies. Individual countries would have to agree to expand their own domestic demand and forego competition by driving down wages and other measures that repress consumer purchasing power. Major commodity markets would have to be stabilized, both to forestall the wide swings in the price of critical materials that have characterized the last decade and deterred long-term business planning and to stabilize and maintain demand in countries that are dependent on commodity sales for their income. The system would, in addition, probably require some kind of international industrial policy to resolve conflicts among nations over the location of industrial activity and, for the United States, the creation of national institutions that could effectively represent our interests in this process.

The postwar U.S. industrial relations system is readily comparable with an international structure of this kind, and were such a structure to develop quickly, one could easily imagine that the principles and institutional forms that have been compromised in the past several years would be restored. But the role that trade unions have played in the postwar period is not crucial to a Keynesian system of this kind. Mass producers in the United States developed stable labor management relations systems and managed to sustain national purchasing power in the early decade of the twentieth century without unions, and many of the emergent institutional structures in nonunion enterprises are reminiscent of that earlier period. Thus, even an international Keynesian economic order is unlikely alone to restore the system that is currently in the process of degeneration. For that, trade unions would probably have to recoup the power they have lost in the political sphere. The one caveat here is that, in the United States, the economic policies antagonistic to an international Keynesian system are so closely linked to antiunion politics that it is hard to imagine a shift in one without a shift in the other. In other words, a political atmosphere favorable to union growth and development is very likely to induce a reversal in U.S. economic policy as well. In the current climate, however, it is very difficult to imagine either.

The alternative to an international Keynesian economic order could be the adjustment of economic structures and institutions to accommodate more flexible forms of production and heterogeneous products. Very little of the older industrial relations system is likely to survive under these circumstances. This poses a twofold problem for the labor movement. The first is to develop new trade union institutions that are consistent with the emergent economic order and capable of providing worker protection within it. This is a problem labor does not face under international Keynesianism. The second is essentially the same as that which labor faces in mass production: to create a place for these new labor institutions within the emergent economic and social order.

Space does not permit a detailed examination of the institutional problem. There is a definite place for trade unions in a system of flexible production. The economic environment under such a system exerts enormous competitive pressure. These pressures will generate dynamic economic growth only if they are channeled into product-and-process innovation. This is a perpetual temptation, however, for enterprises to respond to competition in the short run by cutting labor costs, reducing wages, and exploiting the work force. Unions foreclose this option. When properly structured, they also create an atmosphere of trust and cooperation in which the on-line experience of the work force can be brought to bear in the perpetual redesign of the product and the production process. Historically, it is much more difficult to find examples of dynamic systems of flexible production without strong work organization than it is to find dynamic systems of mass production.[2]

The actual form that such trade union organization would take depends upon the industrial organization in which systems of flexible production are housed. In the United States, such systems have been found in the past in regional groupings of relatively small firms that continually recombine with each other to form a flexible, shifting productive structure. Among contemporary industries, the vestiges of this organizational form can be found in garments and in construction. Trade unions in these industries have historically achieved their power to protect the work force by assuming critical intermediary functions within the market, providing vocational training, running hiring halls and referral services, managing pensions and unemployment insurance systems, providing technical expertise, and catalyzing technological development. With the advent of industrial unionism in the 1930s, many of these older craft organizations were eclipsed: Most observers came to see them as the vestiges of premodern industry, and little attention has been paid to their continuing activity. They are almost never mentioned when one surveys the current labor scene. Some of these older craft unions, however, have recently begun to revive and strengthen their traditional activities and concerns. The construction unions in particular have been increasingly involved in technological development through joint activities with management. There are signs that the garment unions and the machinists are moving in this direction as well. Such unions have an additional advantage over the newer industrial unions in the current climate: They are much less dependent for their strength on politics. They have not fared much better than industrial unions in recent years because the economic environment has undermined their organizational base. But because their members are skilled, providing resources that management needs and cannot itself develop, and, because

---

[2]See Piore (1985) for an elaboration of the issues surrounding the role of unions in a system of flexible production.

they are large and stable relative to the enterprises that compose the industry, they can often assume critical functions in training, hiring, and the provisions of technical expertise, which lever their inherent economic power. It would be premature to herald a revival of craft unionism, but developments in this area could well provide the fulcrum for the resurgence of labor power in the emergent economic order.

The major reason to be skeptical about the significance of these developments is that so far American industry is still dominated by large corporate enterprises. These enterprises have been seeking to adapt to the new economic climate by the development of more flexible forms of internal organization. To simplify enormously, they have been seeking to create under the corporate umbrella, the capacity to continually reorganize and recombine that the regional groupings of small firms allied through malleable subcontracting arrangements create in construction and garments. One can argue that this is likely to be a passing organizational phase. Except in certain industries like ship building and aerospace where the product itself is very large and expensive, the large corporations are basically creatures of mass production. The corporate giants, once they have reorganized and decentralized, may thus dissolve. But to the extent that the corporate organization survives, its justification is likely to be in providing precisely the kinds of community services to its components that the union provides in more decentralized structures. There would thus be no natural role for the labor movement in a flexible system housed in large organizations: Labor would have to insert itself into these organizations through the political process as it inserted itself into the industrial relations systems of these corporations in the 1930s. And this brings politics back to center stage.

To the extent that politics is critical, the future of industrial relations in the United States requires a different kind of analysis than that which has been conducted in the body of this chapter. One would have to examine both the internal politics of the AFL-CIO and the political climate of the country as a whole. I believe that labor achieved the political position that secured its role in the postwar industrial relations system through a kind of double bonding. One bonding was between labor and other progressive forces of American society. The second bonding was between that progressive coalition and the American nation. This second bonding was unusual in American politics. Always before, the U.S. electorate conceived of the society as bound up fundamentally with the protection of the individual. To the extent that a group of any kind was representative of national welfare, it was business. But in the Depression—in part because of Keynesian economics—the national economic welfare became associated in the public mind with organized labor and other groups allied to labor that acted to sustain purchasing power and worked through government to secure individual economic well-being.

For much of recent history, the AFL-CIO has been dominated by leaders with a very different reading of history. They see the power of American labor movement as much more fundamentally economic deriving from the skills of craft workers or the capacity of mass industrial unionism to disrupt the economic system. Since the late 1960s, they have, as argued here, paid only lip service to the importance of the bonds with other progressive forces. And they have sought to restore labor's position by maneuvering, quite unsuccessfully, for a new social compact with big business. They see their failure in this regard as due to the weakness of the overall economic climate and its impact upon labor's economic strength. They continue to expect that an economic recovery will revive that strength and force big business into the kind of pact that will restore the postwar system. This, however, is not the only view represented within the labor movement. Trade union membership, moreover, consists increasingly of blacks, women, and other minorities, the very people with whom the progressive alliance must be struck, and this, too, makes the internal policies of the labor movement more open to the alternative than it has been in the past.

But even if the bond with other progressive forces were to be reconstructed, the bond with the American nation would remain problematic. That second bond depends very much on the fate of Reagan's economic policies. In the early 1980s, when those policies were pushing the economy deeper and deeper into recession, it seemed reasonable to hope that events would create anew the opportunity for labor to identify its fate and its policies with the national welfare, as it had in the 1930s. More recently, in the midst of a recovery, Reagan seems more likely to make that identification himself and to use it to preach the lesson that labor is responsible for the ills of the past.

ACKNOWLEDGMENTS An earlier version of this paper was presented to a Conference on Labor Markets, Industrial Policy, and Economic Growth, Stresa, Italy. A large part of the research upon which this paper is based was funded by a fellowship from the International Labour Organization. The argument of the paper has been developed in collaboration with my colleague Charles Sabel and is elaborated further in our book, *The Second Industrial Divide* (Basic Books, 1984). I have also drawn heavily upon the work of my colleagues in the Industrial Relations Section of the Sloan School of Management in a project whose major sponsor is the Sloan Foundation and which has been organized and directed by Thomas Kochan and Robert McKersie. The views expressed here are not necessarily shared, however, by the research sponsors or by my colleagues and collaborators.

V. REFERENCES

Cappelli, P., & McKersie, R. B. (1985). Labor and the crisis in collective bargaining. In T. A. Kochan (Ed.), *Challenges and choices facing American labor* (pp. 227–245). Cambridge, MA: MIT Press.

Dunlop, J. T. (1982). Working towards consensus. *Challenge, 25* (3), 26–34.

Farber, H. (1985). The extent of unionization in the United States. In T. A. Kochan (Ed.), *Challenges and choices facing American labor* (pp. 15–43). Cambridge, MA: MIT Press.

Freeman, R. (1985). Why are unions faring poorly in NLRB representation elections? In T. A. Kochan (Ed.), *Challenges and choices facing American labor* (pp. 45–64). Cambridge, MA: MIT Press.

Katz, H. C. (1985). Collective bargaining in the 1982 bargaining round. In T. A. Kochan (Ed.), *Challenges and choices facing American labor* (pp. 213–226). Cambridge, MA: MIT Press.

Klein, J. A., & Wanger, E. D. (1985). The legal setting for the emergence of the union avoidance strategy. In T. A. Kochan (Ed.), *Challenges and choices facing American labor* (pp. 75–88). Cambridge, MA: MIT Press.

Meltz, N. M. (1985). Labor movements in Canada and the United States. In T. A. Kochan (Ed.), *Challenges and choices facing American labor* (pp. 315–334). Cambridge, MA: MIT Press.

Mitchell, D. B. (1982). Recent union contract concessions. *Brookings Papers on Economic Activity*, No. 1, 165–204.

Piore, M. J. (1980). Unions and politics. In H. A. Juris & M. Roomkin (Eds.), *The shrinking perimeter: Unionism and labor relations in the manufacturing sector* (pp. 173–187). Lexington, MA: Lexington Books, D.C. Heath and Co.

Piore, M. J. (1983). Can the American labor movement survive re-Gomperization? *Proceedings of the 35th Annual Meeting*, Industrial Relations Research Association, 1982 (pp. 30–39). Madison, WI: Industrial Relations Research Association.

Piore, M. J. (1985). Computer technologies, market structure, and strategic union choices. In T. A. Kochan (Ed.), *Challenges and choices facing American labor* (pp. 193–204). Cambridge, MA: MIT Press.

Piore, M. J., & Sabel, C. (1984). *The second industrial divide*. New York: Basic Books.

Verma, A., & Kochan, T. A. (1985). The growth and nature of the nonunion sector within a firm. In T. A. Kochan (Ed.), *Challenges and choices facing American labor* (pp. 89–117). Cambridge, MA: MIT Press.

4

The Restructuring of the Labor Market, the Labor Force, and the Nature of Employment Relations in the United States in the 1980s

Samuel Rosenberg

The global economy, in general, and the American economy, in particular, have experienced serious difficulties in the 1980s. Reflecting this situation, a restructuring is occurring in the labor market, the labor force, and the nature of employment relations in the United States. To some degree, a sociopolitical regulation of the labor market and employment relations is being replaced by market forces.

Since the 1960s, the American economy has undergone an important transition. There has been a relative expansion of non-goods-producing industries and a relative decline of goods-producing ones. Employment growth appears to have occurred at the top and bottom of the occupational hierarchy but not in the middle. Although the American occupational structure appears to have become more bifurcated from 1960 to 1980, the story for the 1980s is somewhat different. During this period, there has been substantial unemployment, and there seems to be a proliferation of low-wage employment. In addition, since 1970, interindustry earnings inequality has grown substantially.

Workers are forced to respond, eventually, to changes in the structure of employment. But their speed of adjustment can be influenced by government policy. Such policies can either cushion them from the blows of structural

---

Samuel Rosenberg • Department of Economics, Roosevelt University, Chicago, Illinois 60605.

change or attempt to make them respond quicker to shifts in the nature of the demand for labor in the private sector.

The Reagan administration has taken the latter policy direction. It wants to "knock the props" out from under workers, leaving them with little choice but to accept what employers provide. Unemployment has increased, and the impact of the unemployed on employed workers has become more severe. The effective minimum wage has declined. As the share of low-wage employment has grown, cutbacks in unemployment insurance, the elimination of trade adjustment assistance and public service employment, and changes in welfare programs have likely increased the supply of labor available to take such work. And an expanded labor supply to this sector of the labor market has likely helped to keep wages low.

The state policies aimed at introducing a more competitive mode of regulation of the labor market have served to weaken the labor movement. Government industrial relations policies setting a union-busting tone have done the same. The current National Labor Relations Board (NLRB) is certainly the most antiunion one in the post-World War II period. The deregulation of specific industries has introduced new competition in these areas. In addition, increased foreign competition in some industries and increased nonunion domestic competition in others have also emerged.

The upshot is that the American labor movement is facing tough times. The share of employees who are unionized has steadily declined. Wage patterns are being eroded, and wage settlements have been at record lows. Many firms have aggressively sought and achieved work rule changes. But, at the same time, there are some examples of enhanced job security being provided to workers. Yet the enhanced job security for some may also mean the total lack of security for others.

This chapter is divided into four main sections. The first will describe several of the structural changes that have occurred in the American economy. In light of these structural changes, the second will demonstrate that the Reagan administration's labor market policies and some of its social policies are designed to make workers more responsive to competitive forces in the labor market. The third section will discuss the nature of the industrial relations policies of the Reagan administration. The fourth will link the structural changes and the government's policy agenda up to the changes occurring in the nature of employment relations.

I. STRUCTURAL CHANGE: JOBS AND WORKERS

Employment in manufacturing as a proportion of total employment declined from 28.2% in 1960 to 19.2% in 1987. The relative decline began during the 1960s and quickened in the 1970s and 1980s. In fact, during the 1980s there was an absolute decrease in the number of manufacturing workers. In addition, as corporations have shifted production components abroad, there has been a shift in jobs within manufacturing to nonproduction workers,

Table 1. Occupational Distribution of Employment, 1960–1980[a]

	1960		1980	
Major occupation group	No.	Percentage	No.	Percentage
Professional, technical	6986	11.37	15613	16.05
Managers, administrators	5626	9.15	10919	11.23
Sales	4637	7.55	6172	6.35
Clerical	9126	14.85	18105	18.61
Craft	8945	14.55	12529	12.88
Operatives	11348	18.47	13814	14.20
Laborers, nonfarm	3322	5.41	4456	4.58
Service, except private household	5754	9.36	11918	12.25
Private household workers	1718	2.80	1041	1.10
Farmers, farm managers	2507	4.08	1485	1.53
Farm laborers, foremen	1486	2.42	1218	1.25
Occupation not reported	3184	—	0	—
Total	64639	100.0	97270	100.0

[a]*Sources*: 1960 figures are from U.S. Bureau of the Census, Census of Population: 1970, Vol. 1, *Characteristics of the Population*, Part 1, United States Summary-Section 2 (Washington, DC: U.S. Government Printing Office, 1973), Table 221, pp. 718–724. 1980 data are from *Employment and Earnings*, January 1981, Table 21, p. 178. *Note*: The numbers are in thousands.

including managers, engineers, scientists, clerical workers, and sales personnel.

Taken together, the share of employment accounted for by trade, FIRE (finance, insurance, and real estate), and services increased from 45.4% in 1960 to 58.7% in 1986. Professional services, including health and education, and trade were major gainers in employment.

The shifts in industrial employment have important implications for the occupational structure because job tasks vary across industries. Table 1 presents data on the distribution of employment by broad occupational group from 1960 to 1980.[1] The relative decline of craftworkers and laborers is slight, but operatives who were 18.5% of the work force in 1960 were only 14.2% of total workers in 1980. Professional and technical workers, nonhousehold service workers, clerical workers, and the managerial group gained in relative importance.

A more bipolar job distribution likely developed from 1960 to 1980, with employment growth occurring at the top and bottom of the wage structure and occupational hierarchy. Table 2 presents 1980 data on median usual weekly earnings of full-time nonagricultural wage and salary workers. The median weekly earnings of managers and administrators were $380; for professional and technical workers, they were $341. But for clerical workers, they were only $215, and for service workers they were $180. Earnings in between

[1]Figures are only provided through 1980 because changes in the Census Bureau's occupational definitions make comparisons with earlier years extremely difficult.

Table 2. Median Usual Weekly Earnings of Full-Time
Wage and Salary Earners, 1980[a]

Major occupation group	Median weekly earnings
Managers, administrators	380
Professional, technical	341
Craft	328
Sales	279
Operatives	240
Laborers, nonfarm	220
Clerical	215
Service, except private household	180

[a]*Source*: U.S. Bureau of the Census, *Statistical Abstract of the United States:
1981* 102nd edition (Washington, DC: U.S. Government Printing Office,
1981), Table 681, p. 407.

these two extremes were for craft, sales, operative, and laborer occupations, just those occupations that were growing the slowest.

The evidence provided here in support of a more bifurcated occupational structure is, albeit, crude. The occupational categories are too broad to conclude with certainty that the middle of the job distribution has been shrinking. However, Gordon, Edwards, and Reich, working within a labor market segmentation framework, corroborate this trend, at least for 1950 to 1970. Using information on job and industrial structure characteristics, but not wage data, they divide the occupational structure into three segments—independent primary, subordinate primary, and secondary.[2] From 1950 to 1970, employment growth was more prevalent in the independent primary and secondary sectors than in the subordinate primary sector. The subordinate primary sector fell from 37.2% of the employed labor force to 31.0%. The independent primary segment grew from 27.8% to 32.8% of all workers. The secondary sector, having had 35.0% of total employment in 1950, had 36.2% in 1970 (Gordon, Edwards, & Reich, 1982, p. 211).

And Lawrence (1984) finds a relative decline in the number of middle-income full-time jobs in the economy from 1969 to 1983. This was due to the employment experiences of men, not women. There was a decline in the proportion of women in poor-paying jobs and an increasing proportion in middle- and upper-income jobs.[3]

Although the American occupational structure appears to have become

[2]The independent primary sector includes many professional, managerial, technical, and craft jobs. The subordinate primary sector includes many semiskilled blue-collar and white-collar positions. Jobs in the secondary sector include low-skill positions in small nonunion manufacturing firms; service jobs such as janitors, food service workers, hospital orderlies and welfare service aides; lower level positions in retail and wholesale trade; lowest level clerical jobs such as typists in large typing pools.
[3]For additional information on the polarization of employment, see Mishel (1986).

more bifurcated from 1960 to 1980, the story for the 1980s seems to be different. During the 1980s, there has likely been a proliferation of low-wage jobs. Slow productivity growth and the shift of employment out of manufacturing played a role in generating the relative growth of low-wage positions. All regions of the country experienced the trend toward low-wage employment. But it was most pronounced in the Midwest, reeling from deindustrialization. Though part-time schedules have become more prevalent and temporary work has been increasing, the trend to lower wages also held for year-round, full-time workers (Bluestone & Harrison, 1986, 1988).[4]

Not only are more jobs paying low wages, since the early 1970s there has been increasing interindustry earnings inequality. The rank order stability of the U.S. wage structure has not changed. But there has been a widening of the differential between wages paid to workers in the high- and low-wage sectors (Bell & Freeman, 1987). Working within a labor market segmentation framework, Davidson and Reich (1987) find a widening earnings gap between the primary and secondary sectors.

II. THE LABOR MARKET AND SOCIAL POLICY AGENDA

The Reagan administration has been interested in increasing the average rate of profit throughout the economy, decreasing the rate of inflation, and lessening downward wage inflexibility. A weakened, restructured labor force with lowered expectations is necessary for the achievement of these goals. A weakened, restructured labor force, although necessary, is not sufficient for increasing the average rate of profit. Weakening and restructuring the labor force is designed to lower unit labor costs and thus increase the average rate of profit. However, to the extent that this strategy is successful, problems of underconsumption may eventually emerge.

The restructuring of the labor force requires many former middle-income blue-collar manufacturing workers to shift to the lower end of the wage distribution and for new entrants and reentrants to fill the growing demand for low-wage labor. Government policy initiatives have attempted to facilitate this restructuring.

The policies of the Reagan administration have, in fact, resulted in a weakened, restructured labor force with lowered expectations. In some respects, its actions are an extension of those of the Carter administration. However, on balance, a more conservative direction in social policy has taken hold, both in terms of the debate and the policies being instituted.

---

[4]Danziger and Gottschalk (1986) find a growth of low-wage earners who head households, especially male heads of households, from 1979 to 1984. These household heads could not keep a family of four out of poverty even if they worked all year at their current weekly earnings. McMahon and Tschetter (1986) argue that from 1973 to 1985 there has not been a growth of low-wage occupations. Rather, they find a growth of lower wage tracts within occupations.

A. Increased Unemployment

Large-scale unemployment attacks the bargaining power of employed workers. With substantial unemployment, workers fear for their jobs and know they can easily be replaced if they strike. They are aware that if they are fired, they will be unlikely to find equivalent positions. In such an atmosphere, employees are more responsive to the demands of their employers.

After the 1975 recession, unemployment remained at relatively high levels. When Reagan took office in 1981, serious inflation and extensive unemployment were occurring simultaneously. Priority was placed on reducing inflation. Restrictive monetary policy, together with falling world prices for food and energy, resulted in the rate of inflation dropping from 13.5% in 1980 to 3.2% in 1983.

But American workers paid dearly for this as the unemployment rate reached heights not experienced since the Great Depression. The trough of the 1981–1982 recession occurred at the end of 1982. In December 1982, the unemployment rate was 10.7%, and for the entire year it was 9.7%. In that year, 26.5 million people encountered some unemployment, 22% of those in the labor force for all or part of the year. Of these 26.5 million, 22.5 million worked part of the year. But 4 million did not work at all; the majority of them looked for work only part of the year and then left the labor market (U.S. Department of Labor, Bureau of Labor Statistics, August 9, 1983).

Although unemployment rose throughout the economy, it was centered in mining, construction, and manufacturing, those areas where unions have traditionally been the strongest. For example, within manufacturing, by December 1982 the unemployment rate had reached 23.2% in the motor vehicle industry and 29.2% in the primary metals industry (*Economic Report of the President*, 1983, p. 46). Reflecting these sectoral trends, the unemployment rates of operatives and nonfarm laborers were distinctly higher than those of workers in other occupations.[5]

In 1983, the average duration of a spell of unemployment was 20.5 weeks, the longest in post-World War II history. Slightly less than one in four of the unemployed had been looking for work for more than half a year (Ulmer & Howe, 1988, p. 65). The unemployment rate still averaged 9.6% in 1983. Conditions then began to improve. Yet in 1987, after a lengthy economic expansion, the unemployment rate was 6.2%, still high by historical standards but a major improvement nonetheless. The unemployment rates in construction and mining were still well above the national average. However, improving conditions in manufacturing resulted in its unemployment rate falling to 6.0%.

B. Declining Real Minimum Wage

The growth in the number of unemployed constitutes in and of itself an increase in competition in the labor market. The decline in the real value of

[5]The unemployment data are elaborated upon in Rosenberg (1986).

the federal minimum wage has the same impact on low-wage workers. Their wages are now being set more by market forces than by governmental legislation. And by lowering the wage floor, the wages of many other workers are likely being affected as well.

Federal minimum wage legislation was first enacted by the Fair Labor Standards Act of 1938. The current federal minimum wage is $3.35 per hour for the almost 90% of nonsupervisory civilian workers to whom the law applies.[6] The minimum wage has remained unchanged since 1981. As prices have risen since that time, the real value of the minimum wage has fallen. In 1985, the purchasing power of the minimum wage was less than at any time since the mid-1950s.

In addition, the minimum wage has fallen relative to the average wage. After hovering around 50% of average hourly earnings in private non-agricultural industries during the 1950s and 1960s, the minimum averaged 45% in the 1970s. By 1985, it had declined to about 39% of average wages (Smith & Vavrichek, 1987).[7]

According to President Reagan, the minimum wage "has caused more misery and unemployment than anything since the Great Depression" (Zuckoff, 1988). Although that statement is totally ridiculous, it suggests that the administration would have liked to have gotten rid of the minimum wage entirely if that had been politically feasible. It was not. Thus, as a first step toward eliminating the minimum wage, the Reagan administration (as did the Carter administration) proposed a split minimum wage for teenagers for employment from May to September. This legislation was not passed by the U.S. Congress.

C. Unemployment Insurance

Not only has the number of unemployed grown, there has also been an increase in the potential impact of the jobless on employed workers. Although the number of unemployed workers was rising, the government began cutting back on unemployment insurance (UI). UI provides a cushion for workers as they search for work. That cushion is being withdrawn.

When UI was first established by the Social Security Act of 1935, it was designed to provide support for workers with a history of stable employment. It would enable them to search for and find jobs virtually equivalent to the ones they had lost. Also, it was seen as supporting aggregate purchasing power during slack periods.

As time went on, UI came to be viewed in a different light. The Carter administration claimed to support the initial rationale for UI. However, its actions proved otherwise. Implicitly, it took the position that UI, rather than enabling people to search for appropriate jobs, unnecessarily lengthened the

[6]See Gramlich (1976) for a discussion of the extent of noncompliance with the minimum wage legislation.
[7]In nine states, the state minimum wage exceeds the federal minimum wage (Nelson, 1988).

duration of a spell of unemployment, thus increasing the overall level of unemployment. Policies were implemented, either by action or inaction, lowering these benefits, limiting their duration, and making it more difficult to collect them.

As a basis for understanding the initiatives of the Carter administration and of the Reagan administration to follow, some institutional information on the operation of the UI system will be provided. Depending on the length of previous employment, all workers who lose their jobs for acceptable cause can receive benefits for up to 26 weeks. While collecting, they must show they have searched for work and have not declined a "suitable work" offer. There is no nationwide definition of "suitable work," but it is often defined by states as a job equivalent to the previous one.

In specific instances, 13 additional weeks of "extended benefits" (EB) may be granted. The U.S. Congress has occasionally created temporary programs providing for additional UI beyond the extended benefits. For example, during the Ford administration, the maximum duration of benefits was temporarily extended to 65 weeks.

Under President Carter, the tax-exempt status of UI was ended. Legislation was passed to tax the unemployment benefits of individuals who receive a combination of income and benefits exceeding a base amount ($20,000 for single persons, $25,000 for married persons filing joint returns). The program enabling benefits to be paid for up to 65 weeks was allowed to expire in January 1978. A regulation was implemented making it more difficult for workers to collect EB. *Suitable work* for such workers was defined as a job paying at least the weekly benefit or the minimum wage, whichever was higher. Those refusing such work would lose their benefits.

The Reagan administration has further weakened the UI system.[8] It wants to eliminate what it calls "excess unintended benefits." It has tried to accomplish this by increasing the taxation of UI and limiting the provision of EB.

In August 1982, legislation was passed increasing the taxation of UI. Single persons with a combination of income and unemployment benefits of at least $12,000, rather than the $20,000, and married persons filing joint returns, having a combination of income and unemployment benefits of at least $18,000, rather than the $25,000, would have to pay tax on their UI. The widely heralded tax revisions of 1986 further increased the taxation of UI. Now everyone receiving UI regardless of his or her annual income are taxed on his or her benefits.

The Reagan administration, with the approval of the U.S. Congress, redefined the conditions under which EB are to be paid. The unemployment

[8]The major sources for information on the Reagan policy agenda include *America's New Beginning: A Program for Economic Recovery* (1981), *Economic Report of the President* (1983), Office of Management and Budget (1981a), Office of Management and Budget (1981b), Office of Management and Budget (1982a), Office of Management and Budget (1982b), Office of Management and Budget (1983), Office of Management and Budget (1984), Office of Management and Budget (1986), and Office of Management and Budget (1987).

rate required to trigger EB increased. This made it more difficult for states to provide this assistance.

Previously, EB were based on the economywide level of unemployment or on specific state levels. They were paid throughout the country if the nationally insured unemployment rate was greater than 4.5% for 13 weeks. This rate was measured by the number of people collecting unemployment benefits, including EB, as a percentage of the number of people in the labor force covered by the unemployment insurance system.

When not provided throughout the country, EB were paid in any state with an insured unemployment rate of at least 4% for 13 weeks and at least 20% over the level in the corresponding period of the preceding 2 years. A state could waive the 20% requirement if the insured unemployment rate was at least 5% for 13 weeks.

Now, the national criterion for providing benefits has been eliminated, and the minimum unemployment levels have been increased by 1%. Unemployed workers receiving EB are no longer counted in computing the insured unemployment rate.

The higher minimum rates and the redefinition of the insured unemployment rate make it more difficult for states to pay EB. Furthermore, changes implemented at the state level have also made it more difficult to qualify for UI. Since the mid-1970s, the qualification periods of voluntary job leavers have been lengthened and the earnings requirements needed for eligibility have been increased in many states (Burtless & Vroman, 1985).

As a result of the Reagan reforms and the state-level changes, relatively fewer people received UI during the 1981–1982 recession than in any post–World War II recession. In 1975, when the unemployment rate was 8.5%, approximately 78% of the unemployed received UI. This is in contrast to 1982, with a higher unemployment rate, when only 45% received compensation (Burtless, 1983, p. 226). And one-third of those individuals receiving UI exhausted their benefits in 1982 (Cohen, 1985). The decline in the insured unemployment rate and the changes in the EB triggering mechanism virtually eliminated the EB program.

In August 1982, the U.S. Congress created the Temporary Federal Supplemental Compensation program that went against the thrust of the Reagan agenda. As originally enacted, depending on state unemployment conditions, workers were eligible for up to 10 additional weeks of UI. With worsening unemployment, the legislation was amended to provide up to 16 additional weeks. This program expired in 1985.

It began later and was substantially less generous than the equivalent program enacted by the Ford administration during the 1974–1976 recession. At the same time, the EB program was less generous, and long-term unemployment was much higher (Burtless & Vroman, 1985).

The reasons given by the Reagan administration for its changes in unemployment benefits reflect its desire to create more flexibility in the labor market, by limiting nonwage sources of income. More specifically, it argues that structural shifts have occurred in the nature and location of jobs, though it does not specify these trends in great detail. It claims explicitly, whereas the Carter administration did so implicitly, that overly generous UI lengthens the duration of a spell of unemployment. These payments discourage workers from relocating or from seeking employment in new industries that may initially pay lower wages than workers are used to but that hold out the promise of higher wages in the future. Through its changes in UI, the Reagan administration hopes to force workers to lower their job expectations and to adapt more quickly to labor market conditions.

The cutbacks in UI potentially affect all workers. But those most likely to be hurt are former operatives, nonfarm laborers, and service workers. They are the ones most likely to suffer long-term unemployment. The new developments in the UI system have probably increased, to some degree, the flexibility of these workers as well as the labor supply to low-wage positions.

Although the government claims that its initiatives will reduce structural unemployment, this is unlikely to be the case. Studies have shown that although there is a statistically significant relationship between UI and the duration of unemployment, the quantitative significance is minimal (Moffitt & Nicholson, 1982). In addition, Vickery has demonstrated that in an economy characterized by recessionary periods and imperfect product and labor markets, UI affects the composition of the unemployed more than the rate of unemployment. To the extent that UI increases the unemployment duration of recipients, it allows inexperienced workers, not eligible for UI, a better chance to fill available job openings, thus decreasing their duration of unemployment (Vickery, 1979, p. 15).

The primary problem is an inadequate number of jobs. Abraham (1983) has found that the number of people looking for work has exceeded the number of vacancies whenever the unemployment rate has been greater than 3%. During the latter part of the 1970s, when the unemployment rate was lower than during the 1980s, there was an average of 4 to 5 job seekers for every vacant job.

Thus, the extent to which unemployed workers would be able to quicken their adjustment to the labor market is open to question. However, the example of the unemployed, including their economic pain and limited options in the labor market, has likely weakened the resistance of employed workers to employer demands for concessions in wages and working conditions.[9]

D. Trade Adjustment Assistance

While the UI system is being eroded, the trade adjustment assistance (TAA) program has been eliminated. TAA was instituted as part of the Trade

---

[9]It is likely that the cutbacks in UI have lessened the incidence of strikes (Schor & Bowles, 1987). Measures of work stoppages have declined almost every year beginning with 1980. In addition, the U.S. Supreme Court in March 1988 ruled that the U.S. Congress did not act unconstitutionally in 1981 when it prohibited providing food stamps for a striker and his family even though the striker was sufficiently poor and willing to work. This ruling severely hurts the ability of low-paid workers to strike for more than a short period of time.

Expansion Act of 1962 and was the price set by the AFL-CIO for its support of the trade expansion measure.

TAA was received by workers whose unemployment was deemed to be in part due to imports. The payments were for more per week and for longer periods than people received from UI. In addition, training opportunities and relocation and job search allowances were also provided.

Most of the TAA payments went to unionized industrial workers, mainly steel, automobile, and clothing and textile workers, in the mid-Atlantic and North Central regions. During the Carter years, many workers were certified to receive TAA. In fact, in the fiscal year 1980, $1.6 billion in allowances were paid to 536,000 claimants, reflecting primarily the decline in domestic car sales.

The TAA program ended during Reagan's second term in office. Some money for training and other employment assistance for workers who have lost their jobs due to imports remains available through the Job Training Partnership Act (JTPA). (All displaced workers, not merely those affected by imports, are eligible for JTPA funds.)

Initially, in 1981, the Reagan administration developed, and the U.S. Congress passed, legislation increasing the difficulty of qualifying for TAA, limiting the size of the benefit and shortening its duration.[10] The government argued that it was eliminating "excess unintended benefits." These benefits, rather than helping workers adjust to industrial decline brought on by international competition, enabled them to avoid doing so. Too many received such benefits. Few were interested in retraining, job search, or relocation assistance. After receiving TAA, many returned to their original jobs. Also, as payments were retroactive, workers had sometimes returned to their original jobs before payment of compensation.[11] Labor market rigidity, rather than labor market flexibility was, it was argued, the result of this program.

Eventually the government decided to request the elimination of TAA. On equity grounds, the Reagan administration claimed all workers who lose their jobs should be treated the same. Thus, no workers should receive benefits other than UI.

The effects of ending TAA are apparent. The majority of workers who received TAA were blue-collar manufacturing workers. The impact on them is similar to that caused by the changes in the UI system.

E. Public Service Employment

Not only have alternative sources of income to private sector wages been scaled down, but alternative sources of jobs outside of the private sector have been eliminated. Public service employment programs (PSE), funded by the federal government, providing for positions in state and local governments

---

[10]The specifics of this policy change are discussed in Rosenberg (1983).

[11]These criticisms, although valid, do not necessarily justify the steps taken by the Reagan administration.

and in nonprofit-making organizations, have been ended. The positions had been funded under the Comprehensive Employment and Training Act of 1973.

The Carter administration made PSE a central component of its employment strategy. When Reagan entered office in 1981, 309,000 PSE positions existed, approximately 85% of which were held by people officially considered to be living at or below the poverty line. None remained by the end of the year as the funding was eliminated.

Despite the fact that much of the research on PSE was favorable toward it as a means to lessen cyclical and structural unemployment (Briggs, 1982), the Reagan administration developed arguments to eliminate it. At the time when it ended PSE, officials in the administration were making the case that an expanding private economy was a necessary—and in most cases, sufficient—condition for reducing long-term unemployment (Moran, 1982, p. 402). The private sector was where long-term, career employment opportunities do and should exist. PSE jobs had not, it was argued, provided experience easily transferable to private sector employment.

The end of the PSE hurt the unskilled, less-educated, and unemployed, especially among minority groups. It increased the supply of labor to the low-wage segment of the labor market causing increased competition for such positions and increased unemployment. Also, it probably resulted in low-wage workers becoming, of necessity, more responsive to the demands of the employers.

F. Welfare

Although voluntary PSE programs have ended, mandatory public employment programs for welfare recipients are being developed. Criticisms concerning the ineffectiveness of PSE are conveniently forgotten by federal policymakers responsible for "welfare reform." Mandatory "workfare" plans complement welfare changes that limit the number of people eligible for assistance and the amounts they receive.

Since 1973, there has been no growth in the number of households receiving welfare. Thus politicians must have reasons other than growing welfare rolls for placing increasing importance on welfare reform legislation in the 1980s.

The American welfare system is a complex array of many uncoordinated programs. Aid to Families with Dependent Children (AFDC), the most controversial, is emphasized here. AFDC has its roots in the Aid to Dependent Children program established under the Social Security Act of 1935.

Initially, welfare was viewed as primarily for "deserving" white widows and their children. Eventually more and more recipients were black, and an increasing proportion of cases involved families with divorced or unmarried mothers. As the welfare population changed from the "deserving poor" to the "undeserving poor," work incentives and work requirements were instituted. Beginning in 1967, states were required to exempt earnings of $30 per month plus one-third of additional earnings and to allow itemized deductions for work-related expenses in determining AFDC allowances. Also, a mandatory work-training program for all adult recipients was begun (Lynn, 1977).

Welfare reform ideas percolated during the 1970s. During the Carter administration, AFDC and food stamp benefits did not keep pace with inflation. After adjusting for inflation, real benefits in 1980 were 20% lower than a decade earlier. At the end of its term in office, the Carter administration began proposing cuts in AFDC outlays. The Reagan administration accepted these cuts and added some of its own.

The means test for eligibility for welfare has been tightened.[12] Qualifying families have had limitations placed on the amount of work-related expenses they are able to deduct in determining their net income and, thus, their AFDC needs. The $30 and "one-third" income exemption now applies only for a 4-month period after AFDC recipients find work. After that time, the benefit reduction rate rises to 100%.

These changes limit the incentives to work of those still receiving AFDC. They are consciously aimed at low-income families with an earner or a potential earner. Such individuals should, according to the Reagan administration, be forced to work, rather than be provided with an incentive to work. To guarantee that AFDC recipients work, the Reagan administration has proposed legislation requiring states to develop mandatory "workfare" programs for AFDC recipients. States now have the option to do so. Public jobs would be provided if private sector positions were unavailable. Recipients would do enough work each month, calculated at the minimum wage, to earn their payments. Those unwilling to work would lose their assistance.

Although some of the changes in AFDC may have reduced the incentives to work of some of the recipients, on balance, it is likely that the implemented and suggested policy changes will help to increase the labor supply to low-wage jobs. Those deemed ineligible for AFDC or receiving lessened benefits will be more readily available for such employment.[13] Those forced to work in the private sector at the minimum wage under workfare programs will also be available to be called on if needed by employers. This will help to guarantee that wage levels and employment conditions in this segment of the labor market will not substantially improve, with employers having little or no incentive to respond to worker demands. An existing worker could always be replaced by a participant in a workfare program.[14]

---

[12]The specifics of this policy change are discussed in Rosenberg (1983).

[13]For a discussion of the work incentive effects of the AFDC reforms, see Haveman (1984).

[14]In October 1988, while this book was in press, a welfare reform bill was passed by the U.S. Congress. Its 'workfare' provision, to take effect in 1994, is narrower than the earlier proposals of the Reagan administration. 'Workfare' will only apply to two-parent welfare families in which both parents are unemployed. Very few current welfare families have two parents. Either the father or the mother will be required to work a minimum of 16 hours a week in a government or community service position.

III. INDUSTRIAL RELATIONS POLICY—WEAKENING AND BUSTING UNIONS

The large number of unemployed and the cutbacks in the minimum wage and the social wage have hurt unions. Government policy, setting a union-busting tone, has done the same. In its first year in office, the Reagan administration fired the striking air traffic controllers and had the Professional Air Traffic Controllers Organization decertified. That action sent a clear message to employers; they should feel free to bash unions.

The Reagan administration's appointments to the National Labor Relations Board (NLRB) have been designed to create a majority who would roll back many of the gains made by the labor movement. NLRB rulings have made it more difficult for union-organizing drives to succeed and for unionists to achieve their goals at the bargaining table. Employers are now more able to engage in unfair labor practices designed to stop a union victory in a representation election without suffering negative consequences (Gourmet Foods case, 1984). Previously, the NLRB could certify a union at a company that egregiously violated labor law even though the union had not won a representation election. Now, a company is not required to bargain with a union unless the labor organization has received a majority of the votes in a representation election.

In addition, employer rights during a union-organizing drive have been expanded. Employers may now lawfully question employees about a union-organizing drive in progress (Rossmore House case, 1985). In doing so, they cannot threaten workers. Yet, there is a fine line between an actual threat and implied intimidation.

Recent NLRB decisions have also made it more difficult for unions to gain their demands at the bargaining table. It is now easier for employers to move union jobs to nonunion locations. Previously, the NLRB had found that as long as a collective bargaining agreement was in effect, an employer was prohibited from moving work to a nonunion facility. A company may now move work during the life of a contract unless there is a clause in the contract explicitly prohibiting such action. All the company need do, if the move is designed to lower labor costs, is bargain over the decision and its effects (Milwaukee Spring case, 1984). Yet, there is no requirement that an agreement be reached or that the work remain at the unionized plant. And if the movement of work hinges on factors other than cutting labor costs, there is no requirement to bargain at all (Otis Elevator case, 1984).

It is now more difficult for unions to wage successful strikes. Unions can no longer fine workers who resign their union membership during a strike and return to work in violation of union rules. In upholding an earlier NLRB decision, the U.S. Supreme Court suggested that any union rules limiting the freedom of workers to resign during or just prior to a strike may be illegal (Pattern Makers case, 1985).

It is now easier for an employer to succeed with a lockout. In a lockout, the employer bars union workers from the workplace in order to gain concessions in bargaining. The NLRB ruled that management is allowed to hire "temporary replacements" during a lockout (Harter case, 1986).

For a time it had been easier for a company to declare bankruptcy in order to void a labor contract. This tactic was successfully used by several firms, including Continental Airlines and Wilson Foods. In 1984, the U.S. Supreme Court ruled that a company may use bankruptcy proceedings to rid itself of a collective bargaining agreement (NLRB vs. Bildisco case). The company could void its collective bargaining contract as soon as it filed a bankruptcy petition, even before the bankruptcy had been approved by the Bankruptcy Court. As a result of this decision, the U.S. Congress passed legislation limiting the use of bankruptcy as a tactic in labor relations.[15]

IV. THE CHANGING NATURE OF EMPLOYMENT RELATIONS

The industrial relations and labor market policies of the government have hurt unionists and nonunionists alike. In addition, the relaxation of barriers to entry under deregulation of the transportation and communication industries have created tough times for unions in these sectors. Furthermore, high interest rates resulting from restrictive monetary policy served to substantially push up the value of the dollar and increase foreign competition in the first half of the 1980s.

Yet government policy is not the only factor responsible for the problems currently facing the American union movement. The percentage of workers who are union members continues to fall as it has since the mid-1950s. Now less than one out of every five workers is a union member. In addition, in the 1980s absolute union membership also declined. Reflecting this situation, significant nonunion sectors have developed in many industries, including mining, manufacturing, construction, and transportation, historically viewed as centers of unionism.

Also, employers have become bolder in their demand for concessions. The rising union–nonunion wage premium in the 1970s together with the increased competition, both foreign and domestic, facing many firms during the serious recession of the early 1980s, provided the economic incentives for employers to demand givebacks. The weakened state of the labor movement and the general excess supply of labor have increased the opportunities for employers to gain their demands. Employment relations are changing in the face of this situation.

A. Wage Bargaining

Unprecedented numbers of union members have received modest wage increases or experienced no increases or even wage reductions during the

---

[15]For additional information on the rulings of the NLRB and the courts, see *Business Week* (1984), Diamond (1985), Lewiston and Wise (1987), and Taub and Needleman (1984).

1980s. Between 1979 and 1984, at least 3 million union members, about one out of every six, accepted labor contracts that froze or reduced wages and fringe benefits or altered work rules (Gay, 1984, p. 843). Between one-third and one-half of the workers covered by major collective bargaining agreements experienced a wage cut or wage freeze (Mitchell, 1985, p. 577).

Labor market conditions began improving in 1984. Yet even as the unemployment rate has fallen, many unions have still been forced to sign contracts providing for minimal improvements, at best, in earnings. In fact, major collective bargaining contracts settled in private industry in 1986 yielded record low-wage and compensation adjustments. Wage adjustments under these contracts covering 2.5 million workers averaged 1.2% in the first contract year and 1.8% annually over the contract term. The actual wage adjustments may prove to be higher as lump sum payments, which have become increasingly prevalent, and wage changes stemming from cost-of-living allowances (COLA) clauses are not included. About one-eighth of the workers had their wages frozen, and about one-tenth experienced wage cuts over the term of the contracts (Lacombe & Borum, 1987, p. 11).

Two-tier wage structures have become more prevalent. Approximately 8% of all nonconstruction settlements had some form of two-tier plan in 1984 (Mitchell, 1985, p. 593). These arrangements are either temporary or permanent. Under permanent dual-pay plans, newly hired workers are paid via a separate lower pay structure and never catch up with existing workers. Under temporary plans, newly hired workers are eventually paid on the same basis as existing workers.

There appear to be important structural changes occurring in labor relations in the 1980s. Wage equations overpredict the actual wage settlements negotiated between 1980 and 1984 by between one and three percentage points annually. The overprediction is greatest in more centralized bargaining structures and those that relied on pattern bargaining in earlier years (Kochan, Katz, & McKersie, 1986, p. 111; Mitchell, 1985).[16]

Thus, in addition to providing wage concessions, many workers have seen previous wage-bargaining patterns eroding. Unions want to take wages out of competition by pursuing pattern bargaining. But in the 1980s, many employers have pushed for decentralizing the bargaining structures so that wage settlements become more firm-specific and wages are put back into competition. Concessions that have downgraded master pattern agreements have been made in aluminum, auto, cans, copper, meatpacking, railroad, rubber, steel, and trucking. Also, one or more employers have broken out of the pattern in agricultural implements, aluminum, auto, meatpacking, railroad, rubber, steel, and trucking (Slaughter, 1983, p. 35).

[16]However, the econometric findings are not conclusive. The union–nonunion wage differential appears to have remained relatively constant in the first half of the 1980s as some researchers find that it has slightly grown (Edwards & Swaim, 1986; Linneman & Wachter, 1986), whereas others find a slight decline (Mitchell, 1985). Unlike Kochan *et al.* (1986) and Mitchell (1985), Freeman (1986) concludes that union wage settlements in the early 1980s are a predictable response to economic conditions rather than reflecting a structural shift in wage determination.

The elimination of COLA and the introduction of various contingent compensation schemes also tie wage setting more closely to company performance. In 1977, 61.2% of the workers under major contract agreements had COLA clauses in their contracts, whereas in 1987 only 40.4% had them. From 1977 to 1984, this trend was mainly caused by employment losses in industries where COLA clauses were common. But in 1985 and 1986, COLA coverage was suspended or eliminated in many contracts (Borum, Conley, & Wasilewski, 1988, p. 12).

Contingent compensation schemes vary from profit-sharing and tying future wage levels to improvements in the firm's economic performance, to stock-ownership plans with workers gaining equity in the company where they work. Though contingent compensation arrangements have increased sharply since 1980, relatively few workers are covered by such plans. For example, only about 20% of the employees in medium and large firms had profit-sharing plans in 1985 (Broderick & Mitchell, 1987, p. 161).

Worker stock ownership plans, with the exception of tax-credit ESOPs (employee stock ownership plans), are still quite rare. Such arrangements have occurred mainly in the airline and trucking industries. They are also found in other industries including the steel industry.

B. Changes in Work Rules and Job Security Arrangements

In addition to seeking to change compensation levels and compensation practices, many employers have aggressively sought work rule changes. Their concern with work rule concessions is unprecedented in the post–Great Depression period. Management is looking for increased flexibility so as to lower costs of production. This has taken the form of attempting to gain "broader job classifications, more managerial discretion in the allocation of overtime, more liberal subcontracting rights, and restrictions on voluntary transfers or other movements across jobs" (Kochan, Katz, & McKersie, 1986, p. 118).

It is very difficult to generalize as to the extent to which work rules have in fact changed. Often they are the subject of negotiations at the local level rather than being a subject of national bargaining. But, according to 1983 Conference Board survey data, 63% of the surveyed firms said they had received work rule concessions in recent bargaining (Kochan et al., 1986, p. 118).

The nature of the changes vary across industries. Yet common to many negotiations over work rules are worker desires for increased job security. Workers do not wish to work themselves out of their job. Improvements in productivity may lead to fewer workers being utilized to produce the requisite output.

Worker concerns are twofold. First, if laid off it is unlikely they will ever be recalled. This holds even for those with many years of seniority. Second, previously relatively high paid unionized workers often have great difficulty finding jobs equivalent to the ones they lost. Studies of displaced workers

find that many who lose their jobs during previous recessions receive substantially lower wages on their new jobs, if they are lucky enough to find
work (Flaim & Sehgal, 1985; Horvath, 1987; Mishel, 1986; Mishel &
Podgursky, 1988).

Recent collective bargaining agreements demonstrate the premium that
workers are placing on job security. Unions have won a number of protections including plans limiting layoffs or terminations during sales slowdowns, and in a few instances outright bans on plant closings, restrictions on
subcontracting, and limitations on overtime work (Ruben, 1988). The GM and
Ford contracts with the United Auto Workers and the Communications
Workers' contract with AT&T have new job security/retraining programs.
Although job security is not promised, attempts are to be made to limit
layoffs. Money is to be set aside to train incumbent employees for new positions. In return, the company is given more freedom in deploying labor inside
the firm (Osterman, 1987, p. 309).[17] American Airlines introduced lifetime job
guarantees to existing workers while lowering the pay of new employees
during 1983 negotiations (Kochan, Katz, & McKersie, 1986, p. 125).

Yet these types of contracts are still the exception rather than the rule.
Very few employers are willing to give their workers explicit job guarantees.
At best, they agree not to go ahead, for the time being, with a planned closing
or layoff in return for concessions.

Kochan, Katz, and McKersie argue that "the extent of enhanced employment security has grown significantly in the early 1980s" (Kochan et al.,
1986, p. 121). However, they do not provide substantial evidence to back up
this claim. But to the extent that this is the case, management is interested in a
strategy to guarantee that labor does not become too great a fixed cost. That
strategy includes the increased use of "contingent employees" able to serve
as a buffer against declines in aggregate demand or labor force reductions
necessitated for other reasons. Thus the growth of employment security for
some entails the lack of employment security for others.

C. The Growth of Contingent Employees

Long-term employment relationships between workers and employers
do exist. For example, in January 1987, one-third of workers aged 25 and
above had been with their current employer for 10 years or more (U.S. Department of Labor, Bureau of Labor Statistics, October 22, 1987). However,
the union of the new "lean and mean" corporation of the 1980s and the large
number of unemployed of the 1980s has resulted in the growing importance
of the "disposable employee." As "just-in-time" organization of inventory
and production has spread, so has "just-in-time" personnel management.

The definition of the contingent employee is somewhat arbitrary because
very few workers are guaranteed lifetime employment. Yet, it often com-

---

[17]Moberg (1987) argues that the auto industry's job security programs have not been very effective in guaranteeing job security.

prises those who are part-time or temporary workers as well as those who work for outside contractors. The contingent labor force is estimated to account for approximately 25% of the work force (Pollack & Bernstein, 1986). It is said to be growing. A Bureau of National Affairs survey of more than 400 firms found an increase in the use of agency temporaries, short-time hires, on-call workers, and contracting out from 1980 to 1985 (Bureau of National Affairs, 1986, p. 9).

Part-time employees are the largest share of the contingent labor force. Their share of the total labor force has increased since the late 1960s. Between 1968 and 1985, the proportion of employed people who normally work part-time (less than 35 hours per week) increased from 14.0% to 17.4% (Nardone, 1986). Those working part-time for economic reasons who usually work full-time are not included in these figures for the part-time labor force. From 1973 to 1985, there was a significant secular rise in the percentage of employees in the work force who work part-time but would prefer full-time employment (Ichniowski & Preston, 1986). And, not surprisingly, from 1979 to 1983, as a result of the economic crisis, the number of people working part-time involuntarily increased by 2.8 million in contrast to a .7 million increase in those employed full-time. In years thereafter, as the economy has strengthened, full-time employees have grown in number. Although the number of people working part-time involuntarily has begun to decline, there were still slightly less than 2 million more of these workers in 1987 than in 1979. And over this time period, full-time employment increased by 14% from 74.1 million workers to 84.3 million, voluntary part-time employment by 12% from 12.4 million to 13.9 million, and involuntary part-time employment by 52% from 3.4 million to 5.1 million (*Employment and Earnings*, various issues; Levitan & Conway, 1988).

There are two types of temporary workers—those hired through temporary agencies, like Manpower and Kelly Services, and those directly hired on a temporary basis by private companies. Data are not available on the "direct-hire" temporary workers. But the temporary help supply industry has been one of the fastest growing industries in the 1980s. Though small in terms of total employment—695,000—it has more than doubled in size since the late 1970s (Carey & Hazelbaker, 1986).

Those supplied by temporary help agencies are disproportionately female, young, and black. They are most likely to work in clerical or industrial help jobs (Howe, 1986a). However, many firms utilize "direct-hire" temporaries for many professional and technical occupations (Mangum, Mayall, & Nelson, 1985; Osterman, 1987).[18]

Large firms subcontract a variety of tasks to smaller firms. Data do not exist on the full extent of subcontracting. The federal government does collect information on one type of subcontractor—the business service industry.

---

[18]In 1985, the Reagan administration increased the ability of government agencies to utilize temporary employees. Previously, temporary employees were able to be hired for a specified time of 1 year or less. Now temporary appointments may be renewed for 4 consecutive years.

Employment in this industry doubled between 1974 and 1984. More than 4 million people work in this sector (Howe, 1986b).

V. CONCLUSION

Since 1980, the federal government has implemented many, and proposed even more, changes in employment and income security policies. Its actions foster the labor market restructuring that employers desire. Workers have been forced to become more responsive to competitive forces in the economy.

Unions have been weakened. Unemployment has increased, and the impact of the unemployed on employed workers has become more severe. As the share of low-wage employment has grown, cutbacks in unemployment insurance, the elimination of trade adjustment assistance and public service employment, and changes in welfare programs have likely increased the supply of labor available to take such work. Many people have little choice but to do so. They have become more flexible, more willing to accept what employers have to offer.

And what employers have to offer is often not what workers would have preferred. Concession bargaining has prevailed with minimal wage improvements, at best, and work rule changes more to the liking of employers. As a quid pro quo, some workers may have been able to gain enhanced job security. At the same time, the growth of contingent forms of employment points to increased insecurity for other workers. And these contingent workers are often ready to take the jobs of more permanent workers if they unionize or, if unionized, assert their collective bargaining rights.

Wage inequality appears to be increasing and wage formation becoming more firm specific. Fundamental changes seem to be occurring in the system of industrial relations.

Overall, the labor market in the United States has become more competitive in the 1980s. The floor of the wage structure has fallen, and many workers have found themselves skidding down the occupational hierarchy.

Acknowledgments Earlier versions of this chapter were presented to the Conference on Economic Development and Labor Market Segmentation, University of Notre Dame, South Bend, Indiana, and the International Conference on Regulation Theory, Barcelona, Spain. The comments of the participants, especially Theresa Ghilarducci, at these conferences are gratefully acknowledged.

VI. REFERENCES

Abraham, K. G. (1983). Structural/frictional vs. deficit demand unemployment. *American Economic Review, 73* (4, September), 708–724.

America's New Beginning: A Program for Economic Recovery. (1981). Washington, DC: U.S. Government Printing Office.

Bell, L. A., & Freeman, R. B. (1987). The facts about rising industrial wage dispersion in the United States. In *Proceedings of the Thirty-Ninth Annual Meeting* (pp. 331–337). Madison, WI: Industrial Relations Research Association.

Bluestone, B., & Harrison, B. (1986). *The great American job machine: The proliferation of low wage employment in the U.S. economy.* Joint Economic Committee of the U.S. Congress.

Bluestone, B., & Harrison, B. (1988). The growth of low-wage employment: 1963–86. *American Economic Review, 78* (2, May), 124–128.

Borum, J. D., Conley, J. R., & Wasilewski, E. J. (1988). The outlook for collective bargaining in 1988. *Monthly Labor Review, 111* (1, January), 10–23.

Briggs, V. M. (1982). The revival of job creation programs in the 1970s: Lessons for the 1980s. In *Proceedings of the Thirty-Fourth Annual Meeting* (pp. 258–265). Madison, WI: Industrial Relations Research Association.

Broderick, R., & Mitchell, D. J. B. (1987). Who has flexible wage plans and why aren't there more of them. In *Proceedings of the Thirty-Ninth Annual Meeting* (pp. 159–166). Madison, WI: Industrial Relations Research Association.

Bureau of National Affairs. (1986). *The changing workplace: New directions in staffing and scheduling.* Washington, DC: Bureau of National Affairs.

Burtless, G. (1983). Why is insured unemployment so low? *Brookings Papers on Economic Activity, 1,* 225–249.

Burtless, G., & Vroman, W. (1985). The performance of unemployment insurance since 1979. In *Proceedings of the Thirty-Seventh Annual Meeting* (p. 138–146). Madison, WI: Industrial Relations Research Association.

Business Week. (1984). "NLRB rulings that are inflaming labor relations," June 11, pp. 122–130.

Carey, M. L., & Hazelbaker, K. L. (1986). Employment growth in the temporary help industry. *Monthly Labor Review, 109* (4, April), pp. 37–44.

Cohen, W. J. (1985). Discussion. In *Proceedings of the Thirty-Seventh Annual Meeting* (pp. 171–172). Madison, WI: Industrial Relations Research Association.

Danziger, S., & Gottschalk, P. (1986). Work, Poverty, and the Working Poor: A Multifaceted Problem. *Monthly Labor Review, 109* (9, September), 17–27.

Davidson, C., & Reich, M. (1987). *Inter-industry earnings inequality: Post-war trends and structural explanations,* unpublished manuscript.

Diamond, S. F. (1985). No Friends in Labor's Court. *The Nation,* December 14, pp. 647–648.

Economic Report of the President. (1983). Washington, DC: U.S. Government Printing Office.

Edwards, R., & Swaim, P. (1986). Union-nonunion earnings differentials and the decline of private-sector unionism. *American Economic Review, 76* (2, May), 97–102.

Employment and Earnings, various issues.

Flaim, P. O., & Sehgal, E. (1985). Displaced workers of 1979–83: How well have they fared? *Monthly Labor Review, 108* (6, June), 3–16.

Freeman, R. B. (1986). In search of union wage concessions in standard data sets. *Industrial Relations, 25,* 131–145.

Gay, R. S. (1984). Union settlements and aggregate wage behavior in the 1980s. *Federal Reserve Bulletin, 70* (12, December), 843–856.

Gordon, D. M., Edwards, R., & Reich, M. (1982). *Segmented work, divided workers: The historical transformation of labor in the United States.* Cambridge: Cambridge University Press.

Gramlich, E. M. (1976). Impact of minimum wages on other wages, employment, and family incomes. *Brookings Papers on Economic Activity, 2,* 409–451.

Haveman, R. H. (1984). How much have the Reagan administration's tax and spending policies increased work effort? In C. R. Hulten & I. V. Sawhill (Eds.), *The Legacy of Reaganomics: Prospects for Long-Term Growth* (pp. 91–125). Washington, DC: The Urban Institute Press.

Horvath, F. W. (1987). The pulse of economic change: Displaced workers of 1981–85. *Monthly Labor Review, 110* (6, June), pp. 3–12.

Howe, W. J. (1986a). Temporary help workers: Who they are, what jobs they hold. *Monthly Labor Review, 109* (1, January), 45–47.

Howe, W. J. (1986b). The business services industry sets pace in employment growth. *Monthly Labor Review, 109* (4, April), 29–36.

Ichniowski, B. E., & Preston, A. E. (1986). New trends in part-time employment. In *Proceedings of the Thirty-Eighth Annual Meeting* (pp. 60–67). Madison, WI: Industrial Relations Research Association.

Kochan, T. A., Katz, H. C., & McKersie, R. B. (1986). *The transformation of American industrial relations.* New York: Basic Books.

Lacombe, J., & Borum, J. (1987). Major labor contracts in 1986 provided record low wage adjustments, *Monthly Labor Review, 110* (5, May), 39–45.

Lawrence, R. Z. (1984). Sectoral shifts and the size of the middle class. *The Brookings Review*, Fall, pp. 3–11.

Levitan, S. A., & Conway, E. A. (1988). Part-timers: Living on half rations. *Challenge*, May/June, pp. 9–16.

Lewiston, T., & Wise, T. (1987). Locked out by Lockheed: Seattle workers stand firm. *Dollars and Sense*, December, pp. 17–22.

Linneman, P., & Wachter, M. L. (1986). Rising union premiums and the declining boundaries among noncompeting groups. *American Economic Review, 76* (2, May), 103–108.

Lynn, L. E., Jr. (1977). A decade of policy developments in the income maintenance system. In R. H. Haveman (Ed.), *A decade of federal antipoverty programs* (pp. 55–117). New York: Academic Press.

Mangum, G., Mayall, D., & Nelson, K. (1985). The temporary help industry: A response to the dual internal labor market. *Industrial and Labor Relations Review, 38* (4, July), 599–611.

McMahon, P. J., & Tschetter, J. H. (1986). The declining middle class: A further analysis. *Monthly Labor Review, 109* (9, September), 22–27.

Mishel, L. (1986). *The polarization of America: The loss of good jobs, falling incomes and rising inequality.* Washington, DC: Industrial Union Department, AFL-CIO.

Mishel, L., & Podgursky, M. (1988). The incidence of displacement. In *Proceedings of the Fortieth Annual Meeting* (pp. 118–124). Madison, WI: Industrial Relations Research Association.

Mitchell, D. J. B. (1985). Shifting wage norms in wage determination. *Brookings Papers on Economic Activity, 2*, 575–599.

Moberg, D. (1987). The auto industry's insecurity. *In These Times*, Sept. 16–22, p. 8.

Moffitt, R., & Nicholson, W. (1982). The effect of unemployment insurance on unemployment: The case of federal supplemental benefits. *Review of Economics and Statistics, 64* (1), 1–11.

Moran, D. W. (1982). Human resource implications of the budget cuts. In *Proceedings of the Thirty-Fourth Annual Meeting* (pp. 400–405). Madison, WI: Industrial Relations Research Association.

Nardone, T. J. (1986). Part-time workers: Who are they? *Monthly Labor Review, 109* (2), 13–19.

Nelson, R. R. (1988). State labor laws: Changes during 1987. *Monthly Labor Review, 110* (1), 38–61.

Office of Management and Budget. (1981a). *Additional details on budget savings, Fiscal Year 1982.* Washington, DC: U.S. Government Printing Office.

Office of Management and Budget. (1981b). *Budget of the United States government, Fiscal Year 1982.* Washington, DC: U.S. Government Printing Office.

Office of Management and Budget. (1982a). *Budget of the United States government, Fiscal Year 1983.* Washington, DC: U.S. Government Printing Office.

Office of Management and Budget. (1982b). *Major themes and additional budget details, Fiscal Year 1983.* Washington, DC: U.S. Government Printing Office.

Office of Management and Budget. (1983). *Budget of the United States government, Fiscal Year 1984.* Washington, DC: U.S. Government Printing Office.

Office of Management and Budget. (1984). *Major themes and additional budget details, Fiscal Year 1985.* Washington, DC: U.S. Government Printing Office.

Office of Management and Budget. (1986). *Major policy initiatives, Fiscal Year 1987.* Washington, DC: U.S. Government Printing Office.

Office of Management and Budget. (1987). *Budget of the United States government, Fiscal Year 1988.* Washington, DC: U.S. Government Printing Office.

Osterman, P. (1987). Turnover, employment security, and the performance of the firm. In M. M.

Kleiner, R. N. Block, M. Roomkin, & S. Salsburg (Eds.), *Human resources and the performance of the firm* (pp. 275–317). Madison, WI: Industrial Relations Research Association.

Pollock, M. A., & Bernstein, A. (1986). The disposable employee is becoming a fact of life. *Business Week*, December 15, pp. 52–56.

Rosenberg, S. (1983). Reagan social policy and labour force restructuring. *Cambridge Journal of Economics, 7* (2, June), 179–196.

Rosenberg, S. (1986). The state and employers versus trade unions: Minimal cooperation amidst conflict. In G. Sziráczky (Ed.), *The state, the trade unions and the labor market: Possibilities of and limitations to intervention* (Vol. I, pp. 9–40). Budapest: Hungarian Academy of Sciences, Institute of Economics.

Ruben, G. (1988). A review of collective bargaining in 1987. *Monthly Labor Review, 111* (1), 24–37.

Schor, J. B., & Bowles, S. (1987). Employment rents and the incidence of strikes. *Review of Economics and Statistics, 69* (2, November), 584–592.

Slaughter, J. (1983). *Concessions and how to beat them.* Detroit: Labor Education and Research Project.

Smith, R. E., & Vavrichek, B. (1987). The minimum wage: Its relation to incomes and poverty. *Monthly Labor Review, 110* (6, June), 24–30.

Taub, E., & Needleman, R. (1984). *Introduction to labor law update.* Gary, IN: Division of Labor Studies, Indiana University Northwest.

Ulmer, M. G., & Howe, W. J. (1988). Job gains in 1987; unemployment rate declines. *Monthly Labor Review, 111* (2), 57–67.

U.S. Department of Labor, Bureau of Labor Statistics (1983). "News release: Work experience survey shows that 116.3 million worked at some time in 1982, and 26.5 million encountered some unemployment," August 9. Washington, DC: U.S. Government Printing Office.

U.S. Department of Labor, Bureau of Labor Statistics (1987). "News release: Most occupational changes are voluntary," October 22. Washington, DC: U.S. Government Printing Office.

Vickery, C. (1979). Unemployment insurance: A positive reappraisal. *Industrial Relations, 18,* 1–17.

Zuckoff, M. (1988). "New minimum wage reopens old debate," *Chicago Tribune*, January 17.

5

Employment Policy, the State, and the Unions in the Federal Republic of Germany

Gerhard Bosch and Werner Sengenberger

I. INTRODUCTION

From 1957 to 1973, the Federal Republic of Germany had little unemployment. This changed with the economic crisis of 1974–1975. The number of unemployed increased to more than 1 million and remained at close to that level until the beginning of the 1980s. In the next crisis, 1980–1982, unemployment increased to over 2 million. According to all estimates, the number of unemployed will stay at around 2 million for the next 10 years. The Federal Republic of Germany, has, therefore, become a country with a large reserve army of labor.

The policy reaction to this situation has varied. The Social Democratic-Liberal Coalition Government of 1974–1975 was afraid that the large number of unemployed would lead to political radicalization. Therefore, to preserve social tranquility, unemployment benefits were raised on January 1, 1975, from 65.5% to 68% of previous net earnings. Later in the same year, however, considerable cuts were made in other social expenditures to reduce the rapidly growing federal budget deficit.

In subsequent years, from 1976–1979, some of these cuts were restored; some social benefits were even improved. In addition, some job-creation schemes were financed to increase employment (Hickel & Priewe, 1985). Overall, during the 1970s, the Social Democratic-Liberal Coalition Government reacted to the economic crisis by a contradictory program of stop-and-

Gerhard Bosch • WSI, Hans-Böckler Strasse 39, 4000 Düsseldorf 30, West Germany.   Werner Sengenberger • International Institute for Labor Studies, CH-1211 Geneva 22, Switzerland.

go, where temporary savings as well as social political aims played a part in influencing policy.

In the 1980s, there have been fundamental changes in government policy. The further rise in the number of unemployed caused a substantial increase in the payments of benefits. At the same time, a reduction in tax payments and social insurance contributions increased the federal budget deficit. As a result of three cuts in expenditures (the so-called "actions" of 1981, 1982, 1983), the deficit was reduced again. Reforms were implemented that were designed to limit access to unemployment compensation and lower benefit levels. In addition, expenditures on labor market programs declined. Taxes on employers were reduced at the same time.

The Conservative-Liberal Coalition took power in 1982. Dismantling social policies was no longer explained by the need to reduce budget deficits. Now, the stated aim of government policy was to increase flexibility in the labor market, which, it was said, was prevented by the too favorable safety net protecting the employed.

Since 1984, the budget has been balanced. It was, therefore, no longer necessary to justify further cuts in benefits for financial reasons. Furthermore, even from a conservative point of view, the unemployed had already made adequate concessions given the cuts in unemployment benefits. However, the flexible reserve army of labor could only be used to the extent that the existing legal protection against dismissals was curtailed and the ability to collective resistance reduced. These "gaps" in the reduction of social protection were to be closed by changing legislation dealing with dismissals, the right to strike, the establishment of works councils, and by increasing the flexibility of the wage structure.

The economy expanded from 1984 to 1986, and federal revenues grew. But, unlike at the end of the 1970s, these additional funds were not used for providing jobs but rather were earmarked for tax concessions for the wealthy.

In some respects, the Conservative-Liberal Coalition's policies in the 1980s are an extension of those of the Social-Democratic-Liberal Coalition. But, the Conservative-Liberal Coalition Government pursues this policy direction with more consistency than did its predecessor. Employment policy today is aimed at activating the reserve army mechanism.[1] This necessitates considerable political attacks on the social system in a country where legal protection of dismissals and codetermination had been consolidated. These attacks have taken place in the past few years.

The main opponents of this policy have been the trade unions. Although mass unemployment undermined their power and increased internal tensions within the labor movement, the German Trade Union Federation (DGB) was able to organize a centralized campaign against the government's policy. Its biggest trade union, the engineering and metal workers union (IG Metall),

---

[1]The conservatives put it somewhat differently. An important conservative slogan is "Let more market forces rule the labor market" (Soltwedel, 1984).

was able—in spite of mass unemployment and the united opposition of the government and employers—to win a strike to shorten the work week.

The chapter is divided into five main sections. The first describes the substantial cutbacks in unemployment compensation that have occurred in recent years. The second investigates the governmental assault on legal rules and regulations governing employment security and worker protection. The third discusses the employer demand for increased flexibility in the wage level and the wage structure. Although management has strived for greater flexibility and cost relief from wage and social policies, organized labor has tried to defend existing rules and regulations. But, in the area of work-time reduction, treated in the fourth section, labor has been on the offensive. A scheme for analyzing and interpreting recent changes in West German employment and labor market policies is presented in the fifth section.

II. UNEMPLOYMENT POLICY

From 1981 to 1983, the federal budget cuts were aimed at labor market programs. About 45% of the total savings resulted from cuts in unemployment benefit levels and increases in unemployment insurance contributions. As of 1982, the base from which the unemployment benefit ratio of 68% is computed excludes overtime payments, vacation allowances, and the (widespread) thirteenth month of wage and salary income. The exclusion of these income components lowers the effective replacement ratio to between 57.6% and 63.6% of previous net income, depending on the extent to which the recipient received such allowances and on the number of dependents (Sengenberger, 1984, p. 334).

The disciplining role of the employment agency has been strengthened by redefining "suitable work" for the unemployed. After a short period of time, the unemployed are now compelled to accept jobs with lower skill levels, often requiring relocation. If they refuse such positions, they lose their unemployment benefits. From the workers' viewpoint, the extent of deterioration is not quite clear, however, because the implementation and interpretation of the rules is largely left to the local employment administration. What is clear is that substantial downgrading can occur, especially if a worker is repeatedly unemployed (Sengenberger, 1984, p. 334).

Unemployment benefits have been made more difficult to obtain. The minimum contribution period that would entitle a person to unemployment benefits has been increased from 6 months to 12 months. This change, in effect, excludes many young people and women recently reentering the labor market from these benefits.

Additional cuts in wage replacement levels for the unemployed occurred in Fiscal Year 1984. The center–right federal government coalition lowered the basic unemployment insurance benefit for persons with no children to 63% of previous net earnings.

It has become obvious that unemployment insurance is only viable in protecting the unemployed during a short crisis. However, more of the unemployed are out of work for long periods of time. As of the end of 1986, one third of them had been unemployed for a year or more. Many have experienced a drastic lowering of their income. Unemployment benefits can be collected for only 1 year. Thereafter, unemployment assistance, a lower payment than unemployment insurance, may be requested. This, however, is subject to a means test.

As a result of the increase in long-term unemployment and the elimination of certain groups from unemployment insurance schemes, in 1987 only 37.4% of the unemployed received unemployment benefits as compared to 65.9% in 1975. In 1987, 25.9% of the unemployed were provided unemployment assistance. In that same year, 36.7% of the unemployed did not receive unemployment benefits or unemployment assistance. This is in contrast to 1975 when only 23.9% of the unemployed found themselves in this situation. Although the number of people out of work in recent years is substantially higher than in the early 1980s, the federal government spends less on payments to the unemployed.[2]

The reduction in unemployment benefits can be explained by two factors. First, the government wished to reduce the power of labor relative to capital. Unemployment compensation provides a cushion for workers as they search for work. That cushion has been somewhat withdrawn. With lower replacement ratios, workers are forced into accepting lower paying jobs and less skilled work than they have been accustomed to. Second, during an economic crisis, it is easier to legitimize cutting benefits by citing the large deficits of the unemployment insurance funds.

Political intervention and the increase in long-term unemployment have made the unemployment insurance scheme an "insurance for the unemployed without the right to claim," which in the meantime has accumulated substantial balances (Bosch, 1984). These sums are partly used as a reserve and partly taken to pay for an expansion of job training and for work schemes for the unemployed.

The long-term unemployed are only to a limited degree able to be quickly absorbed into jobs. Many have experienced psychological and physical problems and seen their work skills deteriorate. The government attempts to prepare at least a portion of the unemployed reserve army for employment.

III. EMPLOYMENT SECURITY AND WORKER PROTECTION POLICY

In addition to rolling back social benefits in the 1980s, the federal government launched a major assault on legal rules and regulations governing em-

---

[2]The federal government is compelled to finance the deficits of the unemployment insurance scheme (Bundesanstalt für Arbeit) as well as unemployment assistance payments that are granted to the unemployed when the insurance benefits are exhausted.

ployment security and worker protection. Various types of measures have been implemented, such as allowing longer working hours as well as night work and weekend work (in particular industries) for youth.

All of these measures were justified on the grounds of removing legal barriers to profitable deployment of labor. Unless restrictive legal rules were relaxed or abandoned, it was argued that new avenues would not be opened up for economic growth and employment expansion.

The most significant legislative initiative by the federal government was the Employment Promotion Act, which took effect on May 1, 1985. This law introduced a series of amendments to existing rules designed to "open up new opportunities" for the unemployed. The general aim of the law is to make worker deployment in the firm more flexible.

The law created opportunities for a more flexible utilization of workers. Between May 1, 1985, and January 1, 1990, fixed-term contracts for newly hired workers and apprentices taken over into regular employment upon completion of vocational training could last for up to 18 months (from the previous 6 months) without any need for justification. Between May 1, 1985 and January 1, 1990, the maximum permissible period for the use of personnel leasing (the temporary use of employees of agencies) was extended from 3 months to 6 months.

Working time arrangements and work scheduling were made more flexible. Part-time work was made more attractive. More possibilities were provided for job sharing and the short-run scheduling of working hours in line with labor demand (so-called "capacity-oriented variable working hours").

Small firms and newly established firms were granted special relief from restrictive regulations. It was argued that these rules substantially increased the labor costs of small firms, thus restricting their potential for job creation. Very small firms had hitherto been exempted from most of the protection rules and from works council representation. The changes under this law are geared toward further exemption of the small firm from rules regarding worker protection. Part-time workers are excluded when determining the number of employees and, thereby, allowing more firms to remain below the size threshold for which protection rules apply. Newly established small firms have been given special permission to use workers on fixed-term contracts for up to 2 years. Small firms are no longer obliged to continue wage and salary payments when workers are ill.

Section 112 of the Plant Constitution Act has been altered to relax the requirement for employers to negotiate with the works council a social plan in case of work force reduction or other organizational changes with negative consequences for the employees. Thus, for example, the proportion of workers to be dismissed in an economic downturn that requires negotiation between management and the works council has been increased from 5% to 10% or 20% (depending on the size of the establishment) of the work force. Newly established enterprises are (during the first 4 years) totally exempted from the obligation to conclude social plans.

The legislative process leading to this law was accompanied by strong opposition and protests by unions and the left political spectrum in Germany. Measured against the intended positive employment effects, the results of the Employment Promotion Act have so far been disappointing. According to studies by the German Textile Union and the Trade, Banking and Communications Union, the impact was mainly one of replacement. Full-time jobs were replaced by part-time jobs, and normal unlimited work contracts by fixed-term contracts. There was a substitution of contractural patterns but no significant addition to employment. Consequently, the unions have argued that the Employment Promotion Act does not deserve its name.

The law is likely to increase or speed up a tendency for more casual and precarious employment that began in the 1970s. Thus, for example, according to figures from the Federal Employment Institute, the incidence of personnel leasing (agency labor) increased from 140,000 in 1975 to 380,000 cases in 1981 (when this statistic was discontinued). There were four times as many person-hours worked by agency labor in 1985 than in 1975.

These developments taken together point to a sharpening of intrafirm and intraestablishment segmentation between core and peripheral work forces.

IV. POLICIES TOWARD THE LEVEL AND STRUCTURE OF WAGES

Increased flexibility has also been called for in the wage level and the wage structure. Concerning the wage level, it is downward flexibility that is said to be in order. Regarding the wage structure, employers and many mainstream economists have argued for more variability in wage levels.

A. Wage-Level Policy

The recession of 1974–1975 marked the beginning of significantly higher levels of unemployment. Assuming a rather close connection between wage levels and employment levels, employers and a significant number of economists (led by the German Council of Economic Experts) explained the persistent unemployment as the outcome of a misguided income distribution. The total wage bill was seen as too high in relation to profits so that, as a consequence, investment was falling behind and unemployment rising. According to this view, altering the income distribution in favor of profits would allow industry to step up investments and regain higher employment levels (Sengenberger, 1984, p. 330).

In spite of the employers and professional economists' campaign for low or zero wage increases, real wages continued to rise until 1980. But in the early 1980s, the German unions, being sensitive to the preceding argument, pursued a wage policy with moderate annual wage improvements. Between 1980 and 1984, real wages fell.[3]

---

[3]For a good treatment of wage and incomes policies in West Germany see Flanagan, Soskice, and Ulman (1983, pp. 208–300).

Further income losses to workers were due to increased rates of contribution to social security and, more recently, the extension of the obligation of paying social security contributions on extra payments (like vacation pay and Christmas bonuses). At the same time, profit taxes were reduced. It has been estimated that the total amount of money involved in this redistribution package amounted to 210 billion DM for the years 1982 to 1985 (Adamy & Steffen, 1985, p. 2).

B. Wage Structure Policy

By international standards, West Germany had reached a fairly high degree of wage standardization and fairly uniform rates of annual wage improvement across firms, regions, and industrial sectors. Though there were larger differentials in effective wages, legally enforced contract rates affecting all employers set a minimum pay floor in nearly all parts of the economy. Consequently, there was little opportunity for an employer to escape or undercut the highly institutionalized wage standards (Sengenberger, 1984, p. 331).

But recently the wage structure has become a subject of controversy. Downward wage flexibility has emerged. In some cases, wage drift is being eliminated. In other cases, firms are paying less than the prevailing rates.[4] Though this has occurred, both employers (particularly in the small firm sector) and a large number of professional economists still call for more flexibility in the wage structure. Wages are to be made more responsive to supply and demand and should be allowed to vary much more than hitherto by region, industry, and firm. Recently, the rigid wage structure has been viewed as the major obstacle to structural change and the modernization of the economy.

Various measures have been suggested to allow the wage structure to become more flexible (which would most likely be in a downward direction under present labor market conditions). They include increased skill differentials, lower entry rates for newly hired labor, more profit-sharing and profit-related compensation (in lieu of wage increases), increased freedom for the individual worker to choose what form the annual improvement should assume, that is, whether it should go into wages, more vacation time, higher pensions, or more profit shares, more local and individual bargaining (in lieu of industrywide wage setting), and abandoning the law under which collective contracts may be declared uniformly applicable to all employers in the bargaining district.

The government, as yet, has not become active in the wage policy field. But, pressures from experts and also from members of the coalition parties have increased, opening up the way for more wage flexibility. An obstacle to introducing the various changes proposed may be seen in the industrywide

---

[4]Whereas for some time we witnessed a tendency for greater wage uniformity due to a decline of wage elements above and beyond the contract wage (wage drift), later on we tend to have increased differentiation again due to the erosion of the collective wage standard.

bargaining units and collective contracts, whose maintenance is supported not only by the unions but also by many employers in order to ensure equal terms for competition.

V. WORK TIME REDUCTION[5]

German employers have argued for rolling back social benefits, removing legal barriers to profitable deployment of labor, and cutting wages as means for increasing employment. The German labor movement favors work time reduction for combatting unemployment. Organized labor expects work time reduction measures to significantly increase the number of jobs, reduce the level of unemployment, and, ultimately, move the balance of power in the labor market in the unions' favor.

As the various special factors that stimulated economic growth in West Germany in the post-World War II era (such as rebuilding, integration into the world market, and rearmament) gradually disappeared, the average growth rate of the economy declined continually from the 1950s between one business cycle and another. From 1961, the rate of growth in productivity per working hour began to decline. Although productivity was still growing faster than output, the employment gap could be effectively closed by a relatively rapid reduction in working hours per employed person. However, in the mid-1970s, the gap between output growth and productivity growth opened decisively. Reductions in average working hours per person were not sufficient to offset the shortfall in employment (see Table 1).

From the perspective of employment policy, the need for a rapid cut in average hours of work has increased. But, the rate at which such reductions have taken place has slowed considerably. Although from 1960 to 1975, the actual annual reduction in working hours per employed person averaged 1.1%, between 1975 and 1984 it only amounted to .4%.[6]

The workweek was reduced to 40 hours for the majority of employees by the beginning of the 1970s and has since remained at that level. The majority of the employed population had in the meantime achieved 30 days annual holiday. Employers were not prepared to move beyond these boundaries of a 40-hour week and 30 days of annual holiday for white- and blue-collar workers.[7]

These reductions in working hours were not sufficient to offset the shortfall in employment. Between 1974 and 1984 about 1.2 million jobs were lost.

[5]This section is based on Bosch (1986).
[6]See Bosch, 1986, Table 3, for more information on trends in working hours.
[7]In 1978–1979, in the steel industry, the union for metal and engineering workers (IG Metall), failed, after a long strike, to achieve its objective of a 35-hour week. But it did succeed in gaining considerable improvements in holidays in addition to extra holiday entitlement days for older employees and shift workers.

Table 1. Economic Development in West Germany, 1950–1987 (annual percentage changes)

	1950/55[a]	1955/1960[a]	1960/64	1964/69	1969/73	1973/76	1976/80	1980/84	1981	1982	1983[b]	1984[b]	1985[b]	1986[b]	1987[b]
Real GDP[c]	+9.5	+6.5	+4.7	+4.2	+4.2	+1.3	+2.8	+0.9	+0.2	−0.7	+1.5	+2.8	+2.1	+2.6	+1.5
Productivity per working hour	+7.6	+6.3	+5.3	+5.5	+4.9	+3.6	+3.3	+2.2	+1.8	+0.7	+3.4	+3.2	+2.7	+2.1	+1.5
Working time per employee	−0.9	−1.3	−1.1	−0.9	−1.2	−0.6	−1.1	−0.3	−1.0	+0.4	−0.3	−0.5	−1.3	−0.5	−0.6
Productivity per employee	+6.6	+4.9	+4.2	+4.5	+3.6	+3.0	+2.1	+1.8	+0.9	+1.0	+3.0	+2.7	+1.4	+1.5	+0.9
Number of employees	+2.7	+1.6	+0.5	−0.3	+0.6	−1.7	+0.7	−0.9	−0.7	−1.7	1.5	+0.1	+0.7	+1.0	+0.6
Total volume of working hours (changes in output minus changes in productivity per hour)	+1.8	+0.2	−0.6	−1.2	−0.6	−2.2	−0.4	−1.3	−1.6	−1.3	−1.8	−0.4	−0.6	+0.4	+0.0

[a]Without Saarland and W. Berlin.
[b]Provisional.
[c]1950–1960. Real GDP is measured in 1962 prices; 1960–1985, real GDP is measured in 1980 prices.
Source: Deutsches Institut für Wirtschaftsforschung (DIW), Vierteljährliche volkswirtschaftliche Gesamtrechnung für die Bundesrepublik Deutschland 1950–1960; S. Folge 1960–1986; DIW Wochenbericht 1–2/88.

This fall in employment was relatively larger than the job loss occurring in several other Western European countries.[8]

In addition, from 1977–1978 to 1984, the working population increased following the earlier increase in the birthrates. As a result of all these factors, the number of unemployed rose to 1 million on average from 1975 and above 2 million from 1983.

Estimates suggest that an average annual growth rate of at least 3% must be reached to prevent a loss of jobs. But, it is likely that economic growth will not even average 2% in the near future. The Institute of Labor Market and Occupational Research of the Federal Labor Office has made a number of projections for the labor market up to the year 2000. According to its scenario of the most probable outcome, the number of unemployed will rise further to the year 1990 and will remain on a high plateau up to the year 2000 (Klauder, Schnur, & Thon, 1985). These projections are not only of academic interest: Future expectations have played a decisive role both in the internal trade union discussions and in public discussions connected with employment policy. Labor market projections in fact became an important political issue. Employers who promised full employment brought about by economic growth were generally not believed.

Under these labor market conditions, the demand by the trade unions to reduce working time became more important in employment policy discussions than in most other capitalist countries. But the method by which this desired reduction should be achieved remained controversial.

Most unions wanted the government to reduce the retirement age to 58 years. This seemed to be a safe approach, because the trade union demands would be paid for by the government, and any real conflict with the employers would be avoided. Conflict confidently could be expected if the working week was to be reduced below 40 hours or holidays extended beyond 6 weeks, as the employers had agreed among themselves that they would not negotiate beyond these limits. In practice, they established a taboo (Tabu-Katalog) over even discussing changes to these boundaries.

However, it soon became evident that in most industries the retirement age had been de facto so far reduced, that a further reduction to 58 years would only have a minor effect. In the 1970s, besides the lengthening of holidays, earlier retirement was a central point of discussion. A flexible retirement age starting at 63 years (from 65 years before) was introduced. Furthermore, access to pensions was facilitated for those unfit to work, for particular occupations, and for persons of age 60 after 1 year of unemployment. The lowering of the pensionable age together with social security measures introduced by the Social Democratic-Liberal government were widely supported by the unions and their members and made the demand for an earlier retirement a popular one among the employed. However, this success has reduced the scope for comparable measures now. In 1984, the average retirement age

---

[8]In 1985, the employment index in West Germany was 93.9 (1973 = 100); in France it was 99.8; in Great Britain 98.2; in Italy 107.6; in Japan 110.8; and in the United States 125.8 (OECD, 1985).

for manual workers was 57.9 years and 60.5 years for white-collar ones. Further reductions of the retirement age affected a much smaller proportion of the employed than 10 years earlier because there were relatively fewer older workers in the labor market. This particularly applied to the workers of the IG Metall union (2.5 million members in 1984), which in 1982, after a considerable internal conflict, changed its position and demanded a 35-hour work week. At this point the only other unions demanding a shortening of the working week were "printing and paper" (IG Druck und Papier) (142,000 members) and "timber and plastics" (Gewerkschaft Holz und Kunststoff) (147,000 members).

When the 1983 campaign by these trade unions began, the initial situation was particularly unfavorable. The members were skeptical. There was only limited support from the general public, the academic establishment, churches, and the Social Democratic Party. The employers' organizations had declared publicly that under no circumstances would they agree to a reduction in weekly working hours. The federal government fully supported this hard line. To ensure the success of their policy, the employers had established a central negotiating team and thereby succeeded in concealing their own differences of opinion from outsiders, which they had not been able to do previously. Compared with this centralized opposition, the trade unions were becoming increasingly divided, as high unemployment gave rise to further internal differences. Some of the trade unions belonging to the German Trade Union Federation (the Deutscher Gewerkschaftsbund, which had 17 affiliated trade unions with 7.66 million members in 1984) were prepared to make considerable concessions in order to cooperate with employers and the state and restricted themselves explicitly or implicitly to safeguard only those employed in a single industry or possibly in a single section of an industry. Those concerned were primarily the trade unions for "food-drink-catering" (264,000 members), "mining and energy" (360,000 members), "chemicals, paper and ceramics" (638,000 members), textiles and garment (260,000 members), and "bricks, sand and gravel" (517,000 members). These trade unions called for a lowering of the pensionable age and vehemently criticized, sometimes publicly, the demand for a reduction in weekly working hours.

The federal government and the employers placed their hope in splitting the unions. Although in 1982 both had expressed their opposition to any further reduction in the retirement age, when the strike ballot in the engineering industry took place, a law was passed allowing a transition pension (Tarifrente). This law makes retirement possible at the age of 58. Up to the normal (statutory) retirement age (in general 63 years), those opting for early retirement get 65% of their previous gross earnings. The federal government pays a supplement of 35% of this prepension if an unemployed worker is thereby employed. However, such employment is not controlled. Payment of the remainder was to be subject to collective bargaining. In this way, through the support of the state, the conflict over distribution was to be defused and— as the federal government declared officially—an alternative to the 35-hour week offered to the trade unions, so that the "united front called for by the IG

Metall to fight for the 35-hour working week would not be achieved"
(Spieker, 1984).

The employers offered to conclude an agreement about the Tarifrente
plus a wage increase of more than 3% (slightly above the expected rate of
inflation), intending thereby to buy off the trade unions. Beyond that, they
demanded individually agreed flexible part-time work and flexible annual
contracts (which would allow them to schedule working hours in line with
seasonal demand). Furthermore, capital-intensive and expanding companies
were interested in an extension of the weekly working hours and a reintroduction of Saturday work.

In Spring 1984, the defeat of the IG Metall Union seemed to be inevitable.
Yet, the conflict had its own dynamic. First, the IG Metall was able to con-
vince a large proportion of its members and officials of the necessity of the 35-
hour week. Contrary to fears within the union, 80% of all members in the
states of Hessen and Baden-Württemberg in April and May 1984 voted for a
strike. The main reasons for such a high vote in favor of striking were:

The members had understood that the 35-hour week was good for their
own job security and not only an act of solidarity with the unemployed.

The reduction of the retirement age only concerned a few employees and
would, therefore, add only a few jobs.

The IG Metall would not make wage concessions to gain a reduction of
the working time.

Government intervention and the rigid attitude of the employers made
clear that a defeat of the IG Metall union would mean a defeat for the labor
movement as a whole for a long time to come.

Second, the mood among the unions had changed. The majority of the
unions demanded the 35-hour week. It was a result of the efforts of powerful
and well-organized unions in those sectors threatened by major job loss due
to rationalization. It was, furthermore, a result of left-wing influence in the
unions. In addition, all public sector unions (with the exception of the police
union) joined the demand for the 35-hour week. This was surprising insofar
as the proportion of older workers in the public service is almost twice as high
as in the entire economy (entire economy 4.4%, public service 8%). However,
civil service jobs were particularly threatened because of the government's
policy of cuts and privatization. The unions feared that with a further rise of
unemployment, the pressure on public employees would increase. They regarded shortening weekly working time as the only effective means to reducing unemployment.

The IG Metall union in Hessen and Baden-Württemberg was on strike for
7 weeks from the middle of May 1984, and the IG Druck und Papier was on
strike throughout West Germany for 12 weeks from the middle of April.
Because every striking trade unionist in the Federal Republic receives strike
pay, a general strike (within an industry) is very expensive, particularly when
employers can lock workers out. In the past, the employers in, for example,
printing and paper, have replied to targeted strikes (or guerrilla strikes) with a
general lockout. The dispute in 1978 cost the IG Druck und Papier 15 million

DM in strike pay, compared with a yearly surplus in the strike funds of 1.8 million DM: 80% of these costs were caused by lockouts. According to a decision in 1980 of the Federal Labor Court, employers are only allowed to lock out "within reason." If less than a quarter of the workers in a bargaining area strike, the employers may only lock out up to another quarter. The lockout was allowed (within certain limits) so as not "to threaten the solidarity" of the employers through limited guerilla strikes. However, the employers are not able to burden the trade unions through lockouts to the same degree as in 1980. Because of this restriction, a form of secondary lockout (Kalte Aussperrung) had achieved more significance. This is the closure of enterprises that are unable to continue production because of nondelivery of supplies. In these cases, employers are not obliged to continue to pay wages. The affected workers outside the bargaining area are able, however, to claim short-term benefits at the local employment office. For those inside the bargaining areas, the union paid strike pay.

The IG Metall union first called out workers in enterprises supplying the motor industry. The employers reacted quickly with lockouts. In addition—allegedly because of inadequate delivery of parts—in a short period all important car factories in West Germany were closed, which affected suppliers in areas that had not been called out on strike. We now know that these closures were tactics used by the employers. BMW and Daimler Benz, for example, stopped accepting all deliveries 2 days after the strike started. This led to the halting of production in a large number of supplying firms. According to IG Metall, 57,000 workers were on strike, 180,000 were locked out in Baden-Württemberg and Hessen, and 200,000 were affected by secondary lockouts, most of them outside the bargaining area.

The Federal Labor Office agreed, after consulting the federal government, not to pay short-time benefits to workers who were affected by secondary lockouts, as otherwise it might not be considered to be "fulfilling its duty to remain neutral." In this way—as the president of the Federal Labor Office cynically declared—the pressure on the engineering union would be increased and "the dispute would be shortened." The IG Metall union could not, even if it wanted to, fund the strike for a long period, if it paid strike benefits to these workers as well. The IG Metall union already had to pay 500 million DM strike pay during the conflict. These people would have had to bear the loss of wages themselves and, if need be, apply for social security. The intention was to create internal difficulties for the trade union by means of secondary lockouts. The IG Metall union had no choice but to politicize the dispute. In Bonn, 230,000 engineering workers demonstrated against the decision of the Federal Labor Office. Only toward the end of the strike—after the trade unions had won cases at various labor courts—was the practice altered and payment of short-term benefits permitted, but even then only "with reservations."

The IG Druck und Papier union chose a flexible strike tactic. They called out workers on a rolling scale of a few days at a time and then only for a few days and at specific enterprises. The strikes could not be foreseen by the employers who often only became aware of a strike on the very day it happened.

The IG Druck und Papier union, by using flexible tactics, and despite small financial resources, maintained the strike for some weeks longer than the engineering union. This advantage was also reflected in a more favorable settlement. The unexpected ability of the trade unions to hold out in the dispute, and particularly in the prosperous automobile industry, forced the employers to come to terms. A political arbitrator, the former Defense Minister Leber, was appointed, and the following compromise reached in the engineering industry:

1. A reduction in weekly working hours to 38.5 hours beginning January 4, 1985.
2. Taking into consideration "the needs of an enterprise," individual working hours per week could be set between 37 and 40 hours. But the average per enterprise must be 38.5 hours. Employees who work 37 hours were to be compensated in their wages so that their weekly income remained on the same level as for someone working 38.5 hours. This equalization of wages was to be abolished in four stages within a 4-year period.
3. The weekly hours of work may be spread uniformly or nonuniformly over the 5 working days in the week. The specified weekly hours must be achieved on average every 2 months. The average weekly hours worked would be checked monthly in the firm. If the average exceeded 38.5 hours, an appropriate adjustment would need to be agreed to immediately with the works council.
4. On July 1, 1984, wages were raised by 3.3%. Beginning on April 1, 1985, a wage compensation payment of 3.9% was made for reduced weekly hours. In addition, wages were increased by 2%.

The exact timing of working hours and the individual differentiation of working hours had to be agreed at the enterprise between management and the works councils. The IG Druck und Papier union was able, by prolonging its strike, to avoid the clause allowing for individual differences in working time. However, it was still possible on the basis of an agreement within an enterprise to distribute working time unequally over the whole year. This was, however, already the practice in the printing industry prior to the dispute.

We feel the strikes were a trade union success. In a period of conservative hegemony, it was shown that even under unfavorable political conditions, a confrontation with employers and the state could be attempted and won. The trade unions are thus not compelled to be only on the defensive.

But to be successful in such a confrontation, trade unions need a high degree of internal unity. This unity was not found within all trade unions of the Deutscher Gewerkschaftsbund but was present with the IG Metall union itself. This union organizes white- and blue-collar workers of the most important industrial branches in West Germany (automobile, steel, machine-tool building, and electrical industries), which have about 4 million employees. Each settlement with the IG Metall union provides, therefore, a certain level of generality for the whole industry, so that the competitiveness of single branches is not threatened. Four million employees and their families—a high proportion of the whole population—benefited from a reduction of working time. This gave the trade union demand a political generality as well and made it difficult for the employers and the state to localize the conflict. The strike was certainly helped by the comparatively good economic situation in the engineering industry, particularly in Baden-Württemberg, which made each day of the strike extremely costly for the employers.

With the strike, a process of further reductions of the agreed working hours took place. By December 1985, the 38.5 hours week had spread to 6.7 million employees. Some agreements were only reached through additional strikes, for example in metal working.

The government soon emphasized that it did not want to accept another centrally led campaign and strike for the 35-hour working week by the IG Metall union. It wished to avoid another defeat in such a confrontation. In March 1986, Section 116 of the Employment Promotion Act was changed, although the trade unions mobilized millions of workers against this change. (The Deutscher Gewerkschaftsbund organized ballots on this subject on the plant level. About 7.2 of 7.6 million workers voted against the change of Section 116.)

In the future, short-time benefits will not be paid to workers in enterprises outside the bargaining area that are closed because of inadequate deliveries of parts during a strike, if the workers in these enterprises are organized by the striking union and if the union makes roughly similar demands in all bargaining. Short-time benefits would not be paid to metal workers affected by secondary lockouts outside the striking area if the IG Metall union was demanding a reduction of weekly working time throughout its whole organizational sphere. The government and the employers want the union to split its demands: for example, to ask for more wages in Hessen, for a weekly working-time reduction in Baden-Württemberg, or for more holidays in Nordrhein-Westfalen. The trade unions will have difficulty mounting national campaigns for further reductions in working time.

VI. A SCHEME FOR ANALYSIS AND INTERPRETATION

In the previous sections, we have presented a panoramic picture of recent changes in West German employment and labor market policies. The various changes introduced by the federal government point to a clear-cut logical coherence and direction: Both in terms of intent and effect, they are to produce more flexibility in the labor market. It has to be emphasized, however, that this flexibility is of a particular kind, one that operates through greater differentiation or inequality of wages, labor costs, protective provisions, and income support. It is likely to redirect competition in the economy toward the labor market and particularly toward competition for cheap labor and immediate adjustment to changing market conditions (Sengenberger, 1984). This type of flexibility may also be called "static," in contrast to "dynamic" flexibility, which does not allow competitive advantages through cheap labor, but instead, due to universal labor standards and even labor costs, pushes firms to gain competitiveness through new products and processes, that is, through innovation. Firms have to be more creative because there is no "easy way out."

The search for "static" flexibility in Germany is accomplished by two pivotal processes: One is the rollback of financial support to the unemployed, short-time, sick, disabled, and otherwise disadvantaged worker. In this regard, we have seen over the past 10 years major cutbacks in the compensation schemes for the unemployed and underemployed (downscaling of benefit levels and increasing eligibility criteria) and for the worker undergoing training, with the effect of lowering the income replacement ratio of these workers.

These changes in policy have come on top of already substantially decreased income replacement levels as a result of a much larger share of persons out of work who had exhausted their claims for income support or were not eligible for it.

The other basic process, which has been given emphasis more recently, is the legal deregulation and destandardization of the terms of employment, the result being both a weakening and shortening (in terms of labor force coverage) of worker protection. Protective rules, such as protection from dismissal, have been relaxed or even abandoned for particular groups of workers or particular types of employers (small firms). Measures have been taken to allow for a larger scope for inferior terms of employment.

The cuts in the level of income substitution and the growing proportion of the unemployed who are not eligible for compensation have tended to shift the financial burden of income maintenance to a rapidly growing number of welfare recipients. And, because the municipalities are charged with the financing and administration of social welfare, the cost of unemployment is increasingly localized. Along with the shift of the financial burden, the problem of unemployment tends to be compartmentalized and diffused and, thus, the political sting removed.

Flexibilization is also under way with regard to wage structures and working time. There has been a general movement toward decentralizing the setting of terms and conditions of employment at the level of the individual firm rather than through law or industrywide collective agreement. The major moves in this direction have been taken by employers, but the government has approved of most of these actions and has given assistance.

The flexibilization measures have contributed to reactivating the reserve army and mechanism in the labor market in various ways. This mechanism does not merely rest on the amount of unemployment or the size of surplus labor. In a crucial way, the mechanism depends on the extent to which the jobless worker is forced to sell his or her labor in the market. This need grows with the downscaling of income substitution for the unemployed, sick, handi-capped, and retired worker. Therefore, in order to produce an effective labor reserve, you have to reduce or take away alternative income sources. In this way, you manage to generate the downward pressures on wages and em-ployment that the neocapitalist forces claim to be vital for economic recovery.

Although you need to scale down public worker compensation to rein-force the whip of market discipline you would not want to dismantle public subsistence altogether. You still would want to have a sufficient number of workers who are readily available, employable, and productive. This could explain, inter alia, why public support of adult training has been less retrenched.

In addition to producing a sufficient stock of readily available and pliable reserve labor, the disciplining effect of the mechanism also requires removing restrictive and sticky rules on hiring and firing of workers. The requirement is met by the weakening of employment security provisions, the facilitation of fixed-term deployment of labor, and by personnel leasing. Employers should be permitted the unrestricted exchange of labor, and the exchange should be widely practiced in order to demonstrate the reserve character of a sizable segment of the labor force. Workers should be socialized to accept this status and to make rotation a legitimate practice.

Yet, the story does not end here. There is, next to the legal enforcement of more flexibility and an active reserve army, a third ingredient of critical importance, one that is indispensable for the intended restructuring of the labor market. It is the loss of power and control of organized labor. Collective worker organization is weakened through flexibilization (which removes bar-riers to interworker competition) as well as through the reactivated reserve army. Membership in the unions of the German Trade Unions Federation (DGB) decreased from 7.96 million in 1981 to 7.66 million in 1984 but in-creased again during 1985 to 7.72 million.

The active reserve tends also to impair worker control. The greatly in-creased proportion of casual and peripheral workers tends to be largely out-side the control of unions and works councils. Agency workers, for example, are not counted as employees of the firm and, therefore, are not subject to works council representation.

The move toward decentralized bargaining on wages, working time, and other terms of employment is likely to weaken the influence of unions that in Germany are not allowed to negotiate within the firm. It will place the burden of worker representation more and more on the works council as the agent on the firm level. The shift toward decentralized worker representation will coin-cide with the weakened control of works councils due to growing casualiza-tion of the labor force and the growing significance of employment in small firms that are exempted from the Works Constitution Act and works council representation.

The major attack on union strength, however, has been accomplished through the recent change of the rules on worker compensation during strikes as regulated in Section 116 of the Employment Promotion Act. The new regulation that became effective in the Spring of 1986 leads to a cutoff of workers indirectly affected by strikes and lockouts from public unemployment compensation.

Still another move to weaken unions is under way through a bill designed to strengthen "minority rights" of workers both in the private and the public sectors. This is to be done through giving both rival unions and top executives more influence within the works council.

Finally, deregulation and decentralization of the "governance" of the labor market is likely to engender internal divisions and splits within the organized labor movement for it tends to emphasize, if not strengthen, prevailing disparities in the economic position of different industries, enterprises, and skill groups and, in turn, lower the propensity for concerted solidaristic action. Such divisions have surfaced recently on the issue of working time reduction.

Once organized labor is weakened in its relative power and control, further encroachments into the regulatory framework and lapses of influence are likely to come. A weakened labor movement will be less capable of resisting new efforts by the government to cut back on social spending and deregulate employment. And it will be less equipped to fight an antiinterventionist deflationary course of economic policy leading to persistent unemployment.

We potentially face a kind of vicious circle of social restructuring in the labor market based on the quadrangular and mutually reinforcing relationships between flexibilization policies, a reactivated reserve army with the effect of restoring tight market discipline, heightened structural divisions in the labor market and power relations changed in favor of capital and at the expense of labor (Figure 1).

In our view, the spiral was triggered off by rising unemployment during the economic recession of 1974–1975. As unemployment remained at much

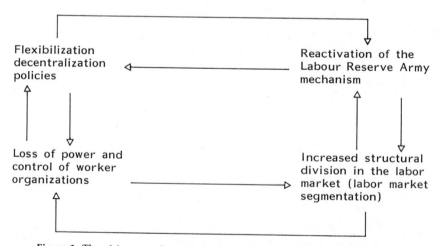

Figure 1. The vicious quadrangle of social restructuring of the labor market.

higher levels than previously, it created strained state budgets and eased the way to cutbacks in social spending that, then, led to the reactivated reserve. These initial forces produced structural divisions in the labor market and concomitant fragmentation of collective worker strength. Although the trigger of the downward spiral originated at a particular point of circular causation, for the feedback process to set in and be maintained, all four forces needed to be at work, and political intervention was indispensible to keep the circular causation going. In other words, the escalation did not come automatically.

The same would apply, however, if one would attempt to revert the spiral of depressive and destructive forces into a reconstructive one. This, again, would likely require more than one of the components to be involved in changing the direction. Thus, for example, unemployment would have to be lowered to strengthen organized labor. In addition, the particular trend toward increased flexibility would have to end. And new stability would be required to break the disciplining effect of the reserve army, and further, to stem the fragmentation of worker organization.

The question remains where in the vicious circle the redirection of forces is likely to be accomplished. Despite the generally adverse economic conditions and a rather hostile political environment, the German trade union movement, as a whole, has so far remained united on key issues and stood firm in defending previously won rights. Though it has lost the battle against conservative antiunion forces on the issue of worker compensation in case of a strike, it has, nevertheless, been able to mobilize millions of workers to openly and forcefully protest governmental action. The extent of this resistance and the widespread public support for the unions was obviously unforeseen by the federal government. Organized labor may have been encouraged by the earlier success of the metal and printing unions. These unions made an important inroad toward shorter weekly working hours, by carrying through strikes almost unprecedented in length and financial burden. Thus, we might say that there are significant counterforces operating against the vicious circle of restructuring the labor market.

VII. REFERENCES

Adamy, W., & Steffen, J. (1985). Zwischenbilanz von Sozialdemontage und Umverteilungspolitik seit 1982, *Schriften des Seminars für Sozialpolitik der Universität zu Köln*.

Bosch, G. (1984). Arbeitsmarktpolikik ohne Arbeitslose: Zur Entwicklung der Überschüsse bei der Bundesanstalt für Arbeit, *WSI-Mitteilungen, 37*, 567–574.

Bosch, G. (1986). The dispute over the reduction of the working week in West Germany. *Cambridge Journal of Economics, 10*, 271–290.

Flanagan, R. J., Soskice, D. W., and Ulman, L. (1983). *Unionism, economic stabilization, and income policies: European Experience.* Washington, DC: The Brookings Institution.

Hickel, R., & Priewe, J. (1985). *Ineffiziente Instrumente oder unzureichende Anwendung? Die Finanzpolitik von 1974–1984 auff dem Prüfstand: Argumente für ein Beschäftigungsprogramm.* Bremen: Progress-Institut für Wirtschaftsforschung, Studie Nr. 3.

Klauder, W., Schnur, P., & Thon, M. (1985). Arbeitsmarktperspektiven der 80-er und 90-er Jahre. Neue Modellrechnungen für Potential und Bedarf an Arbeitskräfften. *Mitteilungen aus der Arbeitsmarkt- und Berufsforschung, 18*, 41–62.

Organization for Economic Cooperation and Development (1985). *Economic Outlook* [Paris], 12.

Sengenberger, W. (1984). West German employment policy: Restoring worker competition. *Industrial Relations, 23*, 323–343.

Soltwedel, R. (1984). *Mehr Markyt am Arbeitsmarkt. Ein Plädoyer für weniger Arbeitsmarktpolitik.* München/Wien.

Spieker, W. (1984). Verbände und Institutionen in der Arbeitszeitpolitik. In H. Mayr, & H. Janßen, (Eds.), *Perspektiven der Arbeitszeitverkürzung,* Köln, pp. 295–306.

6

Reregulating the Labor Market amid an Economic and Political Crisis

Spain, 1975–1986

Lluis Fina, Alberto Meixide, and Luis Toharia

I. INTRODUCTION

The Spanish labor market has experienced important transformations in the last 10 years, not only in terms of its economic performance but also with respect to its institutional framework. Both aspects have to be taken into account if one is to understand not only the general development of industrial relations but also the specific government interventions with respect to it.

The employment situation has sharply deteriorated. Over the past decade, Spain has been the European country with the highest rate of unemployment. The unemployment rate rose from 5.3% in 1977 to 21.9% in 1985. As Table 1 shows, this increase in unemployment has been mainly due to the decrease in the number of employees, notably in manufacturing and construction.[1] The general economic crisis suffered in the Western industrialized world during the 1970s has been compounded in Spain, a process especially felt in the labor market.

The process of political change that started in 1976 after the death of General Franco led to dramatic changes in the institutional framework of the

---

[1]Explaining the decline in the number of employees is beyond the scope of this chapter. For more details, see Fina and Hawkesworth (1987) and Toharia (1988). The specificity of the Spanish case has been recently studied in two papers by two of the authors: Fina (1987) and Toharia (1987).

Lluis Fina • Department of Applied Economics, Autonomous University of Barcelona, Belleterra, Spain.   **Alberto Meixide** • Department of Economics, University of Santiago de Compostela, Santiago de Compostela, Spain.   **Luis Toharia** • Department of Basic and Historical Economics, University of Alcalá de Henares, Alcalá de Henares, Spain.

Table 1. The Evolution of the Labor Market in Spain, 1977–1985
(yearly averages—absolute figures in thousands)

	1977	1985	Absolute variation	Percentage variation Total	Annual
Total population 16 and over	25,685.1	27,916.0	+2,230.9	+8.69	+1.05
Labor force	12,685.1	13,265.8	+ 343.6	+2.66	+0.33
Labor force partial rates:					
Total	50.3%	47.5%	—	—	—
Male	75.2%	68.7%	—	—	—
Female	27.5%	27.8%	—	—	—
Unemployment	682.4	2,910.2	+2,227.8	—	—
Unemployment rate	5.3%	21.9%	—	—	—
Total employment (excluding "marginal")	12,128.3	10,268.5	−1,859.8	−15.33	−2.06
Employees					
Total	8,537.4	7,151.6	−1,385.8	−16.23	−2.19
Public	1,336.5	1,748.2	+ 411.7	+30.80	+3.41
Private	7,201.0	5,403.5	−1,797.5	−24.96	−3.53
Independent workers (nonwage earners):					
Total	3,590.9	3,116.9	− 474.0	−13.20	−1.75
Employers	397.3	311.9	− 65.4	−16.46	−2.22
Self-employed	2,171.3	2,021.2	− 150.1	− 6.91	−0.89
Family helpers	996.7	728.0	− 268.7	−26.96	−3.85
Employment by sector:					
Agriculture	2,499.8	1,786.0	− 713.8	−28.55	−4.12
Mining & Mfg.	3,355.9	2,560.7	− 795.2	−23.70	−3.32
Construction	1,200.3	746.5	− 453.8	−37.81	−5.76
Services	5,072.4	5,175.3	+ 102.9	+ 2.03	+0.25

Source: Ministerio de Trabajo y Seguridad Social, *Boletín de estadísticas laborales,* No. 29, June 1986.

labor market. In April 1977, the freedom of union association was restored. New regulations concerning collective bargaining and many other aspects of industrial relations were subsequently introduced. This meant the end of the old Francoist system in which the state exercised tight control over the labor market, first by means of direct regulation, and later, through a peculiar system of collective bargaining that combined a paternalistic "vertical" trade union organization with outright repression of free unionism and strike activity.

These two processes of economic crisis and political change have occurred at the same time, implying a strong interaction between them. For example, many of the labor market measures adopted by the government have been presented as expedients aimed at fighting the economic crisis, but they have also been strongly influenced by the political transition taking place concurrently: They will probably have a permanent effect on the emerging industrial relations system. Similarly, the new legal framework has deliberately left undetermined many aspects whose concretization will clearly depend upon the dynamics of the economic crisis.

Several interesting issues arise in connection with the impact of government policies on industrial relations during this period. In this chapter, we shall concentrate on two, which we see as particularly relevant: the measures aimed at restraining the growth of nominal wages and the legal regulation of layoffs and dismissals. These are probably the two areas where change has been most dramatic, both in terms of the configuration and the degree of enforcement of the legal framework and in terms of the policies adopted by the government as well as the attitudes of trade unions and employers' associations.

A major contention of this chapter is that these two issues constitute important elements of a new system of regulation of the labor market. New mechanisms of control over the working classes have been established, replacing the older, more overtly repressive ones existing under Franco, whose effectiveness was being increasingly undermined. Thus, under the new system, the self-restraint shown by unions in several nationwide agreements—an attitude partly forced on them by the economic crisis, admittedly—has effectively acted as a check upon money wage increases. This proved to be impossible during the last years of Francoism, when all control devices built into the system of wage regulation broke down under the pressures of workers' demands for higher wages, giving way to an explosive "wage–price sprial." In addition, both individual dismissals and collective redundancies became progressively more expensive for firms in late Francoism, not so much because of changes in legislation as under the pressure of the emerging labor movement. As a matter of fact, this important political weapon of the Francoist regime fully collapsed right after the death of the dictator. In the new situation, by contrast, employers, mainly in an attempt to construct new systems of control at the shopfloor level, have pressed for greater discretion in firing workers. Partly as the result of those pressures, the legal grounds for dismissals and layoffs have been enlarged, and their cost has been reduced and made more predictable.

The Spanish case provides a very interesting case study of institutional changes in the labor market and the system of industrial relations in response to a new social and political situation born in the middle of a deep economic crisis. The actions undertaken by the state have been clearly aimed at establishing a new kind of flexibility (in terms both of wages and employment), consistent with the transition under way at the political level. This should replace the flexibility enjoyed by employers under the Francoist regime, which was progressively lost in the late years of the dictatorship and, especially, in the early period of change toward the new democratic regime.

This chapter is divided into four main sections. The first serves as a background for discussing the new regulatory regime for the labor market by providing some institutional information on worker and employer organizations. The second traces the changes in wage control policy from the old Francoist period to the new system. The third does the same for job security and employment policies. The chapter ends with some general conclusions presented in the fourth section.

II. INSTITUTIONAL BACKGROUND

The two issues investigated in this chapter do not exhaust the whole range of changes experienced by the Spanish labor market and industrial relations system. The process of institutionalization of the trade unions and the role played in it by the state is perhaps the most important issue being left out of the analysis. This process has been discussed elsewhere.[2] We shall merely provide a brief description as necessary background for the rest of the chapter.

There are at present two main union federations in Spain: the Comisiones Obreras (CCOO), which played a quite important (though obviously illegal) role within the Francoist trade union system and which is heavily influenced by the Communist party, and the Unión General de Trabajadores (UGT), one of the strongest federations before the Civil War, which decided not to participate in the Francoist institutions and which is closely linked to the Socialist party. Together, they hold at present about two-thirds of the seats in the legally established works councils. Although in the very early period of political transition trade union unity was an important objective, the different policies and strategies of the two federations (UGT adopting a more collaborative position, whereas CCOO maintained a more militant one) led to a clear-cut separation between them that now seems there to stay, especially since the accession to government of the Socialist party. There are also other, less influential, federations, such as the Confederación Nacional del Trabajo (CNT), the other main federation existing before the Civil War, and the Unión Sindical Obrera (USO), a small union founded by a few Catholic groups in the early 1950s that followed the same strategy as CCOO during its clandestine years. In addition, in some regions, most notably Galicia and the Basque country, there are important union confederations with a nationalistic ideology.

On the whole, even though the percentage of union membership is very low in Spain (ranging between 10% and 20% of wage and salary earners, according to different estimates) and their position at the shopfloor remains rather weak, trade unions are an influential social agent whose policies have affected the development of both the labor market and the industrial relations system in Spain.

The death of Franco left the employers even more unorganized than the

2See Fina and Hawkesworth (1984, 1987).

workers. However, they soon realized the need for organization in the new situation. The result was the creation of the Confederación Española de Organizaciones Empresariales (CEOE), a federation of employers' associations, which represents the great majority of employers, especially large firms. It, together with the Confederación Española de la Pequeña y Mediana Empresa (CEPYME), which represents small and medium-sized firms, has come to be the main voice of employers in public affairs.

These social partners (mainly CCOO, UGT, and CEOE) have played a crucial role in the development of what we have termed a new system of regulation of wages and employment. This has been a dialectical relationship, in the sense that this development has also been an important factor in the evolution and institutionalization of the workers' and employers' associations.

III. WAGE CONTROL POLICY

The Francoist regime established an industrial relations system based on a belief in cooperation rather than class struggle. The main instrument used toward that end was the Organización Sindical (OS) (Syndical Labor Organization) to which all workers as well as firms had to belong. Prior to 1958, the OS did not have many tasks to perform because wages were directly set by the government.

During this period, the main end of all regulations relating to wages was to repress any kind of *collective* pressures to obtain wage increases. Thus, wage levels set by the government were not only minimal but also maximal in the sense that firms had to be authorized should they want to give *general* wage increases. Thus a "paternalistic" system of wage determination was effectively established. Firms could grant wage increases without restrictions, but only in cases where they freely decided to do so without any pressure from their workers. Huge price variations, however, due to fluctuations in agricultural production, forced the government to grant sizable general increases in money wages. Conflicts reappeared within the firms that were paying wages well above the minimum set by government, as to whether or not the increases had to be applied, or whether they could be "absorbed" into the higher levels already being paid by these firms. In 1956, when the government was forced to grant wage increases of as much as 40% to 60%, these conflicts became widespread. As a result, all restrictions on granting wage increases above the minimum were removed, and the firms already paying high wages were allowed to absorb the increases established by the government. This change opened up the possibility of pressing collectively for better wages; conflicts about distribution thus went back into the firms in a climate of high inflation.

By 1958, moreover, the economy was increasingly feeling the strains imposed by its autarchic nature, which was impeding, via the foreign exchange constraint, any sustained economic growth. This led to a process of controlled change and economic liberalization, whose aim was to industrialize the country mostly by using the expected large foreign exchange inflow provided by tourism. This development also included the implementation of a more flexible mechanism for the determination of money wages, which were theretofore to be negotiated through a new system of collective bargaining, tightly controlled by the government and the OS.

Needless to say, there was a contradiction between the intended economic liberalization and the desire to maintain the political status quo: The growing importance of tourism and the related need to be accepted by the international community meant that a new, less visible style of political repression had to be implemented. This contradiction was also reflected in the heavy constraints imposed upon the emerging system of collective bargaining by the inability of the political system to accept the articulation of truly representative workers' organizations.

However, one of the unintended consequences of the new system, despite its many controls and limitations, was to provide the basis for a growing organization of the workers, mostly through the previously mentioned Comisiones Obreras. This, together with the relative prosperity enjoyed by the Spanish economy throughout the 1960s brought about a new wave of workers' demands, which made the emerging contradictions of the regime more acute.

As far as wages are concerned, this process entailed a progressive breakdown of the devices established in the collective bargaining system, which forced the regime to implement new control mechanisms. It made greater use of direct administrative intervention in the final outcome of the bargaining process, particularly through compulsory arbitration and the fixing of legal ceilings to wage growth. These devices were rather effective in the late 1960s, but they became less so in the 1970s. Beginning in late 1973, a series of norms were established, fixing wage ceilings based upon inflation in the previous year plus several additional percentage points to be awarded only exceptionally. In practice, this additional, supposedly exceptional, growth became the general rule in most collective agreements. Thus, in 1974, 1975, and 1976, the governmental guidelines became the minimum increase to be achieved, and actual wage growth always exceeded them. All of this took place in a climate of growing labor conflicts and greater government intervention through compulsory arbitration, the latter reaching in this period, as Table 2 shows, its highest rates ever.

The criteria for wage increases, which were fairly broad, given the economic situation and the antiinflationary objectives proclaimed by the government, were a reflection of the latter's inability to impose more restrictive controls. Thus, weakness also shows up in the several brief periods during which, in a clear recognition of their failure, the controls were temporarily lifted and the parties allowed to negotiate "freely." The breaking of the wage ceilings became, during this period, one of the basic objectives of the still illegal and clandestine unions, not only as an economic demand but also as a political gesture against the Francoist regime.

Table 2. Arbitration Awards in Spain,
1960–1981

Year	Number	Workers affected
1960	1	350
1961	—	—
1962	41	103,162
1963	56	71,900
1964	113	396,466
1965	182	583,253
1966	132	432,103
1967	186	507,881
1968	11	71,764
1969	181	516,958
1970	156	352,722
1971	135	156,360
1972	205	482,922
1973	149	328,243
1974	122	793,111
1975	189	915,491
1976	306	1,473,489
1977	206	613,512
1978	82	374,258
1979	125	904,599
1980	125	517,824
1981	65	701,358

Source: Fina and Hawkesworth (1984), Table 3.

Such was the situation at the time of Franco's death in November 1975. Throughout 1976, with efforts being made to maintain a "Francoist regime without Franco," the situation deteriorated rapidly and irretrievably. Suddenly, the old legal framework became ineffective, and the OS no longer had any control over the workers because everybody was convinced that it was going to be replaced sooner or later. Nobody knew who were the valid representatives of the workers, who increasingly adopted their decisions through general factory meetings. The demands for economic betterment as well as for political change became generalized. The number of days lost in industrial disputes sharply increased in 1976 as compared to previous years.[3]

The following year, 1977, marked a turning point in the political and industrial relations arenas. Political parties, including the Communist party, were legalized, and the first free general elections in 40 years were held on June 15. At the same time, the freedom to unionize was reestablished, the right to strike was recognized, the elections to workers' councils were regu-

---

[3]The quality of the strike data for this period is, at the least, questionable. However, the various estimates available, despite their big differences as to the levels of strike activity, all show a sharp increase in the number of days lost in 1976 as compared to previous years.

lated, and the bases for the new regulation of layoffs and dismissals were laid down.

This process of intense institutional change took place within an economic environment characterized by the explosive wage–price spiral created in the immediate aftermath of Franco's death. (Inflation reached a record high level of 30% in 1977.) The economic policy of the newly elected government had thus necessarily a markedly antiinflationary bias, and wage restraint was one of its major objectives. To that effect, the government proposed that all parliamentary political parties should reach a national agreement aimed at easing the economic situation during the constitutional period already under way. The consequence of this move was the so-called Pactos de la Moncloa (Moncloa Pacts), whose content was very wide and covered economic, social, and political issues and problems. Although neither unions nor employers were invited to sign the pacts, they both participated actively in the public discussions around them and de facto accepted and applied them. The pacts established a pay norm of 20% to 22% for 1978, based, contrary to Franco's pay policies in 1973–1975 and also in 1976, on expected rather than past inflation.

The Moncloa Pacts were not only successful in reducing inflation; they also, and maybe more importantly, set the pattern of centralized agreements between the social partners that established itself in Spain beginning in 1980. Table 3 summarizes the wide variety of agreements (or lack thereof, as was the case in 1979 and 1984) signed in Spain since the Moncloa Pacts. The table also includes the main results of the process in terms of wage and price inflation. A full analysis of the content, implications, and factors affecting the signing of each of these agreements would take us too far afield.[4] We shall merely emphasize here some of the major elements of this post-Franco period, regarding the characteristics and consequences of the wage agreements themselves and the role played by the trade unions and the government in this whole process.

There are three basic features that characterize the Spanish social pacts or national agreements of these last few years. First, wage guidelines are now established in terms of expected rather than past inflation. This change has curbed the wage–price spiral and has paved the way for a reduction in the rate of inflation. These guidelines have usually adopted the form of a range centered around the expected rate of inflation. The only exception has been the Acuerdo Nacional sobre el Empleo (ANE), where the whole range was below that figure. Here, in principle, a real wage loss was being accepted by the unions.

Second, all agreements have established ex-post-cost-of-living adjustment clauses, as a quid pro quo for the elimination of automatic indexation, which was one of the unions' demands in the early transition period (1976–1977). These clauses tended initially to relate to the inflation rate achieved in

[4]See Fina and Hawkesworth (1987) or Toharia (1988) for more details.

Table 3. National Agreements and Wage and Price Inflation in Spain, 1978–1986

	1978	1979	1980	1981	1982	1983	1984	1985	1986
Agreement	Moncloa Pacts	No agreement	AMI	Extension AMI	ANE	AI	No agreement	AES 1st year	AES 2nd year
Signed by	All parliamentary political parties	Decree law December 28, 1978	UGT/CEOE	UGT/CEOE	CC OO/UGT CEOE	CC	OO/UGT/CEOE	UGT/CEOE/government	UGT/CEOE/government
1. Wage range agreed upon	20–22%	11–14%	13–16%	11–15%	9–11%	9.5–12.5%	—	5.5–7.5%	7.2–8.6%
2. Expected inflation	22%	13%	12%	13%	12%	12%	8%	7%	8%
3. Cost-of-living adjustment (CPI threshold)	11.5% by June 30	6.5% by June 30	6.75% by June 30	6.6% by June 30	6.09% by June 30	9% by Sept 30	—	7% by December 31	8% by December 31
4. Length of collective agreements	Free	Free	2 years recommendation	Free (1 year)	Free (1 year)	>1 year if possible	—	2 years recommendation	2 years recommendation
5. Actual inflation	19.8%	15.7%	15.6%	14.6%	14.4%	12.2%	11.3%	8.8%	8.8%
6. Earnings increase	25.4%	22.5%	16.1%	15.4%	14.0%	13.7%	10.0%	9.4%	10.7%
7. Wage rates increase	20.6%	14.1%	15.3%	13.1%	12.0%[a]	11.4%	7.8%	7.9%	8.2%[b]

[a]This figure takes into account the effect of the cost-of-living adjustment clause that was triggered as inflation exceeded the threshold.

[b]Up to September.

Note: Rows 2 and 5: as measured by the growth rate of the average yearly value of the Consumer Price Index (CPI). Row 6: This figure comes from the quarterly survey made by the Spanish Statistical Office (INE) covering firms of 10 employees and over in the industrial and services sectors. It refers to average total monthly earnings per worker. Row 7: This figure is the average wage settlement reached in the collective agreements signed each year. It thus refers to basic pay rates. AMI stands for "Acuerdo-Marco Interconfederal" (Interconfederate Framework Agreement); ANE stands for "Acuerdo Nacional sobre el Empleo" (National Employment Agreement); AI stands for "Acuerdo Interconfederal" (Interconfederate Agreement); AES stands for "Acuerdo Económico y Social" (Economic and Social Agreement).

the middle of each year. To avoid seasonal influences, however, there has been a tendency to move this point toward the end of the year.

Finally, the agreements have also specified how wage increases were to be distributed. This was significant especially at the beginning of the transition period, when workers demanded lump sum rather than proportional increases, adopting a clearly egalitarian attitude. This criterion was soon abandoned, however, in favor of a more traditional, mostly proportional, distribution.

One of the main consequences of these agreements has been a clear deceleration of wage and price inflation, as Table 3 clearly shows. Of course, one could dispute the notion that the national agreements were the main force behind this evolution.

It could be argued that the process of slowing down would have occurred even without them. It is not easy to discriminate between the different possible causes because it all depends on the counterfactual theory one relies upon. Even though this raises difficult issues, we do tend to believe that the social pacts have played an important role. What is clear, at any rate, is the strong correlation observed between the deceleration of wage and price inflation and the existence of the agreements.

This evolution of wages and prices, implying a bare maintenance of purchasing power, has had important consequences for the share of labor in national income, especially since 1980, given the quite high productivity growth experienced by the Spanish economy during this period. As Figure 1

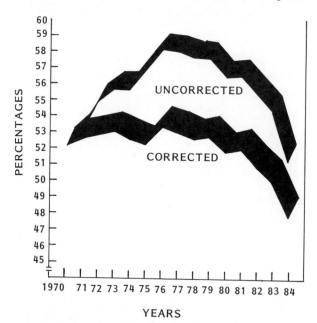

Figure 1. The wage share in the Spanish economy, 1970–1984. The corrected wage share is that which would have been observed if the percentage of wage and salary earners over total employment had remained at its 1970 level. From Fina and Toharia (1986), p. 95.

clearly points out, the wage share, once the change of the composition of the labor force is controlled for,[5] was more or less constant throughout the 1970s but has declined sharply in the last few years. Another important element of this process has been the growing importance of the share of social security contributions within the wage share, a phenomenon to be related to the late development of the welfare state in Spain. As a matter of fact, this could be interpreted as a quid pro quo that unions have accepted in exchange for the limited growth of nominal, and especially real, wages.

A third important aspect is the behavior of the industrial wage structure. Between 1963 and 1975, there was a progressive widening of interindustry wage differentials due to the higher rates of wage growth experienced in those industries that already enjoyed high average earnings. On the contrary, between 1976 and 1978, a strong narrowing took place. Earnings increased more rapidly in low-wage industries, even though these industries were also the hardest-hit by the crisis. This earnings growth was likely the consequence of the new possibilities for organizations that emerged, after Franco's death, in traditionally low-wage sectors composed of large numbers of geographically dispersed firms. After this period of turmoil, however, interindustry wage differentials seem to have remained constant.

The government has tended to give a more prominent role to the bargaining parties (i.e., the employers' associations and the unions). Even in 1979, when no overall national agreement could be reached and the government established a wage-growth ceiling, the latter was only voluntary for the private sector. This trend is reinforced by the legislation concerning the new collective bargaining framework, namely, the Estatuto de los Trabajadores (Workers' Statute) (hereafter quoted as LET) passed in early 1980. It established limits to the use of compulsory arbitration. Later, compulsory arbitration was even declared unconstitutional.

Reflecting the reduced participation by the state and the greater role played by unions and employers, wage demands have lost the political significance they had acquired in the last part of the Francoist period, although, admittedly, the process of wage bargaining has been closely intertwined with the political transition and the process of design of a new industrial relations framework. For example, the Moncloa Pacts of 1977 were meant to provide not only a wage guideline aimed at reducing inflation but also an economic truce that would not endanger the constitutional process. Also, one cannot

---

[5] A short explanation is needed here. The wage share is equal to the gross wage bill over national output. The wage bill is equal to the average wage times the number of workers, whereas total output is equal to output per worker times, again, the number of workers. Now, in very advanced capitalist countries, the number of workers used to compute the wage bill is approximately the same as the one used to calculate total output. This is not so in Spain, however, because the first refers to "wage and salary earners" whereas the second refers to "total employment," the difference being nonwage earning "independent workers" (including employers, family helpers, and the self-employed; see Table 1). The proportion of the latter is sizable in Spain (30% of total employment), but what is most important is that it declined sharply in the 1960s and up until the mid-1970s. Thus, if one wants to use the wage share as a measure of distributive strains, this factor should be controlled for as has been done in Figure 1.

understand the acceptance by unions of a real wage loss in the ANE, signed in 1981 for 1982, without taking into account the political climate that followed the failed coup d'état attempt of February 1981.

In general, the union leaders have adopted a policy of wage restraint with their demands being limited to maintaining purchasing power. The different national wage agreements reached at the top have been followed at all levels of bargaining. In exchange for this moderate attitude, unions, especially the main nationwide federations, have sought to achieve a stronger institutional position within Spanish society as well as the development of welfare provisions, especially unemployment compensation. Also, the worsening unemployment situation has led unions toward a less militantly aggressive position.

IV. THE REGULATION OF LAYOFFS AND JOB SECURITY

Government intervention in the labor market has also changed regarding dismissals and job security. We shall distinguish between two types of dismissals that obey different logics and raise different questions: individual disciplinary dismissals, which are the ultimate sanction that the employer has to ensure effective control over his or her workers, and redundancies, which are mostly a response to the need to adapt production to sales or to adjust to technological change, and are, therefore, more linked to the general economic situation.

The Spanish political transition has brought about significant changes in both types of dismissals. To appreciate the relevance of such changes, it is necessary once again to describe first the situation prevailing during the Francoist regime, stressing the role played by the legal framework both with regard to industrial relations inside firms and to the overall stability of the political system. As we shall see, the individual dismissal was the predominant control device during the Francoist period whereas, in the post-Franco era, both types of dismissals have been used as a mechanism of adjustment to the crisis, leading to an increasingly precarious labor market. We believe, however, that this only partly explains the very strong and general pressures exerted by employers to get a freer and cheaper regulation of firing. A major reason may also have been to reestablish the use of dismissals as a mechanism of control and, in some cases, to prevent or hamper the unionization of their work forces.

During the Francoist period, the absence of any right to unionize implied that the number of situations in which an individual dismissal could be declared fair was much larger than was the case in the political contexts of other Western European countries. In fact, many types of individual or collective activities that in a politically free regime would have been considered a normal right would have led in Franco's Spain to fair dismissals for reasons such as "lack of discipline or obedience" or "voluntary and continued reduction of performance." Even the arrest without charge of a worker for political or union activities, an event that was not at all infrequent, was considered a cause for fair dismissal on the grounds of "unjustified absence from work."

These possibilities had important consequences for the way in which labor relations were organized within firms. Most employers did not make any effort to implement some modern system of "human resources management" that would provide information mechanisms and grievance procedures. Rather, they tended to either act in an authoritarian way, mirroring the prevailing political regime, or adopt a paternalistic attitude, to the point of even protecting the illegal firm-based worker organizations insofar as their demands remained "reasonable." Ultimately, they always had the possibility of resorting to dismissals, or else, should this not be enough, to the repressive powers of the state. Under these circumstances, only the growing organization of the working class could establish some limits to the total discretion of employers. In fact, during the last years of Francoism, there were a large number of conflicts over the dismissal of workers on account of their union activities, especially in the regions and industries where the labor movement had achieved a greater degree of organization. These conflicts began to have some impact on the wider social and political sphere, as suggested by the change that could be observed in the labor courts. The labor judges used various legal arguments to interpret the law more favorably for the workers and began to declare unfair some dismissals resulting from a worker's union activities. When this occurred, the law established that the worker had to receive severance pay if not reinstated. This legal provision ultimately allowed the repression of any kind of union activity, even though at some economic cost to the employer, and it became one of the targets of the illegal trade unions.

As a reflection of the social and political unrest created around this issue, a new law of labor relations was passed in 1976, when Francoism was already in evident decline. In a demagogic move, the law considerably reduced managerial discretion by compelling the employer to reinstate the worker whose dismissal had been declared unfair by the courts. This clause, however, had a very short life, and its repeal signaled a new phase in industrial relations, linked to the new political situation. At the same time, the mere recognition of the basic union rights implied a dramatic limitation of the circumstances in which a dismissal could be considered fair.

Similar changes have also taken place in the case of redundancies based on economic or technological grounds. During the Francoist period, shutdowns and layoffs required a prior authorization from the government (the so-called "expedientes de regulación de empleo" [ERE]). This was consistent both with the interventionist mentality of the regime and with the preoccupation to ensure a climate of social stability. Whenever the redundancy was accepted and no agreement could be reached between the employers and the workers, it was the labor tribunals who determined the corresponding severance pay. With respect to these EREs, the most significant change that took place in the last years of the Francoist regime was the growing participation of workers in the proceedings through the presentation of counterproposals to the arguments of employers and by offering alternative viability plans for the firms in question, thus bypassing the official Francoist unions. In some cases, because of the political relevance, the EREs took a long time to be settled, giving way to important conflicts.

These restrictions applied only to the core group of permanent workers and not to the temporary ones whom the firms could hire to regulate their labor needs in the short term. In this case as well, social reality imposed several important changes even though the legislation was not significantly altered before 1976. Fixed-term contracts provide a clear example of this: It was the judicial interpretation, rather than the legislation, which came to determine that such contracts could only be used when the nature of work was temporary. This implied that, in those industries in which temporary work was significant, this mechanism of flexibility could be used without any restrictions other than those that workers themselves could impose. In fact, through collective bargaining and organized pressures, workers managed to reduce the use of such contracting arrangements. For example, in the early 1960s, the proportions of temporary workers in firms with 10 employees and over in the construction and food-beverages-tobacco industries were 48.4% and 32.3%, respectively. The changes in the economic and social conditions of the labor market since then led to a significant drop in these figures, which reached around 15% in both sectors by 1976.

After Franco's death, the previously mentioned sudden legal vacuum drastically altered the balance of power between capital and labor at the shopfloor. Many employers had to face a problem that they were not prepared to handle—the management of industrial relations. They did not understand the explosion of worker militancy, and they felt defenseless against it. They had lost the dismissal tool not only because many of the assumptions upon which it relied had lost their legitimacy but also because the law itself had made it more difficult to use such a tool. This explains why the employers' associations began to exert stronger pressures to modify a system that no longer was the very flexible instrument of control it used to be and whose nature had by then completely changed. Thus the introduction of a system of unrestricted individual dismissals without any severance payment, which could be used as an effective control mechanism, became one of their top priorities. As a matter of fact, one of the complaints most usually voiced by employers has been the lack of discipline of their work forces under the new system. They have even made an offer of maintaining the employment level in exchange for the possibility of freely firing as many workers as they would see fit (which would obviously be achieved through the higher productivity allowed by free dismissals as a disciplinary instrument).

The result of these pressures has been a process of change in labor legislation that has taken place in two successive, although somewhat overlapping, steps: a first one, aimed at reforming the legal framework of dismissals in the case of workers with an unlimited term labor contract, and a second one, aimed at opening new possibilities for the utilization of the labor force by creating a whole set of new kinds of labor contracts (fixed term, part-time, and so on).

The first set of changes came in parallel with the reestablishment of the freedom to unionize and the institutionalization of the new legal industrial relations framework. Thus, in March 1977, just before the legalization of unions, a decree law introduced a first important reform that eliminated some of the previously mentioned demagogic concessions made just a year before by the Francoist "Parliament." Three years later, some of these changes were consolidated, and some other qualified—in some instances in favor of the workers—in the Workers' Statute (LET), one of the main legislative pieces of the new legal framework. As compared with the situation prevailing during the Francoist period, this first set of changes in labor legislation can be summarized as follows:

Introduction of New Grounds for Fair Dismissals. In particular, dismissals for "objective" reasons, that is, on grounds independent of the behavior of the worker, are allowed, restricted only by the employers' obligation to provide severance pay. Two examples of "objective" reasons, mentioned in the LET, are "problems of adaptation to new methods of production" and "persistent absenteeism for good reason." This implies that employers have been provided with a means of varying their manning levels without having to follow the administrative procedures of the ERE (collective dismissals), thus avoiding interference by the unions in areas that they consider to be their exclusive responsibility.

Reduction in the severance payment to be made for dismissals that have been declared unfair or that have been made on "objective" grounds or those that could follow the resolution of an ERE. At the same time, there has been a substantial reduction in the discretion of the labor tribunals. Thus, before 1976, the severance payment for a dismissal declared unfair could vary between a minimum of 6 months and a maximum of 4 years' wages; since the approval of the LET in 1980, this payment has been established at 45 days' wages per year of tenure with a maximum of 3.5 years' wages, that is, the payment that would correspond to a worker with 28 years of tenure. In the case of the ERE, since 1944 the labor courts could fix, at their discretion, a payment varying between a minimum of 15 days' wages and a maximum of 1 year, depending on factors such as the economic situation of the firm, the family situation of the worker, and the general conditions of the labor market, although, in practice, seniority was the criterion most usually considered. The LET established that this last criterion should be the only one to be used, at the rate of 20 days' wages per year of tenure with a maximum of 12 months.

More rigid deadlines have also been established for the resolution of the ERE, and other provisions have been introduced in order to avoid the previous practice of delaying a decision in politically sensitive cases. For similar reasons, the legal meaning of a "no answer" by the government when an ERE is submitted for consideration has been reversed: Whereas it previously meant that the firm's application was not considered acceptable, it now means exactly the opposite.

A much greater difference between the norms for small and large firms. Thus, in 1980 deadlines were halved, and procedures simplified in the case of small firms. Also, more grounds for "objectively motivated" dismissals could be put forward by firms employing less than 50 workers. Finally, the severance payments in the case of dismissals declared unfair by the labor tribunals to be made by firms with less than 25 workers were reduced to 20% and, of the remaining amount, the firm only had to cover 60%; the rest was paid by the state. The discrimination that this implied for the workers was corrected in 1984, when minimum severance payments were equalized for redundant workers of large and small firms. The state, however, still pays 40% of the payments to be made by small firms, although only in the case of redundancies resulting from a normal ERE procedure.

In 1984, there was a major policy shift that led to the second set of changes we have referred to. Whereas the first set of measures was aimed at facilitating the breakup of the typical, normal (so it was declared in the LET), unlimited labor contract, these second-generation policies have tried to further promote the use of atypical forms of employment contracts, such as part-time work and, most of all, temporary work, first introduced in the Moncloa Pacts of 1977. However, we believe that the introduction of such kinds of special contracts has not been so much the result of the pressures by employers or other political factors but rather of the dramatic deterioration of conditions in the labor market. The unemployment rate has substantially increased and the so-called underground economy is flourishing (although no reliable estimates of the latter exist). The labor market authorities, concerned by these two problems, have argued that these measures would help increase the level of employment. Faced with the critique that labor market segmentation was likely to be reinforced as a result, they have pointed out that a precarious job, with minimum legal protection, is better than no job at all or than a job in the completely beyond the law underground economy, an even worse form of segmentation.

The reaction of trade unions to these policies has shifted from completely opposing them at first because they obviously represent a threat to their bargaining power, to de facto, although grudgingly, accepting them later, more so in the case of Socialist UGT than in the case of the other trade unions (notably CCOO). There were two reasons for this de facto acceptance. First, it was seen as the quid pro quo of the union demand for a reduction of overtime work as a policy of "work sharing" aimed at lowering unemployment. Second, the unions were influenced by the opinions of various groups of workers, most notably the young ones, who suffer extremely high unemployment rates (as much as 50% in 1985 for those aged 16 to 24) and who have seen in these measures a way, as precarious as it may be, of getting a foothold into the labor market.

The employers' organizations, on the other hand, although recognizing that these policies imply an important degree of labor market "flexibility," thus responding to their demands, have criticized them on the grounds that they might discriminate in favor of new or growing firms and against the older firms, with aging work forces. They have also made it clear that this is not the most important kind of "flexibility" for them and that they will keep asking for the removal of the prevailing administrative obstacles to collective redundancies through the ERE. This second set of changes can be summarized as follows:

Introduction of new grounds for fixed-term labor contracts, regardless of the temporary nature of the work to be done. Thus, the only requirement to sign fixed-term contracts of up to 3 years under a "special employment program" is that the worker should be unemployed and that the job should not have been previously occupied by another temporary worker who has completed the 3 year period or by a worker with an open-ended contract who has been declared redundant by a formal ERE or has been unfairly dismissed.

Temporary contracts of up to 3 years can now be signed by any new firm or by any established firm that starts a "new activity" without any other restriction than to give a notice of nonrenewal of the contract 2 weeks in advance of its expiration.

Finally, most restrictions have been removed for hiring young people on a temporary basis. These contracts, moreover, have, as additional incentives, important reductions in social security contributions and, in some cases, generous wage subsidies.

The result of this whole process of change both in the regulation of dismissals and in the establishment of new contractual arrangements can be illustrated by reference to Table 4. As can be seen, hiring increased sharply after the introduction of the new measures at the end of 1984. This flow as a percentage of total wage earners increased from 25.5% in 1984 to 36.0% in 1985. An important effect of the measures has been, as could be expected, to increase labor turnover. The number of people hired under special programs

Table 4. Hires and Dismissals in Spain, 1978–1985
(all absolute figures in thousands)

	1978	1979	1980	1981	1982	1983	1984	1985
1. Total employees	8,404.6	8,200.7	7,917.8	7,661.3	7,602.0	7,492.8	7,169.8	7,151.7
2. Registered hires total	1,311.7	1,556.6	1,908.7	1,966.6	1,607.0	1,471.1	1,830.0	2,571.4
3. (2) as % of (1)	15.6	19.0	24.1	25.7	21.1	19.6	25.5	36.0
4. Hires under the special employment program	138.2	363.9	544.5	483.4	448.9	431.2	448.2	1,014.7
5. (4) as % of (2)	10.5	23.4	28.5	24.6	27.9	29.3	24.5	39.5
6. Dismissals IMAC[a]	—	0.8	195.4	206.9	164.9	151.4	156.4	148.4
7. Dismissals labor courts	151.8	194.8	90.3	84.8	83.8	84.4	78.6	54.9
8. Dismissals ERE	66.2	75.1	60.2	57.5	61.8	60.0	69.0	74.8
9. Total dismissals	218.0	270.7	345.9	349.2	310.5	295.8	304.0	278.5
10. (9) as % of (1)	2.6	3.3	4.4	4.6	4.1	3.9	4.2	3.9

[a]The IMAC (Instituto de Mediación Arbitraje y Conciliación), official body for conciliation, started working in December 1979. When no agreement is reached, the case is forwarded to the labor courts.

against unemployment has also increased substantially, from 24.5% of new hires in 1984 to 39.5% in 1985.

To summarize, the system of dismissals under the Francoist regime was objectively more flexible than has usually been assumed. The restrictions on individual dismissals were almost nonexistent, and there were ample, even if diminishing over time, possibilities to use systems of temporary contracts. Only in the case of collective redundancies was the freedom of employers somewhat limited. In fact, however, given the economic boom of the Spanish economy, especially in the 1960s, this had only a minor effect on costs. At any rate, any assessment from the employers' viewpoint would have to take into account the compensating element of the achievement of their main political objectives.

In the democratic situation, by contrast, given the freedom to unionize, the individual dismissal is no longer the important disciplinary instrument it was in the past. That explains why employers strongly demanded a freer hand in firing workers. They were fairly successful, and the balance of power tilted in their favor at a time when a new industrial relations system was being created. Moreover, the battle against unemployment has become the major ground for government regulation and encouragement of temporary work. The extent to which these new contracting arrangements will give rise to new segmentations of the labor market, through the substitution of fixed-term for permanent employees, remains to be seen.

V. CONCLUSION

In this chapter, we have attempted to describe the process of change in the regulation of the labor market that intervened during the period of political transition from the Francoist dictatorship to the current democratic system. We have focused on two basic issues: the process of wage determination and the regulation of layoffs and dismissals. In both cases, we have seen that the new regulatory framework was by no means predictable in the very early period of transition, not to mention in the last few years of Francoism. Rather, it has been the result of the interplay of economic, political, and institutional forces that have been shaping it. The severe economic crisis was an important constraint on this development, but so was the evolution of the political system and the process of institutionalization of the employers' and workers' associations.

It is likely that the process of change will continue. The national wage agreements, which constitute one of the basic pieces of the new system, have not been institutionalized in any way. They are renegotiated every year (or every 2 years). All social partners (including the government) do not sign them regularly, and their usefulness is questioned at times. In addition, employers are still unhappy about the current regulation of dismissals, especially because of government intervention in the ERE. The new forms of labor contracts, meant initially in many cases to be temporary expedients to fight unemployment, may become part of the normal legal procedures.

Changes are still possible. Any transformations that occur will depend, as we have argued has happened in the past, on the interaction of the different economic, political, and institutional forces at work. The final result is, we believe, unpredictable.

VI. REFERENCES

Fina, L. (1987). Unemployment in Spain: Its causes and the policy response. *Labour, 2,* 29–69.

Fina, L., & Hawkesworth, R. I. 91984). Trade unions and collective bargaining in post-Franco Spain. *Labour and Society, 9,* 3–25.

Fina, L., & Hawkesworth, R. I. (1987). Trade unions and industrial relations in Spain: The response to the economic crisis. In W. Brierly (Ed.), *Trade unions and the economic crisis of the 1980s* (pp. 64–83). London: Gower.

Fina, L., & Toharia, L. (1986). Salarios y costes laborales en España, 1970–84. *Enciclopedia de la economía española* (Vol. 36), May.

Ministerio de Trabajo y Seguridad Social. *Boletin de estadisticas laborales.*

Toharia, L. (1987). Las diferentes explicaciones del desempleo en España y sus consecuencias para la política de empleo. In L. Fina & L. Toharia (Eds.), *Las causas del paro en España: un punto de vista estructural,* (pp. 69–101). Madrid: Fundación IESA.

Toharia, L. (1988). Partial Fordism: Spain between political transition and economic crisis. In R. Boyer (Ed.), *The search for labour market flexibility: The European economies in transition* (pp. 119–139). Oxford: Clarendon Press.

7

The State, the Unions, and the Labor Market
The Italian Case, 1969–1985

Sebastiano Brusco and Paola Villa

I. INTRODUCTION

An analysis of recent Italian industrial relations must begin with the events of 1968–1969. This period was of special importance in the history of all Western countries as well as of the Eastern bloc, but perhaps nowhere was its impact as widely and lastingly felt as in Italy. The industrial relations system, the relations between unions and political parties, and between unions and government were dramatically modified. The changes in the Italian industrial relations system in the past two decades have therefore to be analyzed as a continuous process of adjustment, interrelated with the modifications in the social, economic, and political framework, dating back to the events of the late 1960s. Within the elements of continuity that characterize the whole period under consideration, this chapter identifies three main themes coming to prominence at different times: "pansyndicalism" in the years 1968–1975; "national solidarity government" in the years 1975–1980; and "trilateral bargaining" in the period 1980–1985.

II. PANSYNDICALISM, 1968–1975[1]

The first period runs from the explosion of industrial unrest in the "hot autumn" of 1969 to 1975, the first year—following the oil crisis of 1973—to

---

[1]The literature on the industrial relations system in Italy is extremely rich for this period. Here, the basic characteristics of the evolution in union policy and structure are briefly summarized.

Sebastiano Brusco • Department of Political Economy, University of Modena, 41000 Modena, Italy.   **Paola Villa** • Department of Economics, Catholic University, 20123 Milan, Italy.

Table 1. The Performance of the Italian Economy, 1968–1985

	Real GDP	Real investment	Retail Price Index	Total employed (thousands)	Total unemployed (thousands)	Unemployment rate (%)	Unemployment rate corrected for CIG (%)
	(annual rate of increase)						
1968	—	—	—	19,383	1,172	5.7	n.a.
1969	6.1	7.8	2.8	19,209	1,160	5.7	n.a.
1970	5.3	3.0	5.1	19,325	1,111	5.4	5.5
1971	1.6	− 3.2	5.0	19,295	1,109	5.4	5.5
1972	3.2	0.9	5.6	18,996	1,297	6.4	6.6
1973	7.0	7.7	10.4	19,185	1,305	6.4	6.6
1974	4.1	3.3	19.5	19,539	1,111	5.4	5.7
1975	−3.6	−12.7	17.2	19,635	1,226	5.9	6.9
1976	5.9	2.3	16.7	19,757	1,420	6.7	7.3
1977	1.9	− 0.4	17.0	19,938	1,538	7.2	7.7
1978	2.7	− 0.1	12.1	20,017	1,560	7.2	8.0
1979	4.9	5.8	14.8	20,213	1,686	7.7	8.3
1980	3.9	9.4	21.2	20,488	1,684	7.6	8.3
1981	0.2	0.6	17.8	20,543	1,895	8.4	10.0
1982	−0.5	− 5.2	16.5	20,493	2,052	9.1	10.7
1983	−0.2	− 3.8	14.7	20,557	2,264	9.9	11.9
1984	2.8	6.2	10.8	20,648	2,391	10.4	12.2
1985	2.3	4.1	9.2	20,742	2,471	10.6	12.3

Source: ISTAT, Banca d'Italia.

show a decrease in real income (see Table 1). The hot autumn was much more than the ritual intensification of industrial conflict that occurs when the major industrial collective contracts have to be renewed.[2] It was a mass movement with demands far wider and less defined than those expressed by the unions. The participation of workers was widespread and intense, even though it was concentrated in large companies and metropolitan areas. Among the grassroots, there was a shift of leadership from skilled to unskilled workers. Growing contradictions emerged in social organization and the organization of production, resulting from a decade of intensive internal migration and the disappointment of many of the hopes engendered by the boom of the 1960s.[3] These events occurred in the context of relatively favorable labor market conditions and a student revolt.[4]

For a detailed account, the best known work in Italian is that directed by Pizzorno and published in six volumes. In English, see Regini (1979); Regalia *et al.* (1978); Salvati (1981); Garonna and Pisani (1985); and Lange and Vannicelli (1985).

[2]In Italy, the major sectoral contracts are renegotiated every 3 years at approximately the same time. Several major contracts were due to expire in 1969.

[3]Large internal migration, from the rural southern districts to the industrial northern districts, characterized the economic development of the 1960s.

[4]The recession of the mid-1960s was almost overcome, and industrial employment was approaching the levels of 1963, the previous peak year. But the labor market was not particularly tight, at least not sufficiently to explain the explosion of industrial conflict. In fact, it was the segmenta-

In these years, the trade unions came to play a role that if not a leading one, was equal in importance to that of the party system. The unity and autonomy of the unions was reaffirmed and the union movement became the vehicle for a set of thoroughgoing reforms. To understand the new role of the unions in social policy, it is necessary to take into account: (1) the great increase in union strength, supported by a general mobilization of the working class; (2) the lack of credibility and innovating capacity of the political system; (3) the disappointment of the hopes of an effective social and economic policy that had been raised by the previous center-left coalition;[5] (4) the need of the unions to ensure that rank-and-file mobilization was not dispersed in different and separate struggles, and flowing from this, their desire to aggregate, channel, and coordinate the demands of the rank and file. Encouraged, moreover, by the unexpectedly successful general strike of March 1968 for reform of the pension system (Romagnoli & Treu, 1977, pp. 90–94), the unions sought to take advantage of their new strength by making direct demands on the government for the reform of housing, education, health, taxation, transport, and the development of the *Mezzogiorno* (the southern regions of Italy). These demands were backed by general strikes, by meetings with the political parties, and by frequent meetings with the government. Thus the trade union leadership took on a leading political role that was often more effective than that of the party leaderships themselves. A key word at that time was *pansyndicalism*. Other phrases that became current at the time are equally revealing: the need for *supplenza sindacale*, that is, for unions to do the work of the parties, and for "permanent collective bargaining," that is, continuous bargaining at different contractual levels.[6] It was even maintained that the wage rate was an "independent variable"; the implication here was the absolute independence of collective bargaining and union action from the overall economic framework.

The government—in the early period a center-left coalition with a strong communist opposition—was very sensitive to the changing climate. In 1969, an ex-unionist of the CISL (Confederazione Italiana Sindacati Lavoratori) was designated minister of labor and used to refer to himself as the "minister of laborers." Moreover, the government played an important role in bargaining

---

tion of the labor market, in particular the screening policies followed by modern large firms in the north (who preferred workers neither too young nor too old, male, possibly with some working experience, and so on) that helps to explain the relative shortage of labor in the northern industrial labor markets (see Bruno, 1979).

[5]For a brief discussion of the inability of the center-left coalitions of the 1960s to effect its program of reforms for improving the living conditions of the lowest classes, see Salvati (1981, pp. 338–341).

[6]Toward the end of the 1960s, decentralized bargaining began to develop very rapidly, increasing in number and expanding in scope, with a minimum of institutionalization. This involved several contractual levels (the firm, the plant, the shopfloor) in a sort of continuous process. No formal coordination existed between decentralized bargaining and sectoral bargaining, nor was there any definition or demarcation of bargaining subjects. Union control over decentralized bargaining was established only ex post, by incorporating and generalizing into sectoral contracts (renewed every 3 years) the results obtained at the firm level.

over the renewal of the major national contracts. Some negotiations even took place at the headquarters of the Ministry of Labor. The minister himself was present and proposing solutions for the issues in dispute between unions and employers' associations.[7] Finally, in 1970, an act was passed, best known as the Workers' Charter, which established principles for the regulation of industrial disputes and union organization and, at the same time, for the protection of workers and union activists at the workplace.[8] The charter, which is still in force, recognizes the right to union representation at the workplace and the right of trade union officials to be present at meetings in the factory; it guarantees union representatives against dismissal; regulates individual and collective dismissals; prevents employers from discriminating in employing staff; and, finally, guarantees the right to strike and, by implication, the right to picket.[9] On the whole, the charter stands as an example of advanced labor legislation, safeguarding the rights of workers and promoting union organization. As such, it has acted as a basic point of reference for the Italian industrial relations system ever since.

After the charter was passed, the government ceased to play a significant role in collective bargaining. The focal point of industrial conflict and bargaining activity shifted to the factories. This was made possible by the radical transformations of industrial relations produced by the strike wave of 1968–1970. Where previously the unions had been weak, centralized, and divided, they now became strong, decentralized, and characterized by real unity of action. Lastly, they were in this period much less closely linked to political parties than they had been before.[10]

One of the most remarkable aspects of the new wave of mobilization was the change it brought about in the tactics of conflict. The individual place of

[7]See Giugni et al. (1976, pp. 189–208) for a discussion on the mediating role of the Ministry of Labor.

[8]The idea of a Workers' Charter, as a sort of workers' bill of rights, goes back to the demands of CGIL in the 1950s. However, the act itself was the direct result of the events of the late 1960s. In fact, the political climate was crucial in ensuring its parliamentary approval. Moreover, the final draft of the act incorporated many of the demands raised by the workers' mobilization (see Regalia, Regini, & Reyneri, 1978, p. 152).

[9]The 1970 act does not mention picketing; however, the doctrinal and jurisprudential trend is to regard it as an instrument in support of strikes.

[10]In 1944, under the auspices of the major antifascist political parties, a unified union organization was reconstituted. The events at the end of the 1940s (the outbreak of the Cold War, the exclusion of the left from the Italian national government, the elections of 1948) led to the break up of the union movement into three confederations, broadly reflecting the divisions in Italy's political system. The CGIL, the majority confederation, was linked to the Communist party but included a considerable socialist component; the CISL to the Christian Democratic party and, in general, to the catholic movement; finally, the UIL, the smallest of the three, was supported by socialists, republicans, and social democrats. Thus, since its refoundation in 1944, Italian unionism has been strongly influenced by political events, so that it is usually described as "political unionism" to stress the tight links to the party system. Historically, the labor movement has been weakest when the labor federations' ties with political parties have been strongest. During these times, the ideological and political divisions among the three federations have been most marked.

work, whether factory or shop, became the location where workers conducted their struggles using radical forms of action. Spot strikes, rolling strikes, lightning strikes, and slowdowns were used to disrupt production, with the aim of increasing the damage to the firm and limiting the cost of conflict to the workers. Strikes were regularly extended through time and space—from shop to shop, from line to line, and from worker to worker—and were also used during negotiations.

As Table 2 shows, strike activity increased significantly toward the end of the 1960s. Conflictual activity was intense throughout the 1969–1975 period. It reached a peak in 1969, when over 300 million hours were lost, the equivalent of 23 hours per employee.

What was remarkable in this process was not only the increase in strike activity and the changing nature of the conflicts but also the scope and intensity of rank-and-file involvement. A new type of protagonist was emerging—

Table 2. Strike Activity in Italy in All Sectors of the Economy, 1964–1985

	Strikes originating from the employment relationship			Total strikes[a]		
	Workers involved	Working hours lost through strikes (000)	Index of strike volume[b]	Workers involved	Working hours lost through strikes (000)	Index of strike volume[b]
1964	3,245,000	104,709	8.21	—	—	—
1965	2,310,000	55,943	4.47	—	—	—
1966	1,887,000	115,788	9.35	—	—	—
1967	2,243,000	68,548	5.42	—	—	—
1968	4,862,000	73,918	5.78	—	—	—
1969	7,507,000	302,587	23.67	—	—	—
1970	3,722,000	146,212	11.17	—	—	—
1971	3,891,000	103,590	7.81	—	—	—
1972	4,405,000	136,480	10.11	—	—	—
1973	6,133,000	163,935	11.95	—	—	—
1974	7,824,000	136,267	9.72	—	—	—
1975	10,717,635	181,381	12.86	14,109,732	190,324	13.50
1976	6,974,064	131,711	9.25	11,897,819	177,643	12.48
1977	6,434,445	78,767	5.46	13,802,955	115,963	8.04
1978	4,346,884	49,032	3.38	8,774,193	71,239	4.91
1979	10,519,002	164,914	11.20	16,235,777	192,713	13.09
1980	7,427,601	75,214	5.06	13,824,641	115,201	7.75
1981	3,567,231	42,802	2.87	8,226,626	73,691	4.94
1982	7,490,346	114,889	7.70	10,483,018	129,940	8.71
1983	4,624,874	82,626	5.58	6,844,170	98,021	6.62
1984	n.a.	31,786	2.16	n.a.	60,923	4.13
1985[c]	n.a.	9,969	0.67	n.a.	25,402	1.71

[a]Total strikes include strikes caused by questions not connected with the employment relationship (economic policy measures, demands of social reforms, national events, and so on). It is only since 1975 that these data are recorded.
[b]The index is given by the number of working hours lost per employee in all sectors of the economy.
[c]1985 data are provisional.
Source: ISTAT.

a labor force increasingly concentrated in the cities and the large factories, with the unskilled workers, mostly relatively young and recent immigrants, at the core of the struggles.

The growing wave of mobilization, which had begun among the rank and file, brought to the fore a new generation of grassroots leaders—who had not lived through the divisions of the early postwar period.[11] It also helped to generate pressure for a united union movement that met with enthusiastic support from a union leadership ready to play an active role in the process. A "real unity of action" (among unions affiliated to different confederations) characterized all union activities.

In addition, a plan for the merger of the three confederations (CGIL [Confederazione Generale Italiana del Lavoro], CISL and UIL [Unione Italiana del Lavoro])—the so called *unità organica* ("organic unity")—was set in motion. This process for the unification of union organizational structures started to be realized in the mild form of a unitary federation, not in substitution for but superimposed on the three confederations.

At the same time, a change took place in union structures at the workplace. The existing structures at the plant level (*commissioni interne, sezioni sindacali aziendali*) were divided on the basis of political differences between the three confederations and were weak. They were unable to cope with the growing wave of conflicts, the demand for participation in union activity by the rank and file, and the new wage claims. New structures began to be created in a more or less spontaneous fashion in the strike-prone factories. "Delegates," "factory councils," and "workers' assemblies" were progressively introduced, with power to decide on all union policy matters at plant level. Delegates were elected by the work group without prior nomination. Their mandate could be revoked by the group. They had no obligation to join the union. The union confederations declared themselves in favor of the new grassroots structures and decided to adopt them and accept the general method of electing delegates. When the Workers' Charter came into force in 1970, it provided the framework for the final institutionalization and strengthening of these structures.

The decentralization of union organization resulted in the decentralization of bargaining activities. Plants and shops became the focal point of union activity and collective bargaining. In particular, until the mid-1970s, both the sectoral and interconfederal levels of bargaining were marginalized.[12] Very few agreements were signed at the confederal level. Moreover, in each industrial sector, national bargaining progressively lost its role as the setting where unions put forward their objectives. In a sense, therefore, the traditional bargaining process was reversed. In the past, plant-level bargaining had been limited to implementing the decisions made at the national level. It now

---

[11]See note 10.

[12]Interconfederal agreements, concluded between employers' associations and the union confederations, tend to regulate general issues (e.g., dismissals and wage indexation systems) and are valid for several sectors (industrial categories).

established the objectives, whereas national bargaining was used to consolidate what had been achieved in individual plants (in particular, in the largest factories with the most active *avanguarde*) and to extend these gains to the whole sector.

Such a process of continuous bargaining—involving both national collective agreements and plant agreements—was both more egalitarian than earlier practices and disruptive of the traditional organization of production. Wage increases began to be sought as a fixed sum across the board, regardless of skill grades. Other demands included generalized upgrading, a reduction of basic wage differentials, the control, first, and later the rejection of, any form of incentives and piecework, a reduction of the pace of work and work loads, and an end to overtime and to working in dangerous working conditions. The demands for greater equality—seen as a sign of the breakdown of the system of job grades (*sistema delle qualifiche*)—and those for greater control over the organization of the labor process—seen as a critique of the traditional division of labor, unilaterally imposed by management—gradually came together in the proposal for a so-called *inquadramento unico*, a single grading scale for manual workers, foremen, and white-collar workers.

As a result of the changes taking place inside and outside the unions, the labor movement gained an unprecedented degree of power. Membership rates rose (Coi, 1979; Regalia, Regini, & Reyneri, 1978, p. 149). There was a greater union presence in small and medium-sized enterprises, in geographical areas where previously the unions had been insignificant, and finally in sectors in which the "autonomous" unions (i.e., those not affiliated to the three large confederations) were strongest.

Though membership data are only a rough guide to union strength, they are presented in Table 3. Between 1968 and 1975, the total number of union members (including retired workers) grew from 4.7 to 7.7 million, raising the percentage of unionized workers to almost 50% of the work force.

From 1968 to the early 1970s, the unions struggled for social reforms in such areas as education, housing, and health. The potential beneficiaries were not limited to union members. They made use of general strikes and bargaining with the government. Nevertheless, they produced very few results. There was a change in the pension system and a general, and not particularly progressive, new law on housing (Regini, 1979, pp. 58–59). It soon became clear that direct bargaining with the government was a blind alley, and it was tacitly abandoned.

The impact of collective bargaining on wages was by contrast large and lasting—the combined result of high wage settlements at the national and plant level and of the egalitarian policies of the unions.

Table 4 shows that basic wage rates negotiated under national agreements rose quite significantly throughout the 1969–1975 period. At the same time, plant-level bargaining was on the increase. Not only were a larger number of plant agreements concluded, but the scope of plant-level bargaining expanded to include wage increases and upgrading. As a result, actual money earnings (including incentives, bonuses, and holiday rates) rose faster

Table 3. Membership of Main Union Confederations, 1968–1984
(number of members)

Year	CGIL	CISL	UIL[a]	Total membership Including pensioneers	Excluding pensioneers	Union membership rate (%)
1968	2,460,961	1,626,786	648,393	4,731,848	n.a.	n.a.
1969	2,626,388	1,641,289	n.a.	n.a.	n.a.	n.a.
1970	2,942,517	1,807,586	780,000	5,530,103	n.a.	n.a.
1971	3,138,396	1,973,333	825,000	5,936,729	n.a.	n.a.
1972	3,214,965	2,184,279	842,912	6,242,156	n.a.	n.a.
1973	3,435,576	2,214,099	901,916	6,551,595	n.a.	n.a.
1974	3,826,628	2,472,701	965,051	7,264,374	n.a.	n.a.
1975	4,081,399	2,593,544	1,032,605	7,707,548	n.a.	n.a.
1976	4,313,191	2,823,780	1,104,888	8,241,799	7,103,932	48.65
1977	4,475,436	2,809,802	1,160,089	8,445,327	7,162,986	49.02
1978	4,527,962	2,868,737	1,284,716	8,681,415	7,187,839	48.87
1979	4,583,474	2,906,230	1,326,817	8,816,521	7,225,801	48.41
1980	4,599,050	3,059,845	1,346,900	9,005,795	7,299,821	48.66
1981	4,584,611	2,988,813	1,357,290	8,930,714	7,066,163	47.89
1982	4,570,252	2,976,880	1,358,004	8,905,136	6,869,031	44.43
1983	4,556,052	2,953,411	1,351,514	8,860,977	6,668,339	44.43
1984	4,546,335	3,097,231	1,344,460	8,988,026	6,613,103	43.45

[a]The UIL did not make statistics of its membership available until 1976; figures for 1968–1975 were estimated by Coi (1979).

Source: C.E.S.O.S. (various years) for 1976–1984 data; Romagnoli (1980) and Coi (1979) for 1968–75.

than minimum contractual wages, and the wage drift recorded in those years has to be interpreted as the outcome of this process of continuous bargaining (Dell'Aringa, 1983, pp. 14–16). The rate of increase in real earnings reached a peak in 1970 (+18.1%) and stayed at a high level thereafter, with an annual average rate of increase of 10% for the period 1969–1975. To summarize, what is remarkable in the Italian case is not the intense wage push registered in the early 1970s, as this was true of many other industrial countries (Tronti, 1982), but the persistence of this pressure thereafter.

The explicit aim of the unions was to reduce wage differentials, and this they pursued through across-the-board wage increases, the contraction of basic wage scales, a general upgrading of the lowest jobs, and the replacement of the traditional grading system with an *inquadramento unico*. Wage differentials were quite drastically reduced (see Table 5).

Moreover, the pursuit of flat wage increases in central bargaining (through the renewal of industrywide contracts) served to diminish wage differentials between sectors. Wage differentials by sex also declined (Bettio, 1985). Nonetheless, as plant bargaining was particularly intense and effective in the largest firms and in the most industrialized areas, wage differentials by size of enterprise and by geographical area remained the same (Dell'Aringa, 1976, pp. 31–34). And this, in turn, produced some modifications in the industrial structure, and hence in the structure of employment.

Employment conditions changed quite dramatically. The real revolution

Table 4. Minimum Hourly Contractual Wage, Gross Money
Earnings, Real Earnings, and Wage Drift, All Industries 1968–1984
(annual rate of increase)[a]

	Minimum contractual wage	Gross money earnings	Wage drift[b]	Real earnings
1969	+ 7.3	+10.4	+3.1	7.6
1970	+20.7	+23.2	+2.5	18.1
1971	+11.9	+16.7	+4.8	11.7
1972	+ 9.2	+13.8	+4.6	8.2
1973	+23.0	+22.8	−0.2	12.4
1974	+20.1	+26.6	+6.5	2.9
1975	+28.0	+26.4	−1.6	9.2
1976	+20.8	+20.0	−0.8	3.5
1977	+27.4	+30.9	+3.5	12.8
1978	+16.5	+17.1	+0.6	4.7
1979	+19.3	+18.9	−0.4	3.2
1980	+21.9	+21.5	−0.4	0.4
1981	+23.9	+22.9	−1.0	4.2
1982	+17.5	+16.3	−1.2	−0.2
1983	+13.1	+15.5	+2.4	0.8
1984	+ 9.1	+10.4	+1.3	−0.4
1985	+10.6	n.a.	n.a.	n.a.

[a]The data on contractual wage and gross earnings refer to hourly wages of manual
workers in total industry, excluding family allowances. Data on gross earnings include
incentives, bonuses, and holiday rates.
[b]Data given by the difference between gross earnings and contractual wage.
Source: ISTAT (Istituto Centrale di Statistica [Central Institute of Statistics] and Ministero
del Lavoro e della Previdenza Sociale (Ministry of Labor).

in power relations within the factories meant that all issues related to the
organization of work (internal allocation, upgrading, pace of work, safety
conditions, manpower requirements, and so on) were discussed and subject
to negotiation, thus eroding the power of management to take unilateral
decisions. In the large factories, the union movement acquired enough
strength to make redundancies almost impossible, to protect their shopfloor
representatives, to force the employers into plant-level bargaining, to exercise
a certain degree of control over working conditions, and, in some cases, to
impose changes in the organization of work. However, in order to offset the
effects of increased union power within these factories, employers began to
shift production toward smaller firms, in those sectors where technological
and market conditions made decentralization possible. In this sense, the rise
of trade union power in the large factories from the late 1960s onward must be
seen as one of the principal causes of the process of vertical disintegration that
has taken place in Italian industry (Brusco, 1982). Such developments intensified the segmentation of the labor market into a "primary" sector, consisting of enterprises where the unions are strong and able to enforce their
policy, and a "secondary" sector, consisting of small firms where the union
organization is either weak or nonexistent and management is still able to
impose unilateral decisions.

Table 5. Wage Differentials by Classification Grade,
Male Manual Workers, All Industries
(manovali comuni = 100)[a]

	1969	1974	1977
Operai specializzati	155.1	145.1	126.9
Operai qualificati	129.0	124.4	112.4
Operai comuni	124.2	115.0	107.4
Manovali comuni	100.0	100.0	100.0
Other workers (ungraded)	130.9	145.0	119.5
Apprentices	61.8	67.1	71.1

[a]The data (gross hourly earnings) refer to the April survey of every year. With this classification system operai specializzati refer to skilled workers; operai qualificati to semiskilled workers; operai comuni to unskilled workers employed for simple but specific tasks; finally, manovali comuni to unskilled workers employed for general and unskilled tasks. *Source*: Ministero del Lavoro e della Previdenza Sociale (Ministry of Labor).

The year 1975, which marks the end of the first period, was a year of severe recession (see Table 1). In that year, two important interconfederal agreements were reached, the first modifying the system of wage indexation (the *scala mobile*), the second modifying the *Cassa Integrazione Guadagni* (CIG).[13]

Until this time, an increase in the cost-of-living index of one percentage point led, automatically, to an increase in wages and salaries of one point of *contingenza* (cost-of-living allowance). The money value of the allowance (*punto di contingenza*) varied according to the category of employment, by grade, and age. The 1975 agreement replaced this with a flat-rate mechanism. The money value of the point was established equal for *all* employees (for every 1% increase in the cost-of-living wages and salaries rose by 2,389 lire), independent of the employees' level of earnings. This implied that any increase in the cost-of-living index led to an increase in actual money earnings proportionally higher, the lower the level of earnings.[14] Therefore, this agreement intensified the reduction of wage differentials, noted earlier.

The second agreement, which was incorporated into Law 164 of 1975, was concerned with the "guarantee of wages" for workers temporarily made redundant in times of crisis, under the CIG system. The CIG, a national fund financed by the state and by contributions of employers and employees, had

[13]Since 1956, minimum wages have been partially indexed to the cost of living. The indexation system introduced was based on the cost-of-living index for working-class families, whose base value was set at 100 in 1956. At the end of every 3 months, the number of points by which the index had increased was multiplied by the value of a point (*punto di contingenza*) and added to wages. The value of the point was differentiated by geographical area (zones), by sex, by age, by category of employment (manual workers, foremen, and clerical workers), and by grade. In the 1960s, the *scala mobile* was partially restructured. Discrimination based on sex was abolished, and the zones were gradually eliminated.

[14]At the same time, the level of money wages was such that, at least for the lowest wage rates, the coverage of the losses from inflation was almost complete. For a discussion on the coverage of the *scala mobile* see Faustini (1976) and Filosa and Visco (1980).

been set up during the war to stabilize workers' earnings in those factories that—for problems related to bombing or war shortages—had to limit or interrupt production. This was, in essence, a mechanism of subsidized labor hoarding. The workers made redundant maintain their employment relationship and receive a wage subsidy from the CIG. Up to the late 1960s, the CIG intervened only to assure the workers employed in firms in "exceptional" difficulties and of a "temporary" nature a certain level of earnings (lower than their previous wage rates). This intervention, known as CIG *interventi ordinari*, was supposed to act countercyclically, by helping firms and workers to face cyclical downturns. A radical change in the setup of the CIG was recorded in 1968, with the introduction of the CIG *interventi straordinari* (Law No. 1115). This extended the possible cases for the intervention of the CIG to short-time work and redundancies caused by "economic sectoral crisis" in industrial activity. The temporary nature and the exceptional circumstances were no longer required. In 1975, following the confederated agreement, the intervention of the CIG *straordinaria* was further extended (Law No. 164). As a result, the CIG *straordinaria* began to increase quite dramatically (see Table 6), both because it became easier for a wider range of employers to make use of it for longer periods and because the slowdown of the economy meant that more firms were working at less than full capacity.

The two agreements constitute the borderline between the first two peri-

Table 6. Cassa Integrazione Guadagni (CIG), Total Hours Authorized in Industry, 1968–1985 (in thousands)

Year	CIG "interventi ordinari"	CIG "interventi straordinari"	Total CIG manufacturing industry	Total CIG, all industries
1968	27,876	2,367	30,243	71,112
1969	11,898	7,636	19,534	66,219
1970	20,543	7,157	27,701	68,161
1971	58,355	75,206	133,561	199,569
1972	40,182	63,862	104,044	173,958
1973	22,596	35,729	58,325	126,093
1974	52,570	39,023	91,593	158,418
1975	229,624	59,082	288,706	349,036
1976	130,610	77,645	208,256	285,905
1977	117,246	70,359	187,605	255,129
1978	140,905	110,817	251,722	324,502
1979	59,005	146,607	205,612	299,558
1980	109,338	135,853	245,191	307,137
1981	189,014	312,559	501,573	577,744
1982	193,205	370,105	563,310	620,291
1983	229,250	461,566	690,816	746,518
1984	198,280	548,113	746,393	816,497
1985	121,708	512,107	633,815	716,631

Source: INPS (Istituto Nazionale di Previdenza Sociale) data in Ministero del Bilancio (various years). *Relazione Generale sulla Situazione Economica del Paese.* Roma: Poligra fico.

ods. On the one hand, they are the last agreements of the "offensive" type through which the working class ensured some guarantees against the twin threats of inflation and dismissals. On the other hand, they signal the beginning of a new period characterized by a shift in the locus of collective bargaining from the factories to the center. Indeed, the 1975 agreements were designed—on the part of the employers' associations—to reduce the need for shopfloor bargaining and to establish the union confederations as their bargaining partners, in the hope of reducing union power through the increased centralization of the unions.

III. THE GOVERNMENT OF NATIONAL SOLIDARITY, 1975–1980

The second period, which runs from 1975 to 1980, is marked by two major events: the "national solidarity" government of 1976–1979 and a severe recession, which was to last until the end of the decade. The 1976 general election witnessed a sharp rise in the electoral fortunes of the Communist party (PCI), which was in many ways surprising and unexpected. In this period, influenced in part by the experience of Chile, the PCI put forward the theory of the "historical compromise," that is, the coming together at the government level of the PCI and the Christian Democratic party (DC), representing the two major components of Italian politics, the communist and the catholic. On the basis of a common program, designed to combat the recurring threat of terrorism and the—by then—chronic stagflation, the PCI became part, if not of the government itself, at least of the pro-government parliamentary majority. This in itself had an important impact on the attitude of the unions, because the PCI enjoys the support of the majority of the members in the CGIL, by far the largest of the three union confederations (see Table 3). Moreover, the PCI is the party that encompasses the majority of the politicized grassroots, and above all, workers employed in medium-sized and very large firms and those prepared to take part in conflict.

At the same time, the economy had rapidly and drastically deteriorated, with the worst recession and the highest rate of inflation in the postwar period. Table 1 shows the trends in real gross domestic product (GDP), real investment, inflation, and unemployment, over the period 1968–1985. In the late 1960s, the economy was slowly recovering from the recession of the mid-1960s. The macroeconomic policy adopted by the government (tight monetary policy and restrictive fiscal policy) to deal with the new wave of industrial conflict stopped the recovery in its tracks. However, despite stagnating levels of industrial production, wage settlements remained high throughout the first period. There was a protracted squeeze on profits, and a small acceleration in the rate of inflation. The relaxation of this deflationary monetary and fiscal policy that followed the oil crisis of 1973 and the devaluation of the lira boosted internal inflation. The rate of inflation increased from around 5% to over 10% in 1973, and almost to 20% by 1974. For the rest of the 1970s, the rate of inflation remained high. The world recession of the mid-1970s caused increased unemployment. Up to 1975, the unemployment rate fluctuated around 5% to 6%, but in the second half of the 1970s, it increased steadily, reaching 7.6% by 1980.[15] Finally, there occurred a far-reaching transformation in Italy's productive structure. Large firms were in serious crisis, whereas small and very small firms were growing. The underground economy was considerably expanding. Both economic recession and restructuring were sharply felt by the unions that, with the changes in the political and economic framework, moved from an "offensive" to a "defensive" approach.

With the end of the period of "pansyndicalism," organizations and parties returned to occupy the center of the stage and were more able than before to influence single and collective protagonists (rank and file, union militants, decentralized union structures). Union cadres and union militants once more pledged loyalty to their respective parties; and, at the same time, the process of organic unification between the unions came to a halt.

As the relations between unions and parties changed, the relations between unions and government also changed, with the government no longer a mere mediator but a leading actor in the social conflict. In the previous period, the unions had been the vehicles for a global project, worked out independently, on the basis of the demands of the rank and file, and with frequent recourse to conflict. Now the confederations recognized a "mutual interdependence" with the government. Bargaining activity and social conflict shifted away from the factories. The government began to take part directly in negotiations with the confederations. A pattern of collaboration (or, as it has been called, "bargained corporativism") came into existence. Negotiations began on an agreement by which the government would sanction the authority of the unions (confederations) and make available to the workers increasing amounts of public resources. The unions, in exchange, were to acquiesce in keeping down the cost of labor. To this period belong, on the one hand, certain general provisions of great importance and certain measures in support of workers' wages, and, on the other, certain measures aimed at containing labor costs.

In the first group, the most important is Law No. 903, enacted in 1977, on equality between the sexes. This law stipulates that employers shall not discriminate between the sexes, either in taking on staff, or as regards payment and promotion. Except for a few cases listed in the law, job advertisements or offers must not specify sex. Payment should be determined by the employee's duties, not according to his or her performance. Finally, job ladders and promotion schemes should be similar for male and female workers.

Among the measures passed to protect wages, Law No. 675 of 1977 introduced some modifications into the administration of the CIG, by further extending the applicability of the CIG *straordinaria*. Under the previous law, it was possible to ask for CIG only for the labor force of firms belonging to

---

[15]However, the level of employment was maintained with minor fluctuations. Major crisis-ridden firms did not dismiss their workers; rather they asked for the intervention of the CIG.

industrial sectors previously declared in a state of crisis. But, from 1977 onward, recourse to the CIG became possible for any individual firm, provided
that the actual need was confirmed by the Ministry of Labor. Moreover, the
1977 law removed the obligation for employers to pay 8% of the CIG they
claimed, thus removing any disincentive to the request for state support.

No less relevant for the emerging pattern of industrial relations was the
ruling of the Constitutional Court and the ordinary judiciary concerning the
right to strike. Political strikes in response to trends in government policy
were recognized as legal, provided they did not aim to subvert parliamentary
democracy. Strikes over time and space (such as "spot" strikes and "rolling"
strikes) could occur provided they did not involve damage to property or
persons.

For their part, the unions accepted explicitly or implicitly (i.e., without
real opposition) certain provisions passed by the government to limit the cost
of labor. In 1976, the unions accepted Law No. 796 that, for the highest
salaries only, changed part of the cost of living allowance (the *contingenza*
acquired over the period 1976–1977) into a forced loan to the state. A year
later, with government consent, an agreement on the cost of labor was drawn
up between the Employers' Association (*Confindustria*) and the union confederations. The agreement—later incorporated into two separate laws—stip-
ulated that increases in the cost-of-living allowance, which would have come
about since then, were to be excluded from the calculation of *liquidazione* (a
bonus received at the end of every employment relationship and related to
the length of service). Moreover, the agreement reduced the number of public
holidays and thus the number of days when factories were compulsorily
closed.

More generally, the unions explicitly accepted a policy of wage restriction, as will be explained in more detail later. Here, it will be sufficient to
note, in the language of the period, that at the meeting of the union delegates
in Rome (at EUR [Rome Congress Center]), in 1978, the CGIL openly contra-
dicted its previous line, declaring that wages could no longer be thought of as
an "independent variable."

In 1978, the CGIL launched its new policy of self-restraint, formalizing
the changes that had begun to emerge, more or less explicitly, in the past few
years. This new strategy, known as the "EUR line" (after the Rome Congress
Center where it was accepted by delegates of the three confederations), set
out the unions' willingness to moderate their wage demands and allow for
more flexibility in management's use of labor.[16] Thus, the unions moved from
a strategy of continuous bargaining toward a cooperative attitude, albeit in
the face of internal opposition. The turnaround was presented to the workers
as a necessary sacrifice, in the interests of economic recovery. The unions set
as their own goal a certain degree of restraint in labor costs, with an explicit
target both on wages and on productivity. In return, they demanded an

---

[16]See the speech given by Lama, at that time General Secretary of CGIL, at the delegates' meeting
in Rome in 1977 (Lama, 1978, pp. 272–78).

economic policy that would protect real incomes, particularly those of the lowest paid, and encourage employment.

In fact, a certain moderation in union policy can be seen as far back as 1976. Union demands for the renewal of the sectoral contracts of 1976 and 1979 were rather low, compared with those of 1969–1970 and 1973. In 1977, the unions opened negotiations with the Employers' Association on the problem of labor costs. They allowed the two laws to be passed by the government on the wage indexation system, the first against moderate union opposition and the second with union approval. The new moderate line, however, reflected the view of the union leadership, not that of the rank and file, and, moreover, did not produce the expected results. Unemployment continued to rise (as shown in Table 1).

As unions became more involved in the management of the economic crisis, a process of progressive recentralization took place, both in the general definition of union policy and in bargaining activity. Interconfederal bargaining was now given constantly higher priority than national and plant-level bargaining, and not only were the triannual sectoral contracts (of 1976 and 1979) characterized by relatively poor wage gains and long delays, but bargaining policy was increasingly defined by the center.

As a result, the decentralized structures that had emerged within the factories in the previous period progressively lost their power, and plant bargaining was either restrained or controlled by the union apparatus. Now, too, when important negotiations took place in the enterprises, union officials, other than those at plant level, would usually take the lead. Moreover, in the smaller enterprises or in negotiations on day-to-day issues, a process of recentralization took place even within the factory. Most of the time, only the small "executive body" of the factory council was directly involved in bargaining. The delegates, the factory council, and the workers' assemblies were left with the formal power of ratifying decisions already taken.

The process of unification between the three confederations also ground to a halt. The *unita' organica*, of the early 1970s, met with increasing difficulties not from the rank and file, but at the center. In particular, this was due to the renewed loyalty of union leaders to their closest political parties and to the reemergence of differentiated (if not diverging) positions between the three confederations and the greater difficulties they experienced in overcoming them.

The wage restraint policy set out in the EUR document had an impact on wage increases. Despite the fact that some formal or informal wage bargaining was still taking place at the plant level, the rate of increase in real wages began to slow down significantly, for the first time since the "hot autumn" of 1969 (see Table 4). But wage increases—in real terms—were still high if compared with the other industrialized countries (see Tronti, 1982).

Moreover, since the 1975 interconfederal agreement on the *scala mobile*, the most dynamic component in the rate of increase in wages was no longer the balance of power between unions and management, that is, the outcome of collective bargaining at national and plant level, but the cost of living allowance. Thus by improving the system of wage indexation, the interconfederal agreement of 1975 had reduced the need for direct confrontation on the issue of wages and, at the same time, secured a better defense of real wages, both as compared with the past and to other countries.

Finally, the shift to a more egalitarian wage indexation system began to produce an effect on the wage structure as inflation throughout the period remained high. Thus, wage differentials, already flattened by the effects of union strategy of the previous period, continued to shrink (see Biagioli, 1982).

IV. SUCCESS AND FAILURE OF TRILATERAL BARGAINING, 1980–1985

The pattern of collaboration between the unions and government lasted until 1979 when the PCI, tired of being kept on the mat—of upholding the majority without being in the government—brusquely offered the choice: "either in government or in opposition." A few months later, the national solidarity government fell and was replaced by a center-left coalition. The third period was characterized by a succession of governments: all five-party coalitions. The first government was led by the Christian Democrats; the second by the PRI, a small non-Catholic party; the third, under the leadership of the socialist Craxi, took office in August 1983.

These governments obstinately pursued a dual policy of attacking inflation (which had risen higher and higher compared to other Western countries) and of isolating the PCI by trying to force it into a role of sterile opposition. Thus, the government set out to come to an agreement with the unions that would guarantee consensus and recognition and simultaneously permit a wage freeze. The PCI, for its part, did all it could to prevent this, playing on the loyalties of the communist elements in the CGIL and on the propensity for conflict still present in a large part of the working class.

As the arena of confrontation was shifted to the political-institutional level, to the center, the protagonists of this confrontation became the union leadership, the government, and the employers' organizations. Party loyalty grew more marked among the unions and, by the same token, interunion solidarity showed clear signs of falling off. At the same time, government intervention in negotiations between management and unions took on an increasingly authoritarian character until, for the first time, negotiations were formally conducted between the three parties. As a consequence, the story of industrial relations in this last period is the story of the successes and failures of trilateral agreements negotiated at the central level.

The period opened with an abortive attempt at an agreement between the government and the union confederations on the setting up of an investment fund (*Fondo di solidarietà*), financed by workers' savings. Immediately after the breakdown of the national solidarity coalition, the government tried to introduce a wage cut, suggesting that workers pay a compulsory contribution of 0.5% of their wages to an investment fund, which would also be subject to union control. But the proposal was defeated by the combined opposition of the Communist party and the workers in large factories. In the months that followed, there was a serious clash between management and unions at FIAT, in which the government played a subsidiary role. It ended, for the first time since 1968, in a strong defeat for the workers: 25,000 employees went on CIG. The outcome marked a weakening of the union movement and the reemergence of an aggressive attitude on the part of management. It also pointed to a traumatic separation between the fate of middle and lower working-class elements, on the one hand, and technicians and white-collar elements, on the other hand, which forcibly brought to the unions the problem of wage differentials.

But, on January 22, 1983, under Spadolini's government (PRI leadership), an important trilateral agreement was signed. This agreement—the outcome of a long process in which the government figured as mediator, guarantor and participant—provided for an overall regulation of the entire setup, with the reduction of inflation to 13%, by the end of the year, as the central goal. Employers and unions agreed to renew the wage indexation agreement of 1975, but with the cost-of-living allowance reduced by 15%; to put a ceiling on negotiated increases in sectoral contracts for 1983–1985; to freeze plant wage bargaining for 18 months, after the renewal of national contracts; and finally, to reduce annual working hours by 40, within the year. The government, for its part, agreed to introduce some fiscal measures to reduce the tax burden for employees, and to introduce a set of new laws dealing with employment, the pension scheme, the CIG, and the national health system. It was clear that the government wanted to centralize bargaining to the point where it could control the entire dynamic of wages, leaving very little room for plant bargaining.

The trilateral agreement of January 22, 1983, made provisions for renewed discussion of all the issues involved in it at the start of the following year. Under Craxi's government, this soon changed into wide-ranging negotiations. The government, also under pressure from employers (who demanded a drastic cut in the mechanism of *scala mobile*), asked the unions to agree to a further reduction in the cost-of-living allowance, payable in 1984.[17] In exchange, it offered to the unions a package including a brake on the price of public services, the freezing of rents, a program to revise the tax system, which would limit tax evasion and tax erosion, and a program of intervention in favor of employment. As before, but this time more openly, the unions' positions drastically diverged: whereas the CISL, the UIL, and the socialist element in the CGIL supported the agreement, the communist element in the CGIL opposed it. Indeed, the CGIL's communist leadership, though obviously sensitive to pressures coming from the PCI, was also conditioned by its involvement in the defense of middle and lower income workers who would be hardest hit by a freeze on the cost-of-living allowance. Moreover, the CGIL leadership was well aware that many middle-ranking union offi-

---

[17]More precisely, the government proposed the predetermination of the points of *contingenza* in relation to an inflation rate forecast at 10% (i.e., the government inflation target).

cials, as well as the rank and file, were likely to put up some kind of resistance, or even rebel. As a result, the CGIL split on the *scala mobile* issue,
with the communist component strongly opposing the government proposal.

However, the opposition by the communist element in the trade union
movement did not stop the government from pursuing its course. By a decree
issued on February 14, 1984 (known as the St. Valentine's law decree) the
proposal that had been approved by the CISL, UIL, and the socialist element
in the CGIL was resolved into a law by Craxi. The most important clause in
the decree stated that in 1984 a maximum of 10 points of *contingenza* would be
paid. This became the object of a bitter political struggle. The task of converting the decree into law held the Italian Parliament in stalemate for several
months.[18] Government consensus was damaged to such an extent that the
PCI obtained a relative majority, for the first time, in the European Parliament
elections of June 17, 1984. But, above all, the extreme left opposed the government's intervening in a matter that had hitherto been regulated by collective
bargaining and called for a referendum to cancel the contested clause. For the
reasons already mentioned, the PCI also associated itself with this initiative.
The referendum was held in the spring of 1985. The majority voted for the
government, and the PCI and extreme left were defeated.

For many reasons, this referendum may be seen as the final stage in the
trilateral bargaining period. The difficulties of converting the St. Valentine's
decree into law, the adverse influence exerted over 12 months on Italian
politics by the referendum, the waste of energy, and the severe wounds
occasioned thereby all demonstrate the impossibility of trying to involve the
CGIL in the management of the economy with the aim of isolating the PCI.
Also, the outcome of the referendum proves that, even in questions of industrial relations, the country views Parliament as the natural seat of proposals
and decisions. The result of the referendum cuts the role of the trade unions
down to size. Whereas previously the unions had their say in all matters, now
their influence is restricted to more or less visible bargaining on the regulation
of the labor market.

In addition to witnessing attempts to bring about agreement on holding
down labor costs, the early 1980s saw substantial modifications in the institutional set-up of the labor market. These innovations were introduced by laws
Nos. 79/1983 and 863/1984, which gave legislative force to the agreements of
January 1983 and February 1984. In a climate dominated by the urgency of
reaching an agreement on halting the rise in wages, the unions ended up
allowing institutional reforms that they had always previously opposed.

In particular, the previously mentioned laws have made it much easier to
implement temporary contracts. Part-time contracts have become more prevalent. Firms now have more discretionary power in hiring. Finally, a new
type of temporary contract, namely the *contratto di formazione-lavoro,* has been

---

[18]A first law (No. 219)—regulating the *scala mobile*—was passed in June; and a second law (No.
863)—modifying the institutional set-up of the labor market—was passed only in December.

introduced. Aimed at reducing youth unemployment, this contract allows employers to hire young people (under the age of 29) on temporary contracts (up to 2 years), at a low cost.[19] This type of contract is subject to one condition only, namely that the firm shall, to some extent at least, be responsible for the professional training of the young employees.

These innovations are certainly of great importance. They are partial attempts at deregulating the labor market by eliminating or lessening some of the constraints imposed on management by previous legislation. Although the effect of these provisions on the level of employment is in doubt, their impact on the labor market structure will be wide and lasting.

From the foregoing, it can be seen that the early 1980s witnessed an intensification of the pattern of industrial relations that emerged in the years 1975–1980. Union organization and activity was further centralized and placed outside the factories. The space left for wage bargaining at the plant level was further reduced. But whereas national negotiations at the highest level (between government, confederations, and employer organizations) were acquiring a primary role, and the union movement at levels below was sliding into second place, the differences between the confederations were growing sharper. In effect the union movement was being weakened at *all* levels.

These changes brought with them a further centralization of union structure. In particular, the trilateral agreement of 1983 can be seen as the institutionalization of changes in the bargaining structure that had developed in the previous period of national solidarity government. The very structure of the agreement confirmed the centrality of the interconfederal level as the primary locus for negotiations on general employment conditions and economic policy and the regulation of employee benefits not directly related to the employment relationship. Thus, although the agreement did not modify the general bargaining structure (still based on three levels of bargaining: interconfederal, national, and plant), it defined more precisely the relations between the different levels, giving the interconfederal level the general function of defining the principles and objectives pursued at the lower levels.

Now that the arena of confrontation had shifted away from the workplace to the political-institutional level, the main actor in the labor movement was no longer the rank and file but the union leadership, which bargained directly with government and employers. At the same time, the plant union structure began to lose its capacity for mass mobilization. There was a decline in factory militancy reflected in low worker participation in rallies and demonstrations organized in support of union strategy. Moreover, on some occasions, the gap between the union leadership and the rank and file resulted in open rejection of the leadership by the workers on the shopfloor.[20] Finally,

---

[19]These contracts allow the employer to reduce welfare payments when hiring people under 29 years of age, which enables a reduction in labor costs on the order of 25%.

[20]See Garonna and Pisani (1985) on the struggles at FIAT and ALFA.

union membership dropped steadily since 1980 (see Table 3), and there was some reemergence of autonomous unions, particularly in public administration.

But to fully understand the unions' diminished capacity for mass mobilization and shrinking membership, it is necessary to consider, along with the changes that occurred in the political framework, (1) the determined effort of the union leadership to shift the conflict from the shopfloor to the political arena; (2) the deterioration in labor market conditions and the changes occurring in the employment structure (with an increasing number of large firms in crisis); and (3) the increasing aggressiveness of management.

With the failure to reach agreement in February 1984, the situation tended to change. The split between the confederations, and that within the CGIL itself, further weakened the unions. Any initiative at confederational level was prevented by the long battle for the referendum fought from different positions. From February 1984 to May 1985, all the unions were paralyzed by the split. Slowly, the idea of an all-embracing centralized bargaining faded into the background, and the union rank and file regained something of the role they had lost.

It is especially difficult to identify and measure the impact of the period of "trilateral bargaining" on employment conditions. In the early 1980s, the crucial problems for the management of the labor market were the outcome of those institutional mechanisms—in particular the wage indexing system and the CIG—which had been put in place in the previous period and whose effects had been exaggerated by the high rate of inflation and the worsening economic recession. Undoubtedly, the agreements of January 1983 and February 1984 have had some effect, in particular in controlling wages. However, general economic conditions in recent years have largely contributed to solving the problems posed by the *scala mobile* and the CIG.

Wage indexation had already produced a reduction in wage differentials in the second half of the 1970s. With the rate of inflation still high in the 1980s, it created not only a further compression of wage differentials but also a change in the structure of money earnings. The amount of *contingenza* (wage indexing allowance) over total actual earnings progressively increased, accounting on average for over 50% of money earnings.[21]

All this made wage bargaining more difficult. The presence of such a strong automatic adjustment mechanism, together with the economic recession, made it harder for the unions to gain wage increases. In addition, the unions now became aware that the egalitarian policy had gone too far and that some groups of workers (white-collar professionals and highly skilled workers) had been heavily penalized. The situation was further complicated by the fact that the squeeze on contractual wage differentials, together with a chronic shortage of skilled labor, had induced management to unilaterally readjust wages, leaving the unions out.[22]

[21]See Dell'Aringa (1983, pp. 17–20) and Biagioli (1982).
[22]This has been shown in a study on wage differentials by Biagioli (1985).

Thus the problem of the "reform of the structure of wages" stood out in the early 1980s more vigorously than in the past. The confederations, the rank and file, and the employers' associations were feeling the need to halt the automatic compression of wage differentials. However, the debate on this subject did not last long. The reform of the wage structure occurred, almost unnoticed, as the indirect outcome of the legal changes in the wage indexing system in the context of a lowering of the rate of inflation.[23]

Another way in which institutional mechanisms established in the 1970s displayed their effects in the early 1980s was through the CIG. Unemployment benefits and CIG both provide some sort of income security. But they apply to different categories of workers and involve very different sums of money. Unemployment benefits are paid to workers who have lost their jobs. The CIG is paid to employed workers who are involuntarily and temporarily redundant, due to short-time working. These workers are not dismissed: They cease working, but they keep their employment relationship with the firm. Unemployment benefits vary with each economic sector and category of benefit and tend to be extremely low. In industry, the "normal unemployment benefit" consists of 800 lire (equivalent to about half a dollar) per day.[24] The CIG, by contrast, was conceived from the very beginning as guaranteeing a significant percentage of earnings. The tendency has been to increase the coverage of earnings, as well as to enlarge the scope of the program.

Up to 1968, the CIG was granted only in cases of temporary suspension from work and was approximately equal to two-thirds of earnings. The 1975 and 1977 agreements increased the coverage of the CIG, so that now it guarantees almost 100% of earnings and applies to far more workers.[25] Employers are now entitled to request CIG intervention in almost any case of excess labor, including long-term layoffs with little chance of reemployment. The only limitation left, although it remains implicit in the law, is the size of the firm. Indeed, only large- and medium-sized firms are capable of handling all the stages of the administrative procedure necessary to gain access to the CIG. For small firms in economic difficulties, the only possible solution is to dismiss workers. This is quite easy to do because unions are weak in these firms.

During the economic crisis of the early 1980s, major crisis-ridden firms reacted to the need for restructuring by asking for the intervention of the

---

[23]The changes introduced in the wage indexing system have contributed to a widening of wage differentials and to a contraction in the inflation protection rate but in conditions of slowing down of inflation.

[24]The workers entitled to receive "normal unemployment benefits" are the involuntary unemployed (i.e., dismissed) who had been previously working and paying the social contributions for at least 52 weeks in the last 2 years. "Special unemployment benefits" are relatively greater in amount (up to a maximum of the equivalent of 350 dollars per month). The workers entitled to receive special unemployment benefits are those dismissed due to closure or reduced activity of the firm.

[25]More precisely, the CIG guarantees 80% of previous net salary, and this goes up to approximately 93% as a result of a different system of deductions.

CIG.[26] The contraction in manpower requirements was realized while reducing to the minimum the cost of social conflicts. In fact, the unions did not resist these plans. Rather, they engaged in plant-level bargaining aimed at gaining a guaranteed wage for the labor force involved in restructuring. And because the recourse to the CIG did not imply, in many cases, the possibility of reemployment, the total number of workers in CIG increased steadily and very rapidly. The total number of hours of CIG recorded in 1979 was approximately 300,000,000 (equivalent to 124,000 employees), and in 1984 was approximately 816,000,000 (equivalent to 438,000 employees) (see Table 6).

The steady increase in the number of workers in CIG raised a serious financial problem. The social contributions paid by employers and workers were insufficient to pay for it, and the burden was by and large on the government budget. However, when the situation seemed to have gone out of control and an urgent need for a drastic reform of the CIG was called for, the evolution of general economic conditions, again, helped to solve the problem.

The overcoming of the economic recession and the massive restructuring of the manufacturing industry in the 1980s (which produced a considerable contraction in total employment) have led to a turnabout. In 1985, for the first time since the introduction of the CIG *straordinaria*, a contraction in the total number of hours of CIG has been recorded (see Table 6).

In the early 1980s, partial attempts for a deregulation of the labor market were passed by law. Temporary and part-time contracts were introduced, and their field of application extended. The Italian unions had long been opposed to these kinds of contracts. They feared that the rate of unionization would drop and workers' militancy would be weakened. In spite of pressure from employers, the unions refused throughout the 1970s to create conditions for a more refined segmentation of the labor market. As a result, at the end of the 1970s, Italy was, for instance, the country with the lowest number of part-time workers in Europe.

In 1983 and 1984, this institutional anomaly at last disappeared. With the labor movement weakened and isolated and industry urgently in need of restructuring, this partial deregulation of the labor market was implemented. It is these new provisions, more than the failure of trilateral bargaining, that will influence the labor market in the years to come. It is likely that as a result of these institutional changes, the segmentation of the labor market in Italy will become more complex and less dichotomized and the core of the labor force smaller and weaker.

V. CONCLUSION

To conclude, it is useful to make explicit the model on which our analysis has been carried out. In light of that model, we will briefly summarize the main points of our argument.

---

[26]Thus, some workers were suspended from work but kept their employment relationship with the firm. They received from the state a subsidy that was almost equal to their previous net

In describing the changes in the industrial relations regime from 1968 to 1985, we have referred to three main variables: (1) the institutional framework, (2) the state of the economy, and (3) the efficacy of union action. The institutional framework was viewed through the relations between trade unions and parties, the relations between unions and government, and those between the three trade union confederations. An additional element of the institutional framework is the levels at which collective bargaining occurs: plant level, sectoral level, and interconfederal level. The state of the economy was represented by the rate of economic growth, the rate of inflation, and the rate of unemployment. Also, some attention, though not as much as the topic deserves, was focused on structural changes in the economy, in particular the decentralization of the productive structure fostered by the industrial relations regime. The efficacy of union action was measured in terms of the rate of increase of wages, the impact on wage differentials, and the degree of control that workers manage to exert over the organization of work.

Following these lines, we can retrace the events of those years. The first period, from 1968 to 1975, saw the trade unions highly autonomous. Strong in the unity of the confederations, the union movement declared its autonomy from the political parties and bargained with the government over matters that lay well outside its field of competence. Negotiation was continuous at all levels. There were large wage increases, and wage differentials were reduced. There was strong economic growth and the rate of inflation remained low until the latter part of the period.

The second period, from 1975 to 1980, was one of stagnation. Large firms were in crisis, decentralization increased, and inflation accelerated. The union movement was still powerful and allied itself with the government to tackle the crisis. In order to enable the unions to exercise their powers of coordination, bargaining was concentrated at the confederal level. As a result, wages rose only slowly. Wage differentials, governed by the automatic mechanisms determining wage increases, eluded the control of the unions and dwindled almost to the vanishing point.

The last period, from 1980 to 1985, was a contradictory one, more so than the other two. The rate of inflation, at first very high, was brought under control. The large enterprises were initially in great difficulty. But following the occurrences at FIAT, they set about a restructuring that laid the basis for the economic expansion of the final years of this period. The union movement was divided and weak. The rate of increase of wages was low, and union control over the organization of work was minimal. At the end of the period, the government took a decisive step. It did not attempt to reduce the level of unemployment that was still on the rise. Action was taken, instead, to redistribute the burden of unemployment among a larger number of workers. The aim was to soothe the tensions that might be caused by unemployment being concentrated among particular social groups.

---

salary, whereas others lost their jobs and received a subsidy that was about 1/40 of their previous earnings.

There is a lesson to be learned from these events. In particular, they suggest that there is no obvious connection between the strength of the Italian union movement and the condition of the economy. The EUR policy was imposed by strong unions in a period of recession. The years 1984–1985, a period of strong economic growth, saw a much weakened union movement. Rather, the strength of the Italian union movement derives from the institutional framework, in particular the extent of unity among the confederations, the extent of autonomy from the political parties, and the various levels at which collective bargaining occurs.

VI. REFERENCES

Bettio, F. (1985). The secular decrease of sex-linked wage differentials: A case of noncompetition. *Economia e Lavoro, 3,* 31–56.

Biagioli, M. (1982). Inflazione e struttura delle retribuzioni nell' industria milanese. In M. Biagioli (Ed.), *Inflazione, struttura del salario e contrattazione* (pp. 56–109), IRES-CGIL. Milano: Franco Angeli.

Biagioli, M. (1985). Contrattazione aziendale e differenziali retributivi interaziendali. *Economia e Lavoro, 3,* 75–110.

Bruno, S. (1979). The industrial reserve army, segmentation and the Italian labour market. *Cambridge Journal of Economics, 3,* 131–151.

Brusco, S. (1982). The emilian model: Productive decentralisation and social integration. *Cambridge Journal of Economics, 6,* 167–184.

C.E.S.O.S. (various issues). *Le relazioni sindacali in Italia.* Roma: Edizioni Lavoro.

Coi, S. (1979). Sindacati in Italia: iscritti, apparato, finanziamento. *Il Mulino, 28,* 201–242.

Dell'Aringa, C. (1976). *Egualitarismo e sindacato.* Milano: Vita e Pensiero.

Dell'Aringa, C. (1983). Inflazione e distribuzione del reddito. *Rivista Milanese di Economia, 5,* 7–26.

Faustini, G. (1976). Wage indexing and inflation in Italy. *Banca Nazionale del Lavoro, Quarterly Review, 119,* 364–377.

Filosa, R., & Visco, I. (1980). Costo del lavoro, indicizzazione e perequazione delle retribuzioni. In G. Nardozzi (Ed.), *I Difficili anni '70* (pp. 107–139). Milano: Etas Libri.

Garonna, P., & Pisani, E. (1985). Italian unions in transition: The crisis of political unionism. In R. Edwards, P. Garonna, & F. Todtling (Eds.), *Unions in Crisis and Beyond.* (pp. 114–172). London: Auburn House.

Giugni, G. et al. (1976). *Gli anni della conflittualità permanente.* Milano: Franco Angeli.

Lama, L. (1977). *Il sindacato nella crisi italiana.* Roma: Editori Riuniti.

Lange, L., & Vannicelli, M. (1985). Strategy under stress: The Italian union movement and the Italian crisis in developmental perspective. In P. Lange, G. Ross, & M. Vannicelli (Eds.), *Unions, Change and Crisis: French and Italian Union Strategy and the Political Economy, 1945–1980.* (pp. 98–206). London: Allen & Unwin.

Regalia, I., Regini, M., & Reyneri, E. (1978). Labour conflicts and industrial relations in Italy. In C. Crouch & A. Pizzorno (Eds.), *The resurgence of class conflict in Western Europe since 1968.* (pp. 101–158). London: MacMillan.

Regini, M. (1979). Labour unions, industrial action and politics. *West European Politics, 2,* 49–65.

Romagnoli, U. (1980). *La Sindacalizzazione fra ideologia e pratica.* Roma: Edizioni Lavoro.

Romagnoli, U., & Treu, T. (1977). I sindacati in italia: Storia di una strategia. Bologna: Il Mulino.

Salvati, M. (1981). May 1968 and the hot autumn of 1968: The response of two ruling classes, in S. D. Berger (Ed.), *Organizing interests in Western Europe.* (pp. 329–363). Cambridge: C.U.P.

Tronti, L. (1982). Produttività e salari nei principali paesi industriali, 1973–81. Un esame comparativo. *Prospettive del mercato del lavoro, 4,* 71–78.

8

State Regulation, Enterprise Behavior, and the Labor Market in Hungary, 1968–1983

Peter Galasi and György Sziráczki

I. INTRODUCTION

In Hungary the centralization of economic management began in the late 1940s. Most enterprises were nationalized, small-scale industry and retail trade were practically abolished, and peasant farms were collectivized. The enterprises were directed by an hierarchical state apparatus. The main instrument of economic management was the system of obligatory plan targets. These were disaggregated to the enterprise level and prescribed the input and output levels as well as product mixes. The centralization of economic management and the plan targets were aimed at the forced industrialization of a predominantly agricultural country with significant labor reserves, at the expense of the population's living standard. The rush for growth and the system of plan targets led to low efficiency and to poor quality goods and services.

As a result of economic troubles and tensions in the early 1960s, politicians and planners generally agreed that it was necessary to carry out radical changes in the system of economic management, and in 1968, economic reform was introduced. Plan targets were abandoned, and a normative system based on financial regulators was introduced to control the economy. It was a commonly held view that this normative regulation, which meant identical

Reprinted from *Cambridge Journal of Economics*, 9(3), 203–219, with updating of several references. Copyright 1985 by P. Galasi and G. Sziráczki.

Peter Galasi and György Sziráczki • Department of Labor Economics, Karl Marx University of Economics, 1828 Budapest, Hungary.

treatment for all enterprises and indirect means of controlling market processes, would improve the efficiency of the enterprises and increase their responsiveness to the market. The autonomy of enterprises increased, they were allowed to determine their input and output levels and their product mix and to retain part of their profits for investments and wages. The price system became more flexible and, although some prices continued to be set centrally, the scope of free prices was extended. However, along with the decentralization, the revitalization of the market and the normative central regulation, devices were also built into the system aimed at maintaining the role of the state as the main resource allocator.

The postreform history of the economy can be divided into three periods (Table 1 and Figure 1). The first period (1968–1971) was characterized by a rapid increase in national income and in living standards and a slight increase in the price level. Employment continued to rise, but with the gradual exhaustion of labor reserves, labor shortages began to appear in large cities and industrial centers. The performance of the economy and the quality of the products undoubtedly improved. Nevertheless, the original ideas for reform only partially materialized. As a result of the uncertainties of central financial regulation, state intervention increased, and a partial recentralization of economic management was gradually introduced. At the same time, external

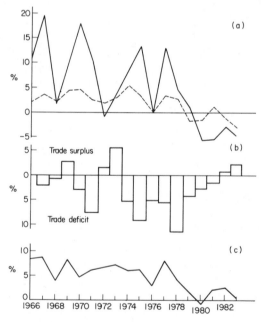

Figure 1. Investment, real wages, foreign trade balance and national income. (a)—: Yearly growth rate of volume of investment; ---: yearly growth rate of real wages. (b) Foreign trade balance expressed as a percentage of national income. (c) Yearly growth rate of national income. *Sources: Statistical Yearbooks,* Central Statistical Bureau, Budapest.

Table 1. National Income, Employment, Living Standards
(Annual Average Growth, shown as a Percentage)

	National income	Number of active earners	Manual and white-collar workers			Population	
			Nominal average wages	Consumer prices	Real wages	Real per capita income	Per capita consumption
1968–71	5.7	1.6	4.5	1.0	3.5	6.0	5.1
1972–78	5.8	0.2	6.6	3.6	3.0	3.8	3.7
1979–84[a]	0.8	−0.2	6.7	7.4	−0.7	0.7	0.9

[a]The data for 1984 are estimates.
Sources: Statistical Yearbook 1981, Central Statistical Bureau, Budapest; *Statistical Handbook 1982 and 1983*, Central Statistical Bureau, Budapest.

conditions worsened. The price explosion in the world market and the consequent adverse terms of trade added to the trouble of the open Hungarian economy. However, fast economic growth also continued in the second period (1972–1978) but was now accompanied by an accelerating rate of inflation and a slowdown in the rise in living standards, while labor shortages became general.

The third period (1979–1984) has been characterized by high inflation, slow growth, and declining real wages. Yet, unlike in capitalist economies, full employment has been maintained, demand for labor has fallen only slightly, and enterprises have hoarded labor. Protracted stagnation and the inflexibility of the economy have induced the leadership to search again for a way out of the difficulties in reform.

This chapter analyzes state regulation, enterprise behavior, and the operation and characteristics of the labour market in these three periods.

II. THE EFFECTS OF THE ECONOMIC REFORM ON ENTERPRISE BEHAVIOR IN THE LABOR MARKET, 1968–1971

A. Profit-Oriented Enterprises and the Liberalization of the Labor Market

The 1968 reform aimed to make enterprises profit-oriented by linking investment and earnings to profits. For investment, the principle adopted was that of a division between enterprises and the central authorities (Kornai, 1980a). Enterprises were allowed to spend some part of their profits on investment and the more efficient they were, the larger the part of the profit retained for investment. The increase in the enterprise wage level was to be dependent exclusively on enterprise profit, a part of which was used to supplement basic wages. This measure was expected to give employees an incentive to increase enterprise performance and to act as an inducement for workers to move from enterprises with low profitability to more efficient and more dynamic enterprises, able to pay a higher profit share.[1]

The logic of the reform required greater autonomy in the labor market. Legal provisions preventing free job changes were abolished, the central determination of enterprise manning was abandoned, and the shaping of independent enterprise wage policies was made possible by the use of the incentive fund to determine individual wages. Thus, the demand–supply relations of the labor market could operate freely to allocate labor and determine earnings differentials.

The effect of the reform was to expand the "second" economy: those small-scale plants, businesses, and forms of income redistribution that lie outside the state-controlled system of production and income distribution. The most important areas for the second economy are small-scale agricultural production on household plots and farms, private house-building activity, legally operating private small-scale industry, and small shopkeeping and nonlegal service and repair activities. There the enterprises were comparatively cost-sensitive and profit-oriented relative to the hierarchically organized state-owned and cooperative sector, even after the reform.

The development and expansion of the second economy can be explained by the advantage it offered to the population and also to the economic management center. It helped to reduce the chronic shortage of consumer goods and made it possible for the workers employed in the state sector to earn supplementary income after regular working hours (Galasi, 1983; Gábor, 1989).

The freedom to change jobs and the growth of the second economy improved the position of workers. They were able not only to choose freely among the job opportunities offered by the units of the state sector but were also able to move into the second economy, where they became small-scale producers or employees. However, the migration from the socialist sector to the second economy was limited by the nature of the second economy and its structural position in the system. We shall return to this question later; here it is sufficient to say that for the broad mass of workers the second economy became important mainly as a source of income supplementary to that from the state sector. The combination offered both employment security and income maximization (Kertesi & Sziráczki, 1987) and for this reason, multiple job holding (moonlighting) became widespread in Hungary.

B. Enterprises' Labor Market Strategies—Adjustments to Competition

The liberalization of the labor market and the emergence of labor shortage caused fierce competition for labor among firms in the state sector, and in

---

[1]The central economic authority prescribed how the gross profits of firms should be divided between taxes and payments to central and local authorities, and investments, welfare and incentive (payable by way of wage increases and profit sharing) funds remaining with the firm.

1968–1969 labor turnover increased by 74%. This situation forced enterprises to adopt different strategies to improve their labor market position.

The cooperatives and the small- and medium-sized state enterprises, which had been relatively disadvantaged under the regime of centralized control, attempted to exploit their market flexibility by rapidly increasing their profits so as to raise wages and improve their labor market position. This strategy was only temporary, whereas the cooperative sector gained strength relative to large-scale enterprises in the state sector.

The main reason for the temporary weakening of the position of large-scale state enterprises after the reform lay in their poor ability to adapt to market conditions: a legacy of overcentralization and the inflexibility of bureaucratic managerial control. They tried to improve their labor market position by lobbying and bargaining for central subsidies, by making use of their position, informal connections, and political capital, by referring to their "importance to the national economy" as they had done before the reform. Under the 1968 reforms, subsidies were intended as emergency measures, to be restricted to communal services; but the pressure of large firms resulted in a quick increase in wage subsidies, from about 125 million forints in 1968 to 600 to 700 million forints in 1970.

A third strategy adopted by firms was the establishment of enterprise labor markets. By using a system of internal labor allocation, wage fixing, and training, firms tried to reduce the mobility of key workers and to restrict labor demand to the lower levels of the job hierarchy. This provided a degree of security against the competition of other enterprises. Enterprises had adopted such methods earlier, but their organization into a consistent labor policy was made possible only by the greater independence gained after the reform.

Internal labor markets are widely recognized as important in capitalist economies (Doeringer & Piore, 1971; Osterman, 1984; Wilkinson, 1981). But their counterparts in the socialist economy have two characteristics that distinguish them from those in the capitalist economies. One is the significant upgrading of the workers' firm-specific skills, and the other is informality.

Firm-specific skills are needed in the socialist economy not only because of firm-specific technology but also because of the frequent shortages resulting from the system of economic organization (Kornai, 1980b). Adaptation at the enterprise level to the production problems caused by the chronic shortages of materials, components, tools, and the like often devolves upon the workers. Consequently, firm-specific skills are highly esteemed and include intrafirm informal relations and practical experience that enable workers to overcome difficulties in the production process and to adjust more easily to unexpected situations. These firm-specific skills increased in importance with the emergence of the overall labor shortage in the early 1970s and the greater risk that the enterprise might lose its elite workers.

The need to retain such employees played a role in the establishment of the mainly informal internal labor markets, structured by hidden power relations, inherent customs, and unwritten laws. Promotion, for example, often manifested itself in an increased opportunity for overtime, for obtaining bonuses and better paid tasks rather than in upward mobility in the formal hierarchy (Kövári & Sziáczki, 1985). The informality is also explained by the absence of collective bargaining at the establishment level; wages were regulated centrally, and consequently at the local level the employees' side became fragmented. Only a restricted group of elite skilled workers substantially endowed with firm-specific skills and occupying key positions in the production process were able to enter into informal bargaining with the management over reward for effort to raise their income—usually at the expense of other groups. Thus, the internal labor markets were based on a consensus between the management and the elite workers. Employees in a weaker bargaining position—and they constituted the overwhelming majority—could attempt to improve their income level only individually by, for example, promotion, increased work intensity, participation in the second economy, or by taking advantage of interfirm competition by frequently changing their jobs.

Thus, typically, small- and medium-sized firms responded to the reforms by market adaptation, whereas the majority of large enterprises simultaneously exploited opportunities for bargaining with the economic management center over wage subsidies and built their internal labor market to meet the competition for labor.

C. Weak Market Mechanisms and Enterprises Bargaining with the State: Impediments for Reform

The picture drawn of the first postreform period would not be complete without a discussion of the difficulties that arose from the uncertainties of normative regulation, from the effect of the weak profit orientation of firms that hampered the working of the price mechanism and market competition, and from the social tensions attributed to the reform.

The problems had already appeared in several sectors by the beginning of 1969. Cooperation between enterprises on, among other things, deliveries tended to decline, and this gave rise to difficulties in the fulfillment of the export tasks laid down in interstate contracts. Free prices and hence costs increased rapidly, and this squeezed enterprises producing export goods at fixed prices. Investment control was unable to put a brake on the tendency to overinvestment. Normative regulation also proved inadequate to deal with such matters as the settlement of the position of loss-making enterprises, the assessment of enterprises' tax liability and subsidies, which required action at the enterprise level.

When the reforms were introduced, those of state subsidies and taxation were postponed as were the termination of monopoly practices and the reorganization of the overcentralized enterprise structure with its predominance of large companies. The former impeded the operation of the price mechanism and the latter the development of market competition.

The incentive power of profit making was weakened from the outset by the large-scale and steeply progressive withdrawal of profits by the state that reduced net profit differentials between enterprises and the funds at their disposal. The growth of enterprises was only slightly dependent on their own profitability as only one quarter of overall investment was self-financed and from bank credits granted according to profitability. The overwhelming majority of investment resources were allocated centrally in the form of long-term credits and state subsidies, decisions about which were at best only marginally dependent on enterprise profitability.

Owing to the loose connection between investment and profitability, the enterprises' motivation for profitability depended mainly on the fact that the earnings of both employees and managers were related to the annual profits of the enterprise. This created a short-term motivation for the efficient running of the enterprise, though even this was undermined by the growing amount of wage subsidies from the state. In addition, state regulation also contained irrational elements. Enterprises were primarily interested in hiring the largest possible number of low-paid workers, in order to be in a position to pay more to their elite employees. Thus wage regulation increased the competition between firms in an already tight labor market.

The problems of wage control, unequal opportunities for profit sharing, and growing earnings differentials caused social tensions, which provided the justification for action against normative regulation. The first opportunity for state intervention was given by the complaints formulated by a group of the workers in large loss-making enterprises. Most criticisms were directed against the allegedly higher earnings in small-scale enterprises and cooperatives, the accelerated labor turnover attributed to these earnings differentials, the labor flow from the large to the small firms as well as against price rises. Many of the criticisms coincided with the interests of the managers of large enterprises, were reinforced by the party and trade union representatives at the enterprise level, and therefore found support in sections of the regional, sectoral, and central authorities. The pressure increased for central intervention to modify wage control, to curb the wage competition of small-scale enterprises and cooperatives in order to reduce labor turnover and to control prices. All this gave impetus to the gradual growth of central economic management.

In 1971, wage control was modified to a form more favorable to large enterprises (Révész, 1978). But this did not solve the problems; on the contrary, it weakened profit orientation further. Under the new system, the annual increase in the wage level depended upon the rise in the profit rate and not on the profit rate itself. Wage controls forced enterprises to increase their profits each year—and to make efforts to utilize and expand their capacities—but only sufficiently to allow a rise in the wage level, while retaining sufficient growth reserves to raise the profit level the next year. At the same time, the practice of central wage subsidies was legalized and extended. Annual budget estimates included subsidies, of which about 75% were granted to large enterprises in 1971 (Böröczfiné, 1976).

Such difficulties undoubtedly contributed to the failure of normative regulation and therefore disrupted the process of reform. The main reason for the failure of the reform lay, however, in the hierarchically organized institutional system of economic management, which impeded the emergence of autonomy and flexibility at the microlevel. After the introduction of the reform, the economy was regulated by both the government and the branch ministries. These used mainly financial and legal controls and price regulation to direct the economic process. The state's rights arose from its ownership of the means of production (foundation, liquidation and merger of enterprises; determination of their profiles; and the appointment and replacement of their directors, etc.), and these areas were also affected by the branch ministries, making it possible for them to intervene at the microlevel beyond the scope of their officially prescribed authority.

The party (the Hungarian Socialist Workers' party) also played a role in the process of economic decision-making. The task of the party established by the reform was one of guiding and controlling rather than one of detailed economic management that was the responsibility of the ministries.

The control of the party over the economy was achieved through a multilevel, multichannel consultation-control and reporting system, supplemented by the cadre-choosing authority of the party committee that decided who should fill a well-defined group of positions. The ministers reported regularly about their ministry's activity not only to the government (Council of Ministers) but also to the party organization within their ministry and hence to the local party as well as to the economic departments of the party's central committee. These channels and those at regional and enterprise level not only provided the means of party control, but they also facilitated a two-way flow of information between enterprises and higher levels in the hierarchy, bargaining over economic management during the economic-political decision-making process. Consequently, the different spheres of political and economic decisions overlapped.

A further characteristic of the institutional system was the ability of some enterprise managers to integrate themselves into the central political–economic management, and therefore to short-circuit the hierarchy, thus becoming the superior of their "superiors" (Csanádi, 1984). For instance, if an enterprise director was elected a member of the central committee of the party, he took part in making decisions related to the development opportunities of his branch that were binding on the relevant branch ministry. The more an enterprise manager was integrated into the central system of political–economic management, the greater was his possible influence on the central decisions concerning his enterprise and the more opportunities there were for improving the position of his enterprise by securing state subsidies, preferences, and special treatment outside market activities and adaptation. Thus, the degree of political integration of the enterprise was an important determinant of its economic behavior.

The enterprise managers' attitudes toward the reform were also largely determined by the degree of their integration into central management. The managers of strongly integrated large companies called for direct state intervention at the expense of normative regulation because they could then expect to improve the position of their firms by state subsidies and preferences to a greater extent than by market adaptation.

As far as the continuation of the reform was concerned, the disposition of central political authority organs toward the reform processes was decisive. Despite the difficulties described, the reform was considered successful because the economy worked more effectively, with steady growth and improved living standards. Consequently, to avoid increasing economic and social tensions by making more radical changes in the institutional system of the economy, they tended to maintain the achievements while encouraging central economic management to eliminate the shortcomings of price and financial regulators. Nevertheless, because of the structural problems discussed, normative regulations and market mechanisms were unable to improve the operation of the economy sufficiently to meet the expectations of the central political authority. Thus political leaders and the managers of large firms put pressure on central economic management to increase direct state interventions. Consequently, the symbiosis of political and economic decision-making and the uneven integration of firms left more and more room for state intervention.

III. RECENTRALIZATION AND THE LABOR MARKET: THE EMERGENCE OF THE SYSTEM OF HIDDEN PLAN TARGETS AND STATE INTERVENTIONS IN THE LABOR MARKET

A. Recentralization and Uncertainty of the Rules of the Game

A marked change toward the recentralization of decision making could be observed in 1972, when some of the largest industrial enterprises were promised special treatment by central economic management to resolve their economic difficulties. Measures were taken to improve their overall as well as their labor market position. For instance, state industry was given a central pay increase, and the industrial activity of agricultural cooperatives was restricted, to reduce the competition for industrial labor.

The recentralization process was speeded up by the country's worsening external economic position and consequent government actions. The government expected the world economic crisis to be short-lived; it therefore considered its main task to be the isolation of the Hungarian economy from negative external effects. As a result, while the world economy stagnated and the Hungarian terms of trade progressively deteriorated, the Hungarian enterprises' propensity for growth did not decrease. Their resource hunger and optimistic expectations gave rise to overinvestment, which resulted in an investment cycle financed at the expense of the foreign trade balance (see Figure 1). As a consequence, Hungary's international indebtedness reached a peak at the end of the 1970s.

Neglecting the fact that enterprises' cost insensitivity and their rush for growth were caused partly by the policy of isolation, most planners and politicians adopted the view that enterprises were unable to use their increasing autonomy properly; they wasted resources, and therefore their freedom of action had to be limited.

The state's direct intervention in enterprise activity manifested itself in ignoring the rules of the game. Faced with the resulting uncertainty, enterprises concentrated their efforts on avoiding the measures unfavorable to their operation either by increasing their staff and productive capacity or by integrating themselves into central economic management. As a result, enterprises were more and more apt to take their decisions in collaboration with central economic management and, by paying increasing attention to its purposes, participated in the centralization of control over enterprise activity.

The rapid increase in direct state intervention reinforced the interdependence between different organs of the state as the operation of one could neutralize the action of another. For this reason, conflicts and negotiations became more frequent between the various parts of the state apparatus, and this could either increase or decrease the enterprises' opportunities for maneuver. To complicate matters, the success or failure of enterprise actions depended on the influence they could bring to bear on the various state agencies, but in practice, the fact that the spheres of authority of these overlapped, facilitated the achievement of the enterprises' purpose. The enterprises tended to push decision making about their problems up to the highest levels possible in the hierarchy of economic management hoping that the more centralized the decision making, the less responsibility the enterprise had to bear.

To the extent that enterprises succeeded in integrating themselves into central economic management, they increased their chances of obtaining resources but at the expense of decreased autonomy. Enterprises that could not be integrated into central economic management had more autonomy but greater uncertainty.

Thus in addition to financial methods of normative central regulation, plan targets were introduced in a disguised form, under the cover of consultation between economic–political bodies and enterprises and by state preferences and subsidies. These latter forms of central regulation brought uncertainty into enterprise behavior.

Central economic management used a third kind of "regulation," the so-called general central expectations, with the intention of reducing uncertainty. Central economic management declared and repeatedly underlined the importance of certain rules of behavior in order to exert influence on the decisions taken at the enterprise level. One example of this kind of regulation was the so-called "responsibility for supply" system, in which government agencies expected enterprises to keep on producing certain goods irrespective of profitability if these goods were judged to be important to the economy as a whole. In return, the enterprises fulfilling these expectations could count on the assistance of the state agencies to meet their pressing needs (for example, the state bank would accept their applications for credit). In order to stimulate the fulfillment of short-term central expectations, state agencies also initiated campaigns as a means of persuasion (Soós, 1984). For example, during campaigns designed to lessen labor market tensions, the government issued, through the official channels of economic management and the mass media, daily declarations about the importance of reducing enterprises' hunger for labor. Various authorities, including party agencies and trade unions, monitored enterprises continuously to see whether they were working in the desired direction, that is, to see if they were genuine in their intention to restrict their hiring of new employees.

These regulations, together with a weak market mechanism and bargaining between central economic management and enterprises over output and subsidies, made the economy work. But this did not mean that the economy could adapt itself to the changing external environment. Thus the economy was operational but by no means efficient.

B. Tensions in the Labor Market, Enterprise Adaptation, and State Intervention

The labor market was characterized by a constant and general overdemand for labor, so that labor reserves were exhausted. As a consequence of the recentralization of economic management, the position of large companies was strengthened and, assisted by state agencies, they could improve their labor market position by merging with smaller enterprises. More and more small- and medium-scale state firms were absorbed into large companies struggling with labor shortages, and this strategy was emulated by the small and medium-scale firms in cooperative industry. These tried to increase their strength by combining in order to resist merger attempts by large state companies. As a consequence, between 1975 and 1978, the number of enterprises dropped by 10.1% in state industry and by 13.6% in cooperative industry, and the size structure of industry changed considerably (Table 2).

Overdemand for labor varied as investment cycles induced periodic fluctuations in the labor market (Fazekas & Köllö, 1985). The tensions caused by the general labor shortage and its periodical intensification induced the authorities to tighten control over the labor market. They tried to allocate labor by intervening directly and from time to time launched campaigns for rational labor management at the enterprise level. In their actions integrating enterprises directly into the economic–political decision-making hierarchy, state agencies showed a preference for large companies over small- or medium-sized ones.

Most actions were initiated by central agencies, but some of them were carried out at the local level, and the most important measures were the following:

1. Attempts were made to reduce the demand for labor by enterprises. The recruitment of workers by enterprises was restricted, and a freeze of administrative and clerical employees was ordered. Wage bill regulation aimed at reducing the number of staff was widely introduced in state indus-

Table 2. Distribution of Enterprises According to the Number of Manual Workers in Both State and Cooperative Industry

	Number of workers employed by the enterprise					Total percentage of enterprises
	−100	101–300	301–1000	1001–5000	5001+	
State industry						
1970	10.7	23.4	30.5	30.1	5.3	100.0
1975	9.1	19.9	34.4	31.5	5.1	100.0
1978	6.7	13.9	34.0	39.4	6.0	100.0
1982	7.4	13.0	37.5	37.8	4.3	100.0
Cooperative industry						
1970	46.5	42.6	10.4	0.5	—	100.0
1975	36.4	50.1	12.9	0.6	—	100.0
1978	13.8	54.9	28.4	2.9	—	100.0
1982	11.0	59.1	27.6	2.3	—	100.0

Source: *Statistical Yearbooks*, Central Statistical Bureau, Budapest.

tries, enabling enterprises to use part of the wage bill freed by staff reduction to raise the wages of the remaining workers. County councils were ordered to determine the permissible number of workers in enterprises operating in their area. Based on their "importance to the national economy" (which again favored large firms), enterprises were classified into three categories—those that were allowed to increase their staff, those that could replace leavers, and those that were ordered to reduce their staff. To achieve planned staffing, county councils tried to make use of the compulsory direction of labor introduced in the mid-1970s.

2. Measures were taken to improve the utilization of the labor force within enterprises: labor discipline was strengthened; action was taken to decrease absenteeism; the practice of giving sick pay was restricted; attempts were made to lessen the loss of working time; and legal provisions setting an upper limit on overtime were relaxed. In the interest of mobilizing internal labor reserves, managers' rights were expanded to allow restructuring of an enterprise's labor force. At the same time, efforts were made to promote in-plant training programs.

3. Some measures were aimed at limiting wage competition. For this purpose, a new wage rate system was introduced that narrowed the wage differentials of workers doing the same kind of job. In addition, measures were taken to reduce the turnover of staff by means of wage sanctions against job leavers and by limiting the free choice of jobs for workers changing their employer more than twice a year.

4. Attempts were also made to influence the allocation of labor among enterprises by administrative means, for example, by "organized redistribution," by the compulsory direction of careers for certain groups of graduates seeking employment and by the introduction of the compulsory direction of labor for certain groups of workers and enterprises.

5. In order to improve the position of large-scale enterprises in the labor market, a campaign was started against the second economy and small-scale enterprises. In many places, local authorities increased the level of taxes imposed on small-scale farming activities, the number of licenses for private industrial activities was restricted, and many official declarations were issued against "unjustified profits" and incomes "disproportionate to work." As a result, the production of small-scale farming and industry decreased (for example, the number of pigs in small-scale farms diminished by 23% in 1975).

These measures were supplemented by various forms of social and political pressures; for example, from time to time enterprises were called upon to reduce their labor demand and to improve their labor management. Managers were also exhorted to extend the piece-rate system and to raise work standards. A press campaign was launched criticizing so-called "job hoppers" and praising those who remained loyally in their jobs. Actions were also initiated at the level of the enterprise. A large-scale state enterprise dismissed a relatively large number of workers, an event unprecedented in the previous 30 years. A number of labor market cartels came into being in the middle of the decade. These were based on interenterprise agreements aimed at reducing labor competition between members. They agreed not to take on each other's job leavers nor to overbid on wages. Such sporadic informal agreements were supported by some regional authorities as well. However, neither the mass dismissals nor the interenterprise cartel agreements gained adherents: they remained isolated occurrences. The attempts at direct state intervention by central and local administrations did not come up to expectations, and they were gradually eliminated toward the end of the 1970s.

The failure of these actions mentioned was due to many factors. Some of them could not really be kept in force because they were neutralized by other elements of state regulation. The obligatory direction of labor could not work because the right to change jobs remained valid, and thus employees could quit their jobs at any time and were not obliged to accept the workplace suggested by labor exchange offices. Other measures, although generally serving the interests of large companies, were actually or potentially detrimental to the operation of many of these large companies, and they put pressure on central economic management either to revoke these measures or to eliminate their negative side effects. Accordingly, large companies applauded the measures taken for restricting the (legal) private sector, but those large enterprises that had cooperative relations with this sector tried to exempt their partners from the restrictions and were generally successful. Large companies also supported the obligatory direction of labor, providing it did not affect their staff, and most of them tried to transgress the rules if they impeded their normal operations.

Attempts at the recentralization of labor management produced only one significant effect: the further consolidation of the enterprises' internal labor market. Enterprises recognized that central and local actions were unable to lessen the overdemand for labor, and mergers had only a temporary effect. Thus the internalization of labor markets increased, and their structuring became more formalized. The most striking sign of this was the rapid increase in the use and reorganization of in-plant training courses (Table 3).

In 1972, the number of people taking part in these courses amounted to 3.1% of all employees and this ratio rose by 6.6% by 1978. The increase was faster among manual workers (136.6%) than among white-collar workers (79.8%), and in-plant training courses for manual workers were radically changed. Training courses for semiskilled jobs decreased, reflecting a decline in demand for such labor, whereas vocational training courses were gradually taken over by the public education system. At the same time, special-purpose further training courses were rapidly gaining ground. The ratio of those attending such courses amounted to 28.6% of all those in training in 1972; by 1978 it had risen to 64.4%. Generally speaking, it was only the enterprise organizing a course that recognized the qualification of the workers successfully completing it and recompensed them, and of the in-plant further training courses 75% to 80% were organized by enterprises for their own workers. In this way, the spread of further training courses diverted the acquisition of firm-specific skills from informal channels to bureaucratic ones and contributed thereby to the stabilization of the labor market internal to the enterprise.

A further important influence on the development of enterprise training was the need to adjust to cyclical variations in economic activity once the external labor reserves had been exhausted in the early 1970s (see Figure 2).

The most important determinant of the cyclical development of the Hungarian economy was the periodical fluctuation of the volume of investment, which affected all sectors of the economy. With the increase in production in the upswing of the investment cycle, the enterprises exploited their existing labor capacity more intensively (by increasing overtime) and rapidly absorbed labor reserves. In the downswing, the intensity of labor utilization was reduced, and the growth of the enterprise slowed or stopped. From 1971–1972 onwards, with the exhaustion of external labor reserves, adjustment to cyclical changes in production came to depend increasingly on the ability of the enterprise to vary the intensity of the use of its own work force. One of the most important means of achieving this was the mobilization of the internal labor slack that existed in the enterprise training courses. It was not by

Table 3. Distribution of Participants (Manual Workers) According to the Type of In-Plant Training Course

Types of in-plant training courses	1972	1978
Training course for semiskilled jobs	49.1	29.1
Vocational training course	24.1	6.5
Further training course	26.8	64.4
	100.0	100.0

Source: *Training courses 1980–1981,* Central Statistical Bureau, Budapest, 1983.

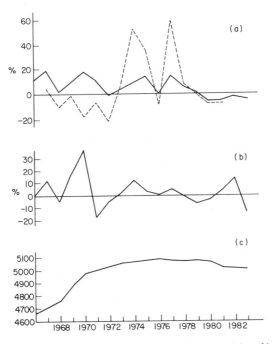

Figure 2. Investment, further training, overtime and employment. (a)—: Yearly growth rate of volume of investment; ---: yearly growth rate of the number of participants in further training courses. (b) Yearly growth rate of overtime hours. (c) Number of employees (thousands). *Sources: Statistical Yearbooks*, Central Statistical Bureau, Budapest.

coincidence that the numbers participating in training courses—especially in further training—increased at an unprecedented rate, and from 1972 through 1978 followed the investment cycle with wide fluctuations.

IV. ECONOMIC STAGNATION AND THE LABOR MARKET, 1979–1983

A. Indebtedness, Restrictions, and Fear of Unemployment

The ailing state of the economy became obvious in the late 1970s and early 1980s. All indicators registered stagnation: Economic growth stopped, the rate of investment fell, living standards stagnated, and external indebtedness increased (see Figure 1 and Table 1). Under these circumstances, state economic policy focused on reducing indebtedness without reducing living standards or increasing unemployment. Central economic management tried to achieve this objective by means that were difficult to reconcile. On the one hand, it continued to recentralize economic control (directives designed to stimulate exports, to restrict imports and enterprises' investment funds, etc.) while, on the other hand, measures were taken to introduce price and currency reforms. A uniform exchange rate of the forint was introduced, and foreign trade prices were adjusted to world market prices. To modify the monopolistic, centralized organizational structure of the economy, some large-scale enterprises were broken up into several small-scale enterprises. Between 1980 and 1983, 25 large-scale enterprises in the state sector were liquidated, and 332 smaller enterprises were founded (Gyurák, 1984).

The economic managers recognized that economic stagnation endangered full employment. To avoid any increase in social tension, the government established a central fund to facilitate retraining. At the same time, recognizing that demand for labor by the state-sector enterprises could diminish, the central economic authority began reinterpreting the concept of full employment. Before the 1980s, full employment meant that every able-bodied person had to be employed in the state sector; now it encompassed all those employed in "socially useful" activities, including activities in the second economy, in households, and so forth (Timár, 1984).

In labor market policy, the avoidance of open unemployment was given priority. For this reason, the compulsory direction of labor ceased, and the agencies for the direction of labor, which formerly had had the function of discipline and "rational labor distribution," were now turned into information centers. Currently, their task is to bring employees and enterprises together and to ensure a satisfactory match between supply and demand.

A normal government reaction to economic stagnation in the socialist countries is the fear of unemployment. However, this fear is not justified by the state of the labor market in Hungary. Despite stagnation, enterprises have no plans to lay off workers; on the contrary, they plan to increase the number of their employees. This paradoxical situation is connected with the continuing excess demand for labor. Under socialism, where the cost of labor does not influence the level of employment, economic stagnation manifests itself in a decline in real wages, as prices rise faster than money wages, rather than in open unemployment. Consequently, economic stagnation is coupled with accelerating inflation generated by the state income policy (see Table 1). State agencies regard an increasing nominal wage level as a condition for successful material incentives. However, this conflicts with the necessary reduction in the purchasing power of the population resulting from the short fall in the supply of consumer goods.

B. The Liberalization of the "Second" Economy

To increase the flexibility of the economy and to offset the effects of diminishing real wages on the standard of living, the central economic authority took various steps to liberalize the second economy.

Several beneficial effects were expected from this policy. The expansion of the secondary sector would, it was assumed, absorb the potential unemployment in the state sector and also make the fall in wages tolerable by widening earning opportunities. Furthermore, the liberalization of the second economy was expected to bring the population's unutilized capital into production and services; to ease the shortage of goods (liable to be exacerbated by import restrictions); and to help establish a flexible small-scale firm sector that would contribute to economic development by supplementing, and cooperating with, the state sector (Laki, 1984).

Although the liberalization process had begun in the second half of the 1970s with the positive encouragement given to small-scale agricultural production, the most rapid progress came in the 1980s. The results were spectacular in terms of the increase in food supplies and exports, and the actions taken served as a model for liberalization in other spheres.

The legal private sector was an important target for liberalization. This sector employs about a quarter of a million people (1978 figures) and consists mainly of small family-run enterprises engaged principally in industrial and service activities where formerly inconsistencies in economic policy led to great uncertainty. Liberalization measures affecting the legal private sector were:

1. The issue of licenses was liberalized. Previously, local councils had been free to decide whether there was any need for tradesmen or retailers in their area; under the new rules they lost this power. They were now obliged to grant a license if the applicant's circumstances satisfied the regulations.
2. It was made easier for tradesmen to buy machinery and equipment, and furthermore—in contrast to previous regulations—they were allowed to deduct investment and modernization costs from their tax bills.
3. Private enterprises were allowed to venture into new fields: first of all, into passenger and goods transport. This was facilitated by a measure allowing private individuals to purchase small vans and permitting them the use of privately owned cars for transport purposes.
4. Licenses were granted to pensioners and to state sector employees.

As a consequence, the number of persons working in the legal private sector increased by about 20% between 1981 and 1983.

The nonstate sector was further expanded by the leasing of state-owned premises to private individuals. Certain state retail and catering trade units could be leased to private individuals for rent against the payment of a security deposit. This system applied mainly to small food retail shops and small restaurants. The lease holders were allowed to employ 6 to 10 employees in addition to their relatives. In June 1983, the number of such units was 8,057, which means that one fifth of all restaurants were leased.

A third area of liberalization was the creation of new forms of small-scale undertaking. While the forms discussed previously predated liberalization, economic units of an entirely new type were now developed. New possibilities of partnership and cooperative management—based on associations of private individuals—were created. These new forms can be grouped into three main types:

1. Partnership leasing: a partnership formed by private individuals to rent a unit from a state enterprise and provide goods and services on contract to state enterprise.

2. Enterprise business work partnerships: These consisted of a state enterprise's employees who concluded a contract with a state enterprise to produce a certain quantity and quality of goods or services after their official working hours using the state enterprise's equipment.
3. Industrial or service partnerships or cooperatives based on their own capital or investments.

Of these forms, the second (VGMK) has become particularly popular. At the end of 1982 the number of participants was 29,331, while 1 year later they numbered 97,200 persons. The peculiarity of this form is that the participants work on contract in partnership with the state enterprise of which they are employees. Hence a worker, who uses the premises and equipment of his state enterprise when producing goods and performing services outside his regular working time, does this as a partner rather than an employee.

This form has brought about significant changes in the labor market. Both the workers and the managers of the enterprise have benefitted from it because their opportunities for open bargaining over wages have been extended. The income paid out for a piece of work done by the partnership does not come from the enterprise wage fund regulated by the state, and so the payment for extra work can be increased without violating state wage regulations. Moreover, the payments for a unit of work done by a partnership member are higher than the earnings of employees doing the same work, even when on overtime. An enterprise employee earning 29 forints per hour might earn 72 forints working on a partnership contract after hours, which is 22% more than for ordinary overtime (Román, 1983). Not surprisingly, within state enterprises, there has been a shift from overtime to business partnership work. This contributed to the slowdown in overtime hours in 1983 (see Figure 2).

The establishment of partnerships has also reinforced the structure in the internal labor markets. It has made it possible for elite workers to get extra income and for enterprise managers to keep their workers (Kövári & Sziráczki, 1985).

The extension of private and semiprivate activities has an important stabilizing role. Although with economic stagnation, the purchasing power of official wages and average living standards declined, opportunities to earn supplementary income exist for the great majority of workers. There is no open unemployment nor a significant shortage of consumer goods. The second economy has made stagnation in the state sector more bearable. But other changes expected from the liberalization of the second economy have not materialized. No significant amount of capital has flowed to the second economy with its improved legal status, and the number of participants having their main jobs in the second economy has not greatly increased. In other words, the second economy has not become entrepreneurial in nature, and its participants have not moved to it from their main jobs in the first or state economy. It has retained its former character, functioning mainly as a source of supplementary income for workers in the state sector.

It is, of course, not by chance that this form has become dominant. The structural position of the second economy is such that in spite of liberalization and legalization it cannot be transformed into a flexible small private enterprise sector based on individual capital investment, for a number of reasons.

In the first place, the state regards the second economy as auxiliary and complementary. Although the output of this sphere is desirable, the fact that levels of income in the second economy are higher than those in the state sector is not. Therefore, when liberalizing the second economy, the state intended that small-scale enterprises based on individual or family effort should be encouraged rather than enterprises using paid workers and high capital investment. This attitude on the part of the state was revealed when during the period of encouragement it maintained the capital "split," a policy that limited the flow of capital between the first and the second economy and prevented the units of the second economy from acquiring the means of production. Similarly, the output of the second economy is important for the state sector in that it is produced by small-scale enterprises that do paid work for state enterprises and are dependent on them for the means of production, the supply of materials, and orders. As a consequence, the legal part of the second economy could not become a sphere of "socialist small private enterprise"; it has become a sector based on small legal capital investment providing workers in the socialist sector with supplementary income.

As for the flexibility of enterprises in the state sector, no improvement can be observed either in their functioning or in their aptitude for rapid adaptation to the market. The measures adopted have not established a rational, working, flexible microstructure to the state sector. Moreover, economic policy has not increased the autonomy of enterprises: They remain heavily dependent on the state, and this impedes their effective management. In Hungary, the state appropriates most of the profit of enterprises with a high profit level and redistributes it among enterprises with a low level of profit (Kornai & Matits, 1983). Thus, the rewards for operating a profitable enterprise are the same as those for an unprofitable one. Loss-making enterprises therefore get nearly the same amount of resources as profitable firms. For this reason, the motivation of enterprise managements to improve performance is rather poor, and without profit-motivated, autonomous enterprises, no flexibility can be injected into the state sector.

V. CONCLUDING REMARKS

The history of Hungarian economic policy and of the labor market in the last 16 years can be described as a partially successful attempt to improve the material incentive system and to make labor allocation more efficient. The "reform" and the other endeavours to revitalize the market have been directed toward creating a flexible, efficient economy in which resources are effectively utilized. Undoubtedly, the flexibility and adaptability of enterprises have improved. Some new structures have also emerged, including the internal labor markets that allow for the retention of the labor force and its mobilization for reallocation within the enterprises. However, profitability and related efficiency have not substantially improved. Cost consciousness among enterprises has not improved, and their resource hunger (including the demand for labor) has remained unchanged. Economic policy relating to the second economy has reduced rather than increased the possibility of material incentives in the state sector by transferring some "profitable" activity from the first to the second economy. Incompatibilities between the two sectors have become more apparent. It is questionable whether efficient, flexible, and adaptive industry can be created without radical changes in the economic system as a whole.

VI. REFERENCES

Böröczfyné, S. K. (1976). *Bérpreferencia rendszer vizsgálata* [Research on the system of wage subsidies]. Budapest: Pénzügykutatási Intézet.
Csanádi, M. (1984). *A gazdaságirányítás és a szelekció néhány sajátossága* [Some characteristics of the economic management and the selection]. Budapest: Pénzügykutatási Intézet.
Doeringer, P., & Piore, M. (1971). *Internal labour markets and manpower analysis*. Lexington, MA: D. C. Health.
Fazekas, K., & Köllö, J. (1985). Fluctuation of labour shortage and state interventions after 1968. In P. Galasi & Gy. Sziráczki (Eds.) *Labour market and second economy in Hungary* (pp. 42–69). Frankfurt: Campus.
Galasi, P. (1983). L'economia sommersa e l'utilizzazione del forza lavoro in Ungheria, *Inchiesta, 13*, 72–84.
Gábor, R. I. (1989). The second economy in socialism: General lessons of the Hungarian experience. In L. Feige (Ed.), *The unobserved economy*. Oxford: OUP.
Gyurák, K. (1984). Az átszervezettek gazdálkodása [The economic activity of the reorganized firms]. *Figyelö, 27*, 4.
Kertesi, G., & Sziráczki, Gy. (1987). The institutional system, labour market and segmentation in Hungary. In R. Taling (Ed.), *Flexibility in labour markets*. (pp. 177–196). London: Academic Press.
Kornai, J. (1980a). The dilemma of a socialist economy: The Hungarian experience. *Cambridge Journal of Economics, 3*, 175–190.
Kornai, J. (1980b). *The economics of shortage*. Amsterdam: North-Holland.
Kornai, J., & Matits, A. (1983). A költségvetési korlát puhaságáról [On the soft budget constraint]. *Gazdaság, 24*, 322–344.
Kövári, Gy., & Sziráczki, Gy. (1985). The old and new forms of shop floor bargaining. In P. Galasi & Gy. Sziráczki (Eds.), *Labour market and second economy in Hungary* (pp. 264–292). Frankfurt: Campus.
Laki, T. (1984). Mítoszok és valóság [Mythos and reality]. *Valóság, 27*, 25–41.
Osterman, P. (Ed.). (1984). *Internal labour markets*. Cambridge, MA: The MIT Press.
Révész, G. (1978). Regulation of earnings in Hungary, *Acta Oeconomica, 21*, 85–97.
Román, Z. (1983). A nagyvállalatok és a VGMK [Large enterprises and the VGMK]. *Társadalmi Szemle, 35*, 65–73.
Soós, K. A. (1984). Tervutasítások, pénzügyi szabályozás, általános elvárások, kampány [Plan directives, financial regulation, general expectations, campaign]. *Gazdaság, 25*, 225–244.
Timár, J. (1984). Problems of full employment. *Acta Oeconomica, 34*, 312–330.
Wilkinson, F. (Ed.). (1981). *The dynamics of labour market segmentation*. London: Academic Press.

III

Youth, Antidiscrimination, and Working-Time Policies

A more detailed look at specific initiatives serves to complement the broad overviews of state policy. The studies by Paul Ryan of youth training in the United Kingdom and by Marilyn Power of affirmative action in the United States demonstrate the limitations of a deregulatory politics. The work of Annie Gauvin and François Michon on working-time policy in France describe an approach to lowering unemployment that did not have as its central component the deregulation of the labor market. Anne Marie Berg, using Norway as her example, analyzes the problems created for women by an employment policy emphasizing part-time work.

Ryan shows that the government's emphasis on youth training reflects a countercurrent to the tide of promarket deregulatory sentiment in the United Kingdom. The need for such a program demonstrates the failure of the unregulated market to provide an adequate supply of skills. Yet, although reflecting a countercurrent to deregulation, the training program has the potential to undermine unions, thus fostering the goal of deregulation.

Ryan analyzes and evaluates union responses to the youth training policies. The trade union movement has been split on this issue with those attacking the government's program fearing the substitution of low-paid youth trainees for regular employees, whereas those supporting it are doing so subject to the regulation of the trainees' roles at the workplace.

The labor movement has been relatively unsuccessful in controlling the youth training policy. There has been a substitution of trainees for other workers. But the negative impact this has had on British trade unions is likely limited. Large unionized employers have not participated to any major degree in the program. The government's youth intervention has proven most popular with the smaller firms and service sector employers who were already relatively unaffected by trade unionism.

Power argues that, as part of its strategy for deregulating the labor market, the Reagan administration has attempted to weaken the federal government's affirmative action policy against racial and sexual discrimination. It called for the formal elimination of goals and timetables that companies must follow to show compliance with the affirmative action order. Yet, somewhat surprisingly, the administration's attempted gutting of affirmative action met with considerable resistance from medium and large corporations. Given this response, the government has not implemented these changes.

Small firms supported the Reagan proposals. Although many large corporations had resisted the civil rights reforms when they were first created in the 1960s, they had successfully adapted to the new regulatory framework. Large firms feared that the alternatives to the federal affirmative action order might be worse for their interests. In addition, they have found that affirmative action increased their relative bargaining power with their white male skilled workers. However, Power concludes that whatever advantages employers may have culled from affirmative action, it is still in the interests of labor to support affirmative action as one step on the path to eliminating racial and sexual inequalities.

Unlike many other European governments, the socialist governments in France in the 1980s have not made the increased use of temporary workers on fixed-term contracts a central aspect of their employment policy. Rather, as Gauvin and Michon show, the reduction and reorganization of working time was crucial in the French approach to lowering unemployment.

In 1982, a law was passed reducing the legal workweek from 40 to 39 hours, lessening the possibility of overtime, lengthening annual paid vacations from 4 to 5 weeks, and lowering the normal retirement age from 65 to 60. In addition, a variety of solidarity contracts were signed between a firm and the government or local authorities, with the approval of the unions representing a firm's workers, providing incentives for shortening the working week, early retirement, partial early retirement, and the hiring of younger workers.

The policy of workweek reduction was a failure. Relatively few jobs were created or existing jobs protected. The program fostering early retirement and forming a younger work force was successful. Many retired early, and most of the retirees were replaced by newly hired workers.

After 1985, the policy focus emphasized partial early retirement and encouraged plant-level agreements concerning the reorganization of working time and modernization. Those who are partially retired are working part-time rather than full-time. These measures are designed to lengthen the operating time of machinery and improve the ability of employers to vary their usage of labor in accordance with variations in product demand and changing conditions of production.

Gauvin and Michon speculate that French employment policy may come to emphasize more the expansion of temporary and part-time jobs rather than the reduction and reorganization of working time for full-time employees. Basing her analysis on the Norwegian situation, Berg analyzes the sociological effect of an employment program centered on increasing the opportunities for part-time work rather than shortening the workweek for full-time workers.

Norwegian men and women disagree over the means for combatting unemployment. Unlike trade unions in other European countries, the Norwegian Federation of Trade Unions has not called for a general shortening of the full-time workday. Rather, it has pushed for a fifth week of vacation and a reduction of the retirement age. However, those unions with a mostly female membership have argued for a 6-hour workday. The women's movement has done the same.

Women are more likely to be part-time workers than are men. The 6-hour workday would place more employees, particularly women, on standard work contracts and thus provide them with higher wages. In addition, a shorter full-time workday would provide more time for men to help with child care and housework.

Yet according to Berg, although men want more leisure time, they do not want it in a way that may lead to additional time spent on household chores. The Norwegian government has pushed part-time work as a means for increasing labor market flexibility. In addition, employers favor part-time work. Encouraging part-time work allows men to keep their privileges in the labor market and in the home, because women are more likely to be part-time workers. Thus Berg fears an unholy alliance forming between the male-dominated labor movement, employers, and the state over the question of working time reforms.

These four chapters further develop the analysis of governmental attempts to "free-up" the labor market presented in the country studies. They focus on matters not handled by those studies. By treating male–female conflicts over working-time reforms encouraging part-time labor, the unwillingness of employers to totally discard affirmative action programs, and the inability of an unregulated labor market to provide an adequate supply of skilled labor, they point out the limitations of a deregulatory approach to the labor market.

9

Youth Interventions, Job Substitution, and Trade Union Policy in Great Britain, 1976–1986

Paul Ryan

> *We do not want to be distracted from creating jobs for young people by simply redistributing the jobs that are there and taking jobs from adults to give to youngsters.*
> —C. H. Urwin, *Trades Union Congress General Council* (TUC, 1978, p. 476)

Prompted by high levels of youth unemployment, British governments have adopted a succession of interventions aimed at the youth labor market. The principal ingredient has been work experience for early (16- and 17-year-old) school leavers. The main line of evolution is unbroken, involving the experimental Work Experience Programme (WEP) of 1976–1978, its replacement, the Youth Opportunities Programme (YOP) of 1978–1983, and YOP's own successor, the Youth Training Scheme (YTS), 1983–present.

Since 1980, a place on YOP/YTS has been guaranteed to all unemployed 16-year-old school leavers. Given the sheer scale of youth joblessness, large numbers of teenagers have consequently been active under YOP/YTS. Since 1981 the annual intake into YOP/YTS has been almost as large as the 16-year-old labor force.[1] By 1985 more than one in every two 16-year-old workers was

---

[1]In 1980/1981 the 360,000 entrants to YOP represented 39% of the 16-year-old population and 98% of the 16-year-old labor force; the analogous figures for the 404,000 YTS entrants in 1985/1986 were 47% and 86% (MSC, 1982b, Table 5; Wells, 1983, Tables D18–D21; Gray & King, 1986, Table 1; *LMQR*, June 1986, Table A). YOP activity among 16-year-old workers in January 1981 could have been as low as 19% (Table 1) despite inflows of this magnitude. Durations of stay on YOP were short (6 months maximum), whereas a significant minority of entrants were 17- and 18-year-olds.

Paul Ryan • King's College, University of Cambridge, Cambridge CB2 1ST, Great Britain.

Table 1. Activities of Young Workers, Great Britain 1980–1985

	16-year-olds			17-year-olds		
Year[a]	YOP/YTS trainee	Unemployment	Employment	YOP/YTS trainee	Unemployment	Employment
1980	10%	10%	80%	3%	12%	85%
1981	19	21	60	6	18	76
1982	26	22	52	7	24	69
1983	36	27	37	11	25	64
1984	44	22	33	7	26	67
1985	52	24	24	5	25	70

[a]Data refer to January.
Source: R. Layard (1986), Table 14.

active on YTS (Table 1). This army of young people has spent most of its time engaged in work experience at a wide variety of workplaces.

The response of trade unions to youth interventions has been ambivalent. Most unions have officially supported, and even promoted, policies targeted at youth unemployment and training. The leadership of the Trades Union Congress (TUC), the federal body to which all major unions are affiliated, has backed YOP/YTS on condition that employers' usage of YOP/YTS trainees be regulated according to union interests. At the same time, many unions have criticized YOP/YTS in general as a second-best response to employment and training problems; and in particular, for allowing the substitution of the "cheap labor" of YOP/YTS trainees for that of regular employees. Some unions have opposed TUC policy and called for the rejection of YOP/YTS, implying the exclusion of work experience schemes from unionized workplaces. This particular manifestation of the broader conflict between strategies of "regulated inclusion" and "exclusion" (Garonna & Ryan, 1986) has involved divisions both within and between trade unions. Abrupt changes of official policy toward youth interventions have occurred in several unions.

The TUC's policy of accepting youth policies as long as their utilization can be suitably regulated finds a historical parallel in the policy of craft unions toward apprentices, particularly in the interwar years. In that earlier period of mass unemployment, unions whose interests were threatened by cheap apprentice labor sought relief in restrictions on the numbers and activities of apprentices, increases in apprentice pay, and recognition of union representation of apprentices. Contemporary equivalents of all three responses can be seen in union reactions to YOP and YTS. In this sense, youth policy in the 1980s revives an issue of importance in an earlier era in the British labor market (Ryan, 1986, 1987).

This chapter analyses and evaluates union responses to contemporary youth policy. Section 1 provides an outline of contemporary youth interventions, followed in Section 2 by an examination of the interaction between trade unionism and youth interventions. Section 3 discusses the YOP/YTS outcomes of relevance to the union regulatory effort, concluding in Section 4 with an assessment of union policy.

I. WORK EXPERIENCE AND YOUTH INTERVENTIONS

The objectives of the WEP/YOP/YTS sequence of youth interventions have been multidimensional. The primary goal throughout has been to reduce youth unemployment. A second objective has been to improve the vocational preparation of young people, through increased training both on and off the job. A third has been to reduce the earnings of young workers, largely as a means to improved performance on the first two objectives. Although the latter two objectives have become increasingly important during the 1980s, the enduring importance of the unemployment goal is indicated by the continued guarantee of a place to all unemployed 16-year-old school leavers.

The principal ingredient in all three schemes has been the provision to 16- and 17-year-olds of work experience at mainstream workplaces. The central position of work experience reflects apprehension lest youth unemployment leads to defective learning of the technical skills and attitudes required for work, as well as to the frustration and anger seen in the urban rioting of 1981. Employer complaints about the attainments and attitudes of young people have also played a part, particularly in the priority given to work experience in the private sector over job creation in the public sector (Department of Employment, 1977; Manpower Services Commission (MSC), 1977, 1982a; Raffe, 1984). A further factor has been the lower fiscal cost of work experience than of vocational education or direct job creation.

Young people have functioned on YOP/YTS under contracts of limited duration. The length of the traineeship increased in 1982/1983 from 6 months to 1 year with the replacement of YOP by YTS; and in 1986 from 1 to 2 years within YTS.

Not all young people active on YOP and YTS have actually undertaken work experience. Both schemes have involved multiple categories of provision, with a minority of young people (particularly those unable to find places on employers' schemes) involved in projects, training workshops, and the like, which offer no contact with workplaces. Nevertheless, the great majority of entrants to YOP and YTS have spent most or all of their time in work experience.[2]

Detailed arrangements have differed from scheme to scheme, reflecting changes in policy priorities. Until 1983, led by the Work Experience on Em-

---

[2]In 1980–1982, 84% of entrants to YOP undertook work experience schemes (MSC, 1982b, Table 5); under YTS, all entrants are required to undergo work experience, but the proportion active under the delivery modes with most orientation to work experience in mainstream workplaces (Modes A and B2) amounted to 79% in 1983/1984 (Gray & King, 1986, Table 1).

ployers' Premises (WEEP) element in YOP, the principal component was simple work experience, with vocational training as a suggested but not required supplement. Under YTS, although the main constituent was stated to be vocational training, work experience was to remain the principal delivery vehicle. Only one quarter of the duration of the YTS contract (13 out of 48 weeks) had to be spent in off-the-job training; the remainder was allocated to work experience. In practice, few YTS trainees have received more than the statutory minimum: the average duration of off-the-job training in 1983/1984 amounted to 14.2 weeks (Department of Employment, 1985). The continuity between YOP and YTS as vehicles for the provision of work experience to school leavers is thus clear.[3]

Schemes built around work experience have not constituted the only medium of intervention in the youth labor market. Direct job creation and recruitment subsidies were more important until 1978.[4] Job creation for young people has, however, remained small scale, whereas recruitment subsidies have been supplanted by employment subsidies linked to low relative pay for young workers (Young Workers Scheme, 1982–). Cuts in youth relative pay have also been encouraged by the removal in 1986 of young workers from coverage by statutory minimum wages and by the progressive curtailment of the access of 16- and 17-year-olds to social security (Bradshaw, Lawton, & Cooke, 1987; Cusack & Roll, 1985). YOP/YTS has dovetailed into these efforts to reduce youth pay. The status of young people active in YOP/YTS is, in the first instance at least, that of trainee rather than employee. The trainee receives from public funds a weekly allowance that has amounted to less than one half the average earnings of 16-year-old employees and that has been promoted as a suitable aspiration for young people.

II. THE CONTENT OF TRADE UNION RESPONSE

Trade union leaders have for the most part supported schemes of work experience and training for unemployed school leavers. The Trades Union Congress was one of the early supporters of work experience, claiming authorship of the original WEP scheme (TUC, 1976). TUC support for WEP and YOP reflected the need to respond to the rapid rise in youth unemployment, as well as to encourage young people to take courses of education and training (TUC, 1976). YOP was seen as a temporary measure, required until macroeconomic reflation had cut unemployment and supported in the belief that it would involve both mandatory education or training and personal counsel-

---

[3]The priority given to work experience contracts for unemployed youths under WEP/YOP/YTS is mirrored in the *contrats d'emploi-formation* and the *contratti di formazione-lavoro* instituted in France and Italy during the last decade (Garonna, 1986; Germe, 1986).

[4]The relevant measures were Community Industry and the Job Creation Programmes (1975–1978), as well as the Recruitment Subsidy for School Leavers (1975–1976) and the Youth Employment Subsidy (1976–1978).

ing (TUC, 1977). Particular importance was attached to the scheme's potential for helping disadvantaged school leavers to acquire employment (TUC, 1979, p. 169).

The advent in 1979 of both a Conservative government and a further severe downturn in the economy altered the basis of support for youth interventions. Youth unemployment was clearly set to become both more severe and more durable than had been anticipated. TUC support for YOP intensified in the face of escalating youth unemployment. At the 1980 annual TUC conference, the TUC's General Council called for the rapid expansion of YOP to deal with mounting youth unemployment and attacked the budgetary cuts imposed by the incoming government upon the Manpower Services Commission (MSC), the public agency charged with administering special employment measures (TUC, 1980, pp. 46, 48). Speeches on behalf of the TUC's Employment Policy and Organization Committee have backed YOP and YTS at almost every annual TUC conference since then. The leaderships of most unions have in turn broadly supported the General Council's policy.

A. The Opposition

The TUC's support for YOP and YTS has not however gone without challenge. Opposition has concentrated upon the work experience component of the schemes. It was initiated at the 1978 TUC conference, shortly after the launching of YOP, by the Civil and Public Services Association (CPSA), representing clerical-grade public employees. The principal reason involved the threatened substitution of YOP trainees for regular employees:

> We have serious reservations about this composite motion, which welcomes the Youth Opportunities Programme . . . the ingredient that is worrying us is work experience. We feel that there is something of a conflict between work experience and, on the other hand, the staffing ceilings and public expenditure cuts that we have experienced . . . the use of young people through work experience would mean—and this is quite blunt—that they would be doing work mainly associated with the clerical area covered by CPSA. This work, we believe, should be done by full time staff who are paid the proper rate of pay and who are members of our association. (TUC, 1978, p. 621)

This critique apart, opposition to youth interventions remained subdued during the first 3 years of YOP. At both the 1979 and 1980 annual TUC conferences, the farmworkers' union (NUAAW) criticized the use of YOP trainees as cheap labor in agriculture. However, the NUAAW's conclusion was not that YOP should be rejected but rather that controls should be imposed upon its usage in agriculture (TUC, 1978, p. 434; 1979, p. 527). By 1981, the mood had changed. A motion put to the 1981 TUC conference by the Society of Civil and Public Servants (SCPS) urged the General Council "to oppose the WEEP scheme and to withdraw trade union cooperation" unless substitution were eliminated, MSC monitoring improved, and union control increased. The motion was carried without formal opposition from the platform (TUC, 1981, pp. 428, 439–42).

The upsurge of opposition to YOP in 1981 was less significant than is suggested by the TUC conference record. Even if the conditions imposed for continued support for YOP-WEEP were demanding, the 1981 conference motion gave ample scope for delays. Moreover, delegates were already aware of the government's proposals to convert YOP into a training scheme (Department of Employment, 1981a). The inception of YTS in 1982/1983, with its emphasis upon training and its enhanced role for union regulation, allayed many of the fears expressed at the 1981 conference. At the 1982 conference, as many as 12 unions spoke in favor of a motion that "welcomes the MSC's Youth Training Scheme," subject to a variety of safeguards, as laying "the foundation for the establishment of proper schemes of further education, training *and work experience* which are needed for all young people in the transition from school to work." (TUC, 1982a, p. 477; emphasis added)

The extensive lineup of support in 1982, far from indicating the absence of opposition, may have been encouraged by TUC leaders to deflect widespread criticism of YTS. At the time only the Furniture, Timber and Allied Trades Union (FTATU) spoke out against YTS, depicting it as the exploitation of youth labor by a government that had deliberately caused youth unemployment (TUC, 1982a, p. 487). However in 1983, when YTS was just getting under way, the TUC conference saw a serious clash between a motion, sponsored by the union of technical college lecturers (NATFHE), which offered YTS a qualified welcome, and a rival motion, sponsored by the craft printers' union (NGA), which condemned YTS as "totally inadequate in quality" and called on the General Council to reconsider its support. The NGA speaker called YTS "nothing more than a sophisticated and cynical rerun of YOP," arguing that union support for it would discredit unions in the eyes of young people (TUC, 1983a, p. 429). This quasi-rejectionist position was supported by two other unions, those of nonmanual workers in engineering (metal products) and journalists (TASS and NUJ, respectively), but it failed in the face of speeches from six other unions and the platform in support of the NATFHE motion.

Minority opposition continued at the 1984–1986 conferences. In 1984, after NATFHE had again moved critical support for YTS, the local government officials' union (NALGO), with the support of the CPSA and the NGA, submitted an amendment calling on the TUC to withdraw support from YTS within 6 months. The principal item of criticism was the government's refusal to increase the trainee allowance. Although the rejectionists' move was beaten back by the General Council, precious little enthusiasm for YTS was expressed even by supporters of the official platform (TUC, 1984). Opposition was muted in 1985, reflecting both the continued efforts of the General Council and the government's recent decision to extend the basic YTS contract from 1 to 2 years, a move consistent with long-standing TUC policy. Even then, the schoolteachers' union, NAS-UWT, had to be persuaded to remit a motion attacking training policy, whereas COHSE, the health workers' union, called for the rejection of YTS as having "miserably failed the young people of this country" and having depressed wages (*Financial Times*, 5 September 1985; TUC 1985).

At the 1986 conference, even NATFHE, the stalwart of earlier defenses of YTS, wavered, sponsoring a motion highly critical of the "serious shortcomings of the two year YTS" and describing the content of YTS as "irreconcileable with the stated objectives of the scheme" (TUC 1986a, p. 38). The NATFHE motion did not, however, call for withdrawal from YTS. It was left to NALGO to maintain the rejectionist tradition by opposing the resolution on youth training (TUC 1986a; *FT*, 4 September 1986).

The TUC conference record is thus marked by fairly continuous opposition to General Council policy. The principal item of criticism has remained the cheap labor/substitution set of issues raised by CPSA in 1978, backed up by concerns over the trainee allowance and health and safety.

Fluctuation in the identity of the opponents of TUC policy reflects conflict within particular unions, frequently between a leadership seeking to follow the TUC line and groups within the membership seeking to overthrow it. The conferences of many unions have seen defeats for the official line in favor of policies of either rejecting YOP/YTS outright or imposing such conditions as to make youth schemes unlikely to get off the ground.

Conference defeats for leadership policy of support for YOP/YTS have been commonplace in unions that organize public sector employees. Examples include the CPSA in 1978, 1982, 1983, and 1984; NALGO in 1983; the Post Office Engineering Union (POEU) in 1983; the Union of Communications Workers (UCW) in 1984; the National Union of Public Employees (NUPE) in 1983; the Inland Revenue Staff Federation (IRSF) in 1985; the Confederation of Health Service Employees (COHSE) in 1985 and 1986; and NATFHE in 1985. In other years and in other unions, rejectionist motions have attracted substantial minority support, notably at all of the 1982–1986 annual conferences of the retail workers' union, USDAW, as well as those of NATFHE in 1983, IRSF in 1984, and NUPE in 1986.[5]

Opposition at the local and workplace level is less readily assessed. Surveys of the attitudes of workplace representatives (shop stewards) toward YOP found less knowledge of it and more suspicion toward it than among senior officials (Eversley, 1986, pp. 215–216; Trade Union Research Unit [TURU], 1980). At the same time, a survey of the difficulties that YTS sponsors had encountered found only a trivial role for "trade union unrest"; whereas only 6% of nonsponsors indicated that trade union or employee opposition had been a reason for their abstention (Sako & Dore, 1986).

A continuing role for local opposition to YTS is, however, apparent in part of the public sector. Although national agreement to set up 4,000 YTS places in central government was reached in 1983, by late 1985 only 1,046

[5]*CSAR* (1978, 1982, 1984); *Health Services*, July 1985, July 1986; *Dawn*, May issues, 1982–1986; *FT*, 16 August, 6 October, 11 November 1983, 15, 17 May 1984, 18 May 1985; *TES*, 20 May 1983; *THES*, 3 June 1983, 31 May 1985.

trainees were in place; the shortfall was blamed by the government on "the opposition of some civil service trade unions, mainly at local and departmental levels" (*Times*, 30 April 1986).

B. TUC Strategy: Regulated Inclusion

The TUC has promoted acceptance of YOP and YTS, subject to regulation of the terms on which trainees function at the workplace. The strategy became fully developed as part of the move from YOP to YTS and was promoted within the union movement by publications and regional conferences to educate union representatives (TUC 1982b, 1983b).

The means of regulation envisaged have been both direct and indirect, national and local. Indirect regulation, the principal method, is pursued through union representation on the Manpower Services Commission, the tripartite public body responsible for the design and administration of youth interventions. At the national level, the TUC nominates one third of the members of both the MSC's governing board and the Youth Training Group (which oversees YTS); trade unionists are similarly represented on both the Area Manpower Boards through which particular YOP/YTS schemes are approved and the Programme Review Teams through which they are monitored.

The content of union regulation was developed in response to criticisms of YOP. The central principle has been that youth schemes be accepted only on condition that employers' use of trainees engaged in work experience be controlled so as to prevent substitution. Under YOP, the original design of its work experience component (WEEP) called upon employers to provide some off-the-job training and at least four types of job tasks during the 6 months that YOP trainees spent with them. Had these requirements been widely implemented, they would have severely constrained substitution, as trainees could have proven productive only in the most rapidly learned (i.e., least skilled) job tasks.

The aspirations for YOP achieved only limited success. In 1980 only 34% of WEEP entrants received off-the-job training, typically for less than a day a week (Department of Employment, 1981b). Only one in three trainees received at least the recommended menu of four tasks (Bedeman & Harvey, 1981, Table 8). The MSC's own surveys of sponsors suggested that 30% of WEEP places involved substitution for regular employment (Comptroller and Auditor General, 1983, p. 25).

The TUC's initial response to mounting union dissatisfaction with YOP during 1980–1981 was to encourage MSC to bolster quality control in both the approval and the monitoring of particular schemes. In terms of approval, although trade unionists were formally involved through MSC Area Boards, only projects that involved at least 20 WEEP places were actually considered in practice (TURU, 1980). As few WEEP trainees participated in projects that large (11% in one sample; Jackson and Hanby, 1982), small firms interested in substitution faced little difficulty in obtaining approval. A small change was, however, introduced in 1980. The NUAAW's complaints about substitution in agriculture led to a temporary trial procedure in the East Midlands, in which *all* WEEP applications from farmers were to be considered by an Area Board subcommittee on which the NUAAW was represented (TUC, 1980, p. 49).

In terms of monitoring, MSC activity had, by 1981, fallen heavily into arrears, reflecting budget reductions at a time of rapid YOP expansion. Even though 40,000 site visits were abandoned and the criteria for inspection relaxed, a backlog of 30,000 projects remained to be inspected in 1982 (CAG, 1983, p. 26). Partly as a result, the General Council joined the calls from the floor at the 1981 TUC conference for improvement in monitoring in YOP.

The second component of indirect regulation was TUC support for the replacement of YOP by a higher quality scheme, with training aspirations converted into training requirements. The first changes came in 1981, with the MSC's tightening up of YOP-WEEP eligibility rules; the adoption of a quality improvement plan that produced 100,000 year-long "high-quality training places" during 1982/1983; and the announcement of a New Training Initiative, with the conversion of YOP into a scheme of universal youth training as the leading proposal (Department of Employment, 1981a).

As the New Training Initiative emanated not from the MSC but from a government that was actively hostile to trade unionism, the union role in its formulation can have amounted to little more than the voicing of dissatisfaction with YOP. The TUC was however actively involved, through the MSC, in giving detailed shape to the ensuing Youth Training Scheme (MSC, 1982a). The outcome was a set of differences between the designs of YTS and YOP that reflect to a considerable extent the TUC's regulatory strategy.

YTS was intended to involve a shift in the content of youth activity from simple work experience with the hope of training to training based principally upon work experience. Under YOP, employers had been offered the services of young people at zero price and subject to little control. Under YTS, sponsors were required to provide training. YTS projects were to be accepted only if they conformed to eight training-related criteria, including at least 3 months spent off the job. Training was to extend beyond the needs of particular jobs and involve "core skills" transferable within a family of related occupations. Sponsors were to be accepted only if they possessed a "proven record" in training. The quality of training was to be ensured by embodying training plans in legally enforceable contracts with the MSC. Finally, sponsors were provided from public funds with up to £650 per trainee year (in addition to the trainee allowance) to pay for training (MSC, 1982a). To the extent that these requirements were enforced and YTS entrants spent their time in training, their value in production and the threat of substitution would be correspondingly reduced.

The threat of substitution was to be attenuated further by the "additionality" rule, under which sponsors were to be allowed to claim an additional £3700 on behalf of two of their normal intake of school leavers for every three YTS trainees sponsored. This substantial bonus was linked to increases in youth intakes in order to make YTS a supplement to normal recruitment rather than a substitute, as well as to encourage higher levels of training within regular youth employment. No such incentive had been offered under YOP.

In addition to these changes in the design of the scheme, union interests were to be protected by tightening up procedures for the approval and monitoring of projects. Consideration was given initially to making union approval of particular projects a legal requirement. However, as the Employment Act of 1982 banned any clause requiring union approval for a labor market contract, what emerged instead was an informal expectation that Area Manpower Boards would not approve schemes that lacked union support. In unionized workplaces, a signature from a local union official became an informal requirement. On the monitoring side, trade union representatives were to be involved in program review teams for YTS projects (*IRRR* Special Issue, 1983).

The TUC also pursued more direct forms of regulation by building into the design of YTS a role for decentralized bargaining. YOP had made no provision for union involvement at workplace or corporate level. Under YTS, the relevant unions were empowered to bargain over both the trainee allowance ("topping up") and employee status for trainees (TUC, 1982b, 1983b). Success in this area would both increase the incomes of trainees and, by narrowing the differential in labor cost between YTS trainees and regular employees, reduce the incentive to substitution.

Several unions have taken the cue and pursued direct regulation of YOP/YTS content. The General and Municipal Workers' Union actually anticipated TUC policy on YTS in a YOP guide, prepared for local representatives, which included a model agreement explicitly intended to prevent substitution by regulating trainee activities (GMWU, 1982). NALGO adopted, in 1983, a policy of making support for YTS projects conditional upon full topping up of the trainee allowance to normal youth pay levels, retreating a year later to a recommendation to seek partial topping up. The retail workers' union (USDAW) seeks to limit YTS trainees to less than 5% of permanent employment, to veto schemes where employment or hours are being reduced, and to seek topping up and employee status for the trainees themselves (*Dawn*, May 1984). Such regulatory endeavors are clearly intended to curb substitution.

The regulatory issues are different for craft unions. Given the costs of training for the occupations that they represent, they have less to fear from cheap trainee labor. The key issue for them has been the link, if any, to be forged between YTS and the existing rules governing apprenticeship. Some craft unions have sought to use the public subsidy inherent in YTS to offset the decline in apprentice training in the 1980s; others have been more concerned to resist its implications for the incomes of apprentices.

The electricians' (EETPU) and builders' (UCATT) unions have led in adapting the existing regulatory structure to YTS. Even before the inception of YTS, the EETPU had concluded a training agreement for the electrical contracting industry in which YTS was to form the basis of the first year of apprenticeship. The trainee allowance was effectively accepted as it stood in return for an increase in training volume. The existing first year weekly wage of £42 was reduced to £28, £25 of which represented the YTS allowance. In return for lower labor costs, employers agreed to increase their apprentice intakes. Similarly, UCATT agreed in 1983 to the replacement of the first year of apprenticeship by YTS as part of the provision of 20,000 YTS places (*IRRR*, 8 Feb. 1983, 22 Oct. 1985).

The craft unions showing least willingness to incorporate YTS into a revised system of training have been those in printing and engineering. The radical revision of craft training in the printing industry in 1983 gave no role to YTS (British Printing Industries Federation/National Graphical Association, 1983). The principal engineering union (AUEW) accepts YTS only where trainees receive regular junior workers' pay and do not replace redundant workers (*IDS* 412, November 1983; *FT*, 15 May 1984). The union has privately instructed its local convenors of shop stewards to insist on the withdrawal of YTS where a plant is on short-time working. Fear of substitution therefore affects craft unions as well.

These avenues for the direct regulation of YTS are irrelevant to the non-union sector. There union interests can be protected only by the quality control activity of the MSC, which might prove no more reliable under YTS than it had under YOP. The TUC therefore sought high levels of takeup of YTS by unionized employers. Trade unionists were encouraged to press their employers to set up YTS projects (TUC, 1983b). A special unit was set up within MSC to encourage YTS schemes in large companies, where union recognition is most common.

Other successes were registered for union interests in the transition from YOP to YTS. The 1981 White Paper had proposed that the trainee allowance be reduced, from £25 to £15 a week, and that participation in the scheme be made compulsory for unemployed school leavers. Both were rejected by the MSC, following the TUC lead. The TUC's major defeats were the failures to raise (a) the overall level of funding for training under YTS and (b) the trainee allowance, toward the TUC's target of £34.

In these varied respects, the transition from YOP to YTS shows several gains for trade union interests. The changes between the two schemes certainly reflect a wider set of interests than those of trade unions. "For the first time there was agreement amongst employers, unions, the education and training services and other interests that all young people entering employment need good quality basic training" (MSC, 1982a, p. 7; see also Raffe, 1984, 1988). However, the role played by union interests in the detailed design of YTS was recognized even in quarters less than friendly to trade unionism.[6]

---

[6]A Conservative MP, Jonathan Aitken, comparing the MSC's plan for YTS (MSC, 1982a) with the 1981 White Paper, concluded that "the TUC has had a very strong influence on this document" and, in urging the "danger that the TUC tail is wagging the MSC dog," made clear his view of the appropriate place for the TUC within the MSC (House of Commons, 1982, pp. 56, 59).

III. THE OUTCOMES OF UNION REGULATION

The results of the TUC's regulatory effort can be assessed at various levels. The first concerns the operational nature of YTS itself; the second, the degree of attainment of particular objectives such as increased trainee allowances and low substitution.

A. YTS in Operation

A substantial difference rapidly emerged in 1983 between YTS on paper and in practice. As had been the case under YOP, the priority given to securing sufficient YTS places to be able to cater fully to unemployed school leavers led to important concessions to employers. Of the eight quality criteria that YTS schemes had been intended to satisfy, only that requiring 3 months' off-the-job training was retained. The linkage of training schemes to occupational families was dropped. Legal enforceability of training agreements was not required, leaving the administrative sanctions used under YOP (closure) as the only recourse in the face of low-quality schemes. Employers were assured that monitoring would be limited in scope, a move consistent with the government's preference to limit public intrusion into employer activities (*IDS* 293, July 1983; Ryan, 1984). The "additionality" rule requiring employers to increase youth recruitment in order to obtain full YTS subsidy appears to have been a dead letter from the outset.

Some of the early concessions on training quality are being slowly clawed back by MSC at present. Under plans for the 2-year YTS, certification as an Approved Training Organization is to be required in order to run a YTS scheme; trainees are to receive an explicit training agreement with, and a statement of achievement from, their sponsor; and progress is claimed toward linking YTS to a coherent set of national vocational qualifications (MSC, 1986). The effectiveness of these moves remains to be seen. A cautious appraisal is suggested by the fact that they formed part of the initial design of YTS. Many employers still oppose them. Moreover, the proportion of time to be spent off the job is less (below 20%) in 2-year than in 1-year YTS; the additional funds provided to encourage better training within the extension to 2 years are also relatively small, the government calling instead for higher contributions from employers.

The effectiveness of monitoring under YTS remains a matter of uncertainty. YTS is organized on a two-tier basis, with managing agents generally subcontracting to a large number of employers for their supply of work experience (Gray & King, 1986, Table 12). Managing agents are held responsible for the quality of their schemes. The MSC claimed that this would make the task of quality control easier than under YOP; there were only 3,500 managing agents as against 150,000 WEEP sponsors. The argument is hardly convincing, ignoring as it does the possibility that subcontracting providers of work experience will be all the more able to conceal low quality by being twice removed from the MSC. The National Audit Office found that the incidence of unacceptable quality declined only marginally between 1983 and 1985, from 35% to 32% of places (*IRRR*, 9 October 1984, 20 August 1985). The large backlog of inspections that built up under YOP has been avoided under YTS, but the feasibility of enforcing quality controls on a host of work experience subcontractors remains dubious.

The disappointing increase in training quality between YOP and YTS has reflected the limited success of the TUC's regulatory plans, thereby promoting continuity of opposition between YOP and YTS.

B. Union Coverage and Bargaining

A central element in TUC strategy has been to capture YTS for unionized workplaces. Only an indirect index of success is available here: the association between youth activity under YOP/YTS and unionization across sectors (Table 2). The industrial distribution of youths undertaking work experience refers to the last year of YOP (1982/1983) and the last year of 1-year YTS (1985/1986). The intensity variables estimate the availability to employers of the services of YOP/YTS trainees in work experience as a percentage of those of regular employees (full-time equivalents).

The economy-wide average intensity of work experience of around 1% for both years indicates that the importance of youth interventions as a source of labor services—and therefore the potential extent of substitution—has

Table 2. Intensity of Work Experience Activity under YOP and YTS and Trade Union Membership Density, by Sector

Sector	(1) YOP-WEEP 1982/1983	(2) YTS 1985/1986	(3) Change (2)–(1)	(4) Union membership density[b]
	Intensity of work experience[a]			
Agriculture	3.01%	1.36%	−1.65	22.6%
Manufacturing: engineering	.48	.54	.06	79.6
Manufacturing: other	.60	.74	.14	59.6
Construction, mining	.67	.55	− .12	47.3
Utilities, transportation, communications	.15	.45	.30	96.1
Distribution	2.48	1.38	−1.10	14.9
Insurance, banking	.72	.61	− .11	54.8
Professional services	.23	.10	− .13	76.3
Personal & miscellaneous services	1.87	2.60	.73	11.5
Public administration	.81	2.53	1.72	62.2
All production industries	.48	.58	.10	
All services and agriculture	1.18	1.39	.21	
All sectors	.92%	1.05%	.13	53.6%

[a]Average numbers of YOP (WEEP only) and YTS (all modes) trainees active at workplaces as a percentage of numbers of regular employees (full-time equivalent).
[b]Union membership as a percentage of labor force attached to sector, 31 December 1979 (Price & Bain, 1983).
Sources and methods: Appendix A.

been marginal overall. Higher levels have been attained in particular sectors. YOP/YTS intensities of 2% or higher prevailed in Agriculture and Distribution in 1982/1983, as well as in Personal Services and Public Administration in 1985/1986. The greatest usage of young trainees by employers was attained in agriculture where, in 1982/1983, approximately 1 in every 33 hours of available labor services was provided by a YOP trainee. Still higher levels appear in particular subsectors.[7]

The takeup of both YOP and YTS has been slanted strongly toward sectors with lower levels of unionization.[8] For YOP, more than three quarters of the variance in intensity is associated with unionization ($r^2 = .77$; $p < .01$). For YTS, an inverse association is also present and statistically significant ($r^2 = .40$; $p < .05$). Although the association with unionization is less close for YTS than for YOP, the difference may partly reflect the age of the data on unionization and is anyway too small to attain statistical significance. Thus the TUC's policy of acquiring YTS for the unionized sector has neither succeeded in the absolute sense nor unambiguously reduced the concentration of work experience in the nonunion sector.

The reason for the limited nature of the change between YOP and YTS can be found in Table 2. Only one of the more highly unionized sectors (Public Administration) sponsored much more work experience under YTS than under YOP.[9] Intensities did increase in three of the four industrial sectors, with their high levels of unionization, but the increases were small in absolute terms. The other major reallocation of trainees between YOP and YTS has been the considerable decline, within sectors with low union density, in the importance of Agriculture and Distribution relative to Personal and Miscellaneous Services. These changes do not suggest much of a role for union regulation, either direct or indirect. Youth activity has proved as heavily slanted toward the service sector, with its preponderance of small enterprises and nonunion employers, under YTS as it was under YOP.

Another indicator relevant to the success of TUC policy is the extent to which the YTS allowance has been "topped up" by union bargaining efforts. In 1983/1984, unions succeeded in bargaining increases in the £25 allowance for only 16% of trainees, the average increase being £19. Regular levels of

---

[7]Work experience intensities in excess of 7% were found in Repairs and Personal Services (Deakin & Pratten, 1987, Table 1).

[8]In the absence of more recent estimates, data on union membership density for December 1979 are used for both YOP and YTS. The large reduction in union membership that has occurred since 1979 creates difficulties for this approach, although its effect upon the broad pattern of unionization appears to have been limited to a slight reduction of the differences between manufacturing and services (Millward & Stevens, 1987, Chapter 3).

[9]The increase in intensity in Public Administration appears surprising in view of the exclusionary attitude of some public sector unions. It reflects low levels in central government, where the CPSA has been hostile to YTS, and high levels in local government, where NALGO has switched from initial hostility to accepting a large-scale YTS effort involving 70,000 places a year by 1986 (IRRR, 3 March 1987).

youth earnings were attained in less than 1 in 10 cases (Department of Employment, 1985, Table 3). Although these figures represent an increase on the zero baseline of YOP, the level under YTS is less than impressive. Moreover, the importance of negotiated increases for first-year trainees has declined slightly under YTS; by 1985/1986 the average was £16, with only 13% of trainees affected (MSC, 1987).

No data are available on the extent to which employee status has been bargained for trainees, nor on the degree to which trainees have joined trade unions. A TUC survey has, however, found widespread indifference or hostility toward unions among YTS trainees, suggesting that union gains on that front have been limited as well (TUC, 1986b).

C. Substitution

A central objective of the union regulatory effort has been to curb the loss of regular employment to YOP/YTS trainees. Fears that substitution would prove extensive reflect the high substitutability of youth for adult labour in the general labour market (Marsden and Ryan, 1986, 1989). They have proven well founded in the case of YOP/YTS. One in every three employers participating in YTS admitted doing so at least partly to reduce labor costs, and, whereas 8% of participants met disappointment on this score, twice as many reported unanticipated savings on labor costs (Sako & Dore, 1986, Tables 3–5). In the work experience component, 70% of 1983/1984 trainees were described by their sponsors as either assisting others to do their jobs or doing regular jobs themselves (Gray & King, 1986, Table 11). Not surprisingly therefore, substitution is estimated to have characterized nearly half (47%) of YTS places in 1985/1986 (Deakin & Pratten, 1987, Table 3). Moreover, substitution appears to have increased between YOP and YTS; the rate estimated for 1981 was 30% (CAG, 1983, p. 25).[10]

Substitution has been concentrated in the youth area. More than three quarters of substitution under YTS has involved other youth jobs, with only one in every eight YTS places involving job loss for older workers (Deakin & Pratten, 1987, Table 3). Intensified substitution within the youth category is also suggested by the marked decline in the youth employment rate and the steadiness of the youth unemployment rate in the face of the rise in YOP/YTS activity since 1981 (Table 1). The implication is that, far from curbing substitution, the TUC's regulatory effort has actually failed to prevent a marked increase between YOP and YTS, particularly within the youth labor market.

---

[10]Substitution may be presumed to have been higher than these estimates as they derive from the responses of employers to questions about their employment policies in the absence of YOP/YTS. Employers may be presumed to be aware that substitution is formally prohibited under YOP/YTS and have therefore reason to downplay its extent. Whatever the size of this bias, it would take an implausibly rapid decline in the rate of underreporting to invalidate the inference that substitution increased between YOP and YTS.

A high level of substitution might be expected of both YOP and YTS in view of the centrality of work experience and the absence of employer payroll costs in each program. In the words of the chairman of the MSC, when questioned about substitution on YOP:

> We were concerned to ensure that there was an element of real work within the work experience programme and that runs with it a risk of substitution . . . you cannot have young people doing a real job of work without running the risk that someone may actually be out of a job because of it. (House of Commons, 1983, p. 58)[11]

Trade union attempts to regulate work experience directly either ignore this logic or pursue essentially unenforceable restrictions, such as the clauses in a model YOP agreement that (a) recruitment be unaffected and (b) when a WEEP youth is doing the tasks of a regular employee, the latter stand by rather than be reassigned to other tasks (GMWU, 1982).

Nor is the increase in substitution between YOP and YTS surprising, particularly in its youth–youth ("deadweight") dimension. The "additionality" incentives intended to make YTS trainees distinct from regular youth recruitment appear to have been quietly discarded at an early stage (MSC, 1984). Most employers have used YTS as a prolonged screening period for the recruitment of young people, a response involving widespread substitution for regular youth employment (Sako & Dore, 1986). The success of MSC's efforts to bring mainstream youth jobs under YTS has led to parallel stratifications in YTS and the wider youth labor market (Lee, Marsden, Hardey, Rickman, and Masters, 1987; Raffe, 1988). Moreover, the increasing importance attached to a high rate of retention of YTS "graduates" within sponsoring firms—an objective at least as highly valued by young entrants and the government as by trade unions—can only be achieved by extensive substitution of trainees for young employees.

The TUC's regulatory program has thus succeeded only in part. Gains have been made in terms of an increase in the priority given to training, of increased trainee allowance, of recruitment of trainees into trade unions, and possibly of a reduced preponderance of nonunion workplaces. YTS continues to evolve and may yet develop into an acceptable system of youth training. However, progress remains limited on all of the criteria that the TUC set out in 1982/1983. Substitution has risen; increased allowances and employee status remain unusual; trainees have proved difficult to recruit; and nonunion workplaces continue to dominate the provision of work experience.

IV. EVALUATION AND CONCLUSION

In contrast to the reactive and incoherent policy often attributed to trade unionism, the TUC has both developed a clear strategy for the regulation of

---

[11]Official rhetoric notwithstanding, the substitution of youths for older workers has been accepted to be an implication of youth interventions. YOP was designed to "give a competitive edge

youth interventions and promoted it vigorously within the union movement. The achievements of the campaign have, however, proved so limited as to suggest that it has largely failed.

The poor return to the TUC's efforts—and in particular the increase in substitution—may nevertheless constitute a less serious loss for trade unions than might be inferred from conference debate. Its importance depends upon the nature of union objectives. Although the content of union goals remains a matter of controversy, it is widely accepted that the employment and pay of existing members both feature strongly therein (Oswald, 1985). Cheap trainee labor threatens both the employment security and the pay of existing union members, both directly through substitution and indirectly through reduced bargaining power (Ryan, 1987).

The effects of substitution appear, however, to have been confined for the most part to both the youth segment of the membership and nonmembers (in nonunion employment). To the extent that the objectives of trade unions are dominated by the interests of the adult majority within the membership (Borooah & Lee, 1987), the effects of substitution should therefore be of limited importance to trade unions.

It would be incorrect to hold that, simply because adult members dominate trade unions numerically and organizationally, unions simply pursue the interests of adult members. Any prospective monopoly for adult interests is qualified by the importance of youth among potential members, attention to whose interests may bolster recruitment[12]; by the sporadic activism of young members; and by altruistic and paternalistic sentiment among adults (Ryan, 1987). The fact that most union leaders have supported YOP/YTS suggests a concern to improve the fortunes of young people, even nonmembers. The importance attached, by the TUC and its opponents alike, to raising the basic trainee allowance and to protecting the health and safety of trainees also indicates an orientation to young workers' interests as neither goal is of any instrumental value to adults.

Thus, to the extent that youth interests have weight in union objectives, the loss of employment security and earning power that substitution means for many young workers represents a significant blow to union objectives— particularly as the offsetting benefits of increased youth activity and of improved training have proved limited and elusive, respectively.

The importance of youth interests within union policy is, however, strictly bounded. Some idea of the limits is provided by the General Council's rejection of the National Society of Motor Mechanics' 1978 call for both increased independence for youth representation in the TUC and statutory youth employment quotas (TUC, 1978, pp. 474, 489; 1979, p. 48). The wide-

---

to young people in the labour market," and it was recognized that "this may . . . affect adversely other age groups" (MSC, 1977, p. 43).

[12]Competition to recruit YTS trainees has been particularly intense in engineering; both the EETPU and the AUEW offer free membership to trainees (*FT*, 19 May 1983; *AUEW*, 12 July 1983).

spread indifference of most union members to YOP/YTS, attributed both to the limited numbers involved and to the distance of trainees from unionized areas of the workplace, points in the same direction (*LRD*, June 1985).

The effects of YOP/YTS upon union objectives thus appear negative; their importance depends upon that of the interests of young workers within unions themselves. However, unions value not only the substantive objectives of pay levels and employment security but also the procedural goal of involvement in decision making (Flanders, 1970). To the extent that trade unionists value participation for its own sake, irrespective of the outcome, the continued activity of union leaders in the MSC, together with the newly created role of union representatives in the design and operation of projects under YTS, represents positive attainments to be set against the substantive disappointments.

The combination of substantive disappointment and procedural success sheds some light upon responses to youth interventions within the union movement. In response to attacks on YOP/YTS, the TUC leadership has urged the importance of its continued participation in the MSC, claiming that the position of young workers would be even worse were the unions to walk away from them.[13] Although outcomes might well have been worse in the absence of union involvement, it is also possible that procedural interests inform the official stance. Procedural objectives tend to be valued more highly by union officials than by members, partly because it is the former rather than the latter who get to participate. For many members, procedural gains appear hollow when they lack substantive counterparts. Indeed, from the perspective of left-wing members, procedural gains tend to be viewed as losses whatever the substantive results, the participation of unions in the MSC constituting cooperation in their own demobilization and incorporation.[14]

The questions posed to the union movement by YOP/YTS are therefore as much political as industrial. If the substantive outcomes have been disappointing, they have also been largely irrelevant to the active concerns of most union members. Procedural outcomes are potentially more significant, but their assessment depends upon wider political and ideological issues. It can, however, be said that the TUC overestimated the prospects for regulatory success at a time of high unemployment, whereas the Conservative government has been able to promote and legitimize its policies more effectively as a result of continued union involvement in the MSC.

The situation may be about to change. The debate within the union

---

[13]"We do understand and we do sympathize with the many trade union criticisms [of YOP]. . . . But it is the view of the General Council that it would be fundamentally wrong . . . to shout out 'YOP is a fraud, please shut it down.' Because then we would have to ask ourselves the question: What would happen to the hundreds of thousands of young people who are on the dole? They will not thank us unless we can immediately offer them something better." (W. Keys, TUC, 1981, p. 428)

[14]A full account of the factors associated with opposition to YOP/YTS would have to take account of the industrial interests of union members, union competition for members, employer attitudes, and wider political conflict.

movement over whether to reject or regulate youth interventions remains unresolved—and has even subsided as far as YTS is concerned. Conflict has, however, been revived by a government move to extend work experience to older members of the youth labor market. The Job Training Scheme (JTS), currently under development, is intended to extend access to publicly funded work experience from 16- and 17-year-olds to 18- to 25-year-olds. The long-term unemployed among these "older" young workers are to receive off-the-job training and work experience, during 6-month contracts along the lines developed under YOP/YTS, in return for their unemployment benefit (or social security).

The threat posed to union interests by substitution is greater under JTS than under YOP/YTS. The potential size of JTS is comparable to that of YTS. Although its restriction to the long-term unemployed will reduce the appeal of JTS work experience to employers, the greater experience of 18- to 25-year-olds suggests greater substitutability for older workers than in the case of YOP/YTS. Divisions within the trade union movement over YOP/YTS have already been intensified by JTS. The TUC has advocated the same policy as vis-à-vis YOP/YTS: support for JTS combined with pressure for improvements in the scheme's quality. However, one quarter of the membership of the TUC's General Council, led by NALGO and NUPE, has already voted for a boycott (*FT*, 26 February 1987). The Wales and Scottish TUCs (along with such supporters of YTS as the general workers' union, TGWU) have also supported rejection. The outcome of conflict on this by now familiar terrain remains to be seen, but TUC sponsorship of the modest Work Experience Programme for unemployed school leavers in 1976 must by now strike many unionists as having been the thin end of a long wedge.

V. APPENDIX: DERIVATION OF WORK EXPERIENCE INTENSITIES

The intensities of work experience under YOP and YTS (Columns 1 and 2, Table 2), are derived from (a) employment in the sector in September 1982 and December 1985. Part-time workers are converted to full-time equivalents on a one half basis. Sources: *Employment Gazette*, November 1983, Table S1.2; Occasional Supplement Number 2, December 1983, Table 3; Historical Supplement Number 2, February 1987, Table 1.4. (b) Numbers of starts on YOP (WEEP only) in 1982/1983 and YTS (all modes) in 1985/1986 (MSC, 1982b, Table 5; Gray & King, 1986, Table 1) allocated to sectors according to unpublished MSC estimates based on the 1983 WEEP Sponsors and the 1986 YTS Providers surveys; converted to an average population active on work experience by using the average durations of stays (26 weeks in 1982/1983 and 35 weeks in 1984/1985, assumed unchanged in 1985/1986) and average access to and time spent in off-the-job training (Department of Employment, 1981b, 1985). The average duration of off-the-job training is assumed invariant across sectors in each year; 48- and 49-week working years are assumed for trainees and regular employees; YTS trainees are assumed to undertake their off-the-job training continuously throughout the duration of their contract.

The sectoral breakdown is based on the industry Orders of the 1968 Standard Industrial Classification; 1985/1986 figures are reallocated from the 1980 to the 1968 SIC. Breakdowns of trainees by subsector for 1985/1986 are derived from the YTS Leavers Survey of 1986 (unpublished).

Acknowledgments An earlier version of this chapter was presented to a conference in Hull, England. Comments provided by William Brown, Brian Deakin, John Gennard, David Lee, Robert Lindley, David Marsden, David Raffe, and Roger Tarling are gratefully acknowledged, as are the suggestions of an official of the Trades Union Congress and the provision of unpublished data by the Manpower Services Commission.

VI. REFERENCES

A. Books, Pamphlets, and Articles

Bedeman, T., & Harvey, J. (1981). *Young people on YOP*. London: MSC.
Borooah, V. K., & Lee, K. C. (1987). *Trade unions, relative wages and the employment of young workers*. Discussion Papers on Structural Analysis of Economic Systems, Number 5; Cambridge Growth Project, Department of Applied Economics, University of Cambridge.
Bradshaw, J., Lawton, D., & Cooke, K. (1987). Income and expenditure of teenagers and their families. *Youth and Policy, 19*, 15–19.
British Printing Industries Federation/National Graphical Association. (1983). *Recruitment, training and retraining agreement*. Bedford: Diemer and Reynolds.
Comptroller and Auditor General (1983). *Special employment measures administered by the Department of Employment and the Manpower Services Commission*. Memorandum. House of Commons, Committee of Public Accounts, Fourth Report, Session 1983–1984 (pp. 1–29). London: HMSO.
Cusack, S., & Roll, J. (1985). *Families rent apart*. London: Child Poverty Action Group.
Deakin, B., & Pratten, C. (1987). Economic effects of YTS. *Employment Gazette, 95*, 491–497.
Department of Employment. (1977). Young people and work. *Employment Gazette, 85*, 1345–1347.
Department of Employment. (1981a). *The New Training Initiative: a programme for action*. Cmnd 8455. London: HMSO.
Department of Employment. (1981b). Furthering their chances of a job. *Employment Gazette, 89*, 125–126.
Department of Employment. (1985). A survey of Youth Training Scheme providers. *Employment Gazette, 93*, 307–312.
Eversley, J. (1986). Trade union responses and the MSC. In C. Benn & J. Fairley (Eds.), *Challenging the MSC* (pp. 201–238). London: Pluto Press.
Flanders, A. (1970). *Management and unions*. London: Faber & Faber.
Garonna, P. (1986). Youth unemployment, labour market deregulation, and union strategies in Italy. *British Journal of Industrial Relations, 24*, 43–62.
Garonna, P., & Ryan, P. (1986). Youth labour, industrial relations and deregulation in advanced economics. *Economia e Lavoro, 20*, 3–19.
General and Municipal Workers' Union (GWMU). (1982). *YOPS: A guide for union negotiators*. Esher, Surrey: Author.
Germe, J. F. (1986). Employment policies and the entry of young people into the labour market in France. *British Journal of Industrial Relations, 24*, 29–42.
Gray, D., & King, S. (1986). *The Youth Training Scheme: The First three years*. YTS Evaluation Series Number 1. Sheffield: MSC.

House of Commons. (1982). *Employment Committee*. Fourth Report from the Employment Committee. London: HMSO.
Industrial Relations Review and Report. (1983). Industrial relations guide to YTS. Special issue. London: IRRR.
Jackson, M. P., & Hanby, V. B. (1982). *British Work Creation Programmes*. Aldershot: Gower.
Layard, R. (1986). *How to beat unemployment*. Oxford: Oxford University Press.
Lee, D., Marsden, D., Hardey, M., Rickman, P., & Masters, K. (1987). Youth training, life chances, and orientations to work: A case study of the Youth Training Scheme. In P. Brown and D. N. Ashton (Eds.), *Education, Unemployment and Labour Markets* (pp. 138–159). Brighton: Falmer.
Manpower Services Commission. (1977). *Young people and work*. London: MSC.
Manpower Services Commission. (1982a). *Youth task group report*. Sheffield: MSC.
Manpower Services Commission. (1982b). Review of fourth year of special programmes. *Special Programme News*, October 1982.
Manpower Services Commission. (1984). *Youth Training Scheme review 1984*. Sheffield: MSC.
Manpower Services Commission. (1986). *Annual Report 1985/1986*. Sheffield: MSC.
Manpower Services Commission (1987). *Youth Training Board*. Progress report on YTS for April 1987. Internal working paper, YTB/87/8.
Marsden, D., & Ryan, P. (1986). Where do young workers work? The distribution of youth employment in various European economies. *British Journal of Industrial Relations, 24*, 83–102.
Marsden, D. W., & Ryan, P. (1989). Youth employment and modes of youth regulation. Forthcoming in Ryan, P., Garonna, P., & Edwards, R. C. (Eds.), *The problem of youth; The regulation of youth employment and training in advanced economies*. London: Macmillan.
Millward, N., & Stevens, M. (1987). *British workplace industrial relations 1980–1984*. Aldershot: Gower.
Oswald, A. J. (1985). The economic theory of trade unions: An introductory survey. *Scandinavian Journal of Economics, 87*, 160–193.
Price, R., & Bain, G. S. (1983). Union growth in Britain: Retrospect and prospect. *British Journal of Industrial Relations, 21*, 46–68.
Raffe, D. (1984). Youth unemployment and the MSC. In D. McCrone (Ed.), *Scottish Government Yearbook 1984* (pp. 188–222) Edinburgh: Unit for Study of Government in Scotland.
Raffe, D. (1988). The context of the Youth Training Scheme; an analysis of its strategy and development. *British Journal of Education and Work, 1*, 1–31.
Ryan, P. (1986). *Apprenticeship and industrial relations in British engineering: The early interwar period*. Paper presented to Workshop on Child Labour and Apprenticeship, University of Essex, May.
Ryan, P. (1987). Trade unionism and the pay of young workers. In P. N. Junankar (Ed.), *From school to unemployment? The labour market for young workers* (pp. 119–142). London: Macmillan.
Sako, M., & Dore, R. (1986). How the Youth Training Scheme helps employers. *Employment Gazette, 94*, 195–204.
Trades Union Congress. (1976). *Report of 108th Annual Trades Union Congress*. London: TUC.
Trades Union Congress. (1977). *Report of 109th Annual Trades Union Congress*. London: TUC.
Trades Union Congress. (1978). *Report of 110th Annual Trades Union Congress*. London: TUC.
Trades Union Congress. (1979). *Report of 111th Annual Trades Union Congress*. London: TUC.
Trades Union Congress. (1980). *Report of 112th Annual Trades Union Congress*. London: TUC.
Trades Union Congress. (1981). *Report of 113th Annual Trades Union Congress*. London: TUC.
Trades Union Congress. (1982a). *Report of 114th Annual Trades Union Congress*. London: TUC.
Trades Union Congress. (1982b). *Youth training: TUC guide and checklist for union negotiators*. London: TUC.
Trades Union Congress. (1983a). *Report of 115th Annual Trades Union Congress*. London: TUC.
Trades Union Congress. (1983b). *TUC handbook on the MSC's Youth Training Scheme*. London: TUC.
Trades Union Congress. (1984). *Report of 116th Annual Trades Union Congress*. London: TUC.
Trades Union Congress. (1985). *Report of 117th Annual Trades Union Congress*. London: TUC.
Trades Union Congress. (1986a). *Agenda for 118th Annual Trades Union Congress*. London: TUC.

Trades Union Congress. (1986b). Recruitment of trainees into trade unions, TUC circular number 167. London: TUC.

Trades Union Research Unit (1980). *Youth unemployment, state intervention and the trade union role: Some emerging issues.* Occasional Paper Number 63, Ruskin College, Oxford.

Wells, W. (1983). *The relative pay and employment of young people.* Research Paper Number 42. London: Department of Employment.

B. Periodicals

AUEW Journal (AUEW), Amalgamated Union of Engineering Workers, London.

Civil Service Annual Report (CSAR), Civil and Public Services Association, London.

Dawn, Union of Shop, Distributive and Allied Workers, London.

Employment Gazette (EG), Department of Employment, London.

Financial Times (FT), London.

Health Services, Confederation of Health Service Employees, London.

Incomes Data Services Report (IDS), London.

Industrial Relations Review and Report (IRRR), London.

Labour Market Quarterly Report (LMQR), Sheffield.

Labour Research Department Bargaining Report (LRD), London.

Times, London.

Times Educational Supplement (TES), London.

Times Higher Educational Supplement (THES), London.

10

The Reagan Administration and the Regulation of Labor
The Curious Case of Affirmative Action

Marilyn Power

The organization and structure of labor markets in a capitalist society at a given point in time is heavily affected by the particular nature of the struggle between capital and labor. Capitalists attempt to shape the labor markets they confront, but they must also respond, to a greater or lesser extent, to the pressure of worker organizations (cf. Milkman, 1983; Rubery, 1978). The outcome, an historically specific organization of labor markets, becomes part of the "regulatory framework" (Boyer, 1979) within which accumulation takes place.

In the United States in the 1950s, the emerging civil rights movement added a new element to the struggle for control of labor markets. Black workers, in their demands for an end to economic discrimination, were confronting *both* employers and certain segments of organized labor, particularly craft and skilled blue-collar unions that had actively discriminated by race. By the mid-1960s, the militance and effectiveness of civil rights organizations had resulted in a series of federal laws and executive orders that forbade discrimination by race and sex (the latter prohibition added as an amendment) in pay, hiring, and promotion. These antidiscrimination provisions have become part of the regulatory framework, despite the initial opposition of segments of capital; and although they have not been consistently enforced, they have nevertheless effected gradual changes in the organization of labor markets. Although inequality by sex and race is still prevalent, women and nonwhite men have been making slow but noticeable progress into traditionally white

Marilyn Power • Department of Economics, California State University-Sacramento, Sacramento California 95826.

male occupations, and black women have moved in considerable numbers into white female occupations, especially clerical work.

Of the antidiscrimination regulations, the most controversial, and perhaps the most directly effective, has been affirmative action. Affirmative action against racial discrimination was mandated in the United States in 1965 by an executive order. It was amended to include sexual discrimination in 1967, and in 1972 was revised to allow the use of goals and timetables to determine compliance with the order. All firms except construction contractors doing business with the federal government are required to submit an affirmative action plan if they have contracts for $50,000 or more and employ at least 50 people. Construction contractors are required to meet affirmative action guidelines if they hold federal contracts in excess of $10,000.

Affirmative action has been extremely controversial from the beginning. Conservative economists complained about interference with the market; employers complained about expensive and onerous paperwork and about being forced to hire less competent employees; unions complained about the threat to seniority rules and, in the case of craft unions, loss of control over admittance to apprenticeship programs; white men (and at times white women as well) complained about reverse discrimination. It comes as no surprise that the Reagan administration, with its emphasis on the free market, sympathy with capital, and lack of concern for discrimination, would be hostile to affirmative action. What may be surprising is that the administration's attempts to weaken the affirmative action order by the formal elimination of goals and timetables met with considerable resistance from the business community, particularly among medium to large corporations.

In what follows, I will first give a brief description of the history and effectiveness of the affirmative action executive order, and chronicle the Reagan administration's attempts to dismantle it. I will then focus on the use of goals and timetables and suggest why large capital may not want them formally abolished. I will argue that corporate commitment to goals and timetables has two aspects: a "protective" aspect and a "positive" aspect. In brief, federally mandated affirmative action may be used by capital to protect itself from more militant civil rights pressure and to facilitate the violation of the (already very shaky) "accord" with white male skilled workers.

I. HISTORY OF AFFIRMATIVE ACTION

The government has required firms with federal contracts to use "affirmative action" in hiring minorities since 1961. However, the definition of affirmative action remained extremely vague throughout the 1960s. In 1965 the Johnson administration issued Executive Order 11246, the order under which affirmative action is currently enforced. Johnson created the Office of Federal Contract Compliance Programs (OFCCP) in the Department of Labor to supervise compliance with the order, but there was still no explicit definition of the meaning of "compliance." In 1967 the affirmative action order was amended to prohibit discrimination by sex.

Throughout the 1960s and early 1970s, there was considerable debate about the proper method of determining compliance with affirmative action goals. Several pilot projects had required contractors to submit affirmative action plans including "manning" tables establishing goals and timetables for minority group hiring, within a range established by the government. Contractors were then required to make a "good faith" effort to meet their goals. If the goals were met, the contractor was considered to be in compliance with affirmative action; if they were not met, the contractor could be subject to a costly investigation and, possibly, sanctions.

The use of goals and timetables was immediately controversial, with some members of Congress arguing that it established hiring quotas, illegal under the Civil Rights Act. The Nixon administration vigorously supported the use of goals and timetables, however, and in 1970 their use was extended to all federal contractors and, for the first time, to the hiring of women as well as racial minorities. In 1972, both the Senate and the House of Representatives concurred and, by allocating the required funds, in effect ratified the executive order, including the use of goals and timetables (Goldstein, 1984, p. 26).

The defense of goals and timetables by the Nixon administration is, on the face of it, surprising, because strengthening affirmative action does not seem consistent with Nixon's "probusiness" stance. In fact, the implementation of goals and timetables was a strategy to *deregulate* affirmative action (Robertson, 1985). As long as a company was in compliance with its stated and approved goals, government investigators could not argue about the structure or adequacy of its specific affirmative action programs. This use of goals and timetables to limit government scrutiny and regulation of corporate hiring and promotion activity is one important reason many companies opposed the Reagan proposals.

II. EFFECTIVENESS OF AFFIRMATIVE ACTION

Although the affirmative action executive order was issued in 1965 and structured around the development of goals and timetables in 1970, the order was not aggressively enforced until after 1973. In fact, effective enforcement of regulations barring *sex* discrimination did not *begin* until 1974 (Leonard, 1984b, p. 445). Even during the period of more aggressive enforcement, both the chances of being reviewed and the penalties imposed were quite low. Between 1973 and 1981, 11,000 establishments were reviewed, about 10% of all federal contractors. Twenty-six of the establishments were barred from bidding on government contracts (the ultimate sanction), and 331 had to give employees back pay totaling $61 million (Leonard, 1984b, p. 447). Since 1981, only two additional companies have been barred (Pear, 1986).

The review process appears to have been chaotic at best, if not downright perverse. Examining the pattern of compliance reviews between 1974 and 1980, Jonathan Leonard found that establishments whose labor force was 100% white male were the *least* likely to be reviewed, whereas establishments with relatively high proportions of female or nonwhite male workers were the *most* likely to be reviewed (Leonard, 1985, p. 378). Leonard offers a number of possible explanations for this counterproductive behavior; for example, firms that are already in compliance may be easier to review, thus improving bureaucratic "efficiency" in terms of quantity of paper pushed. There seems to be a random element to the review process as well: One OFCCP compliance officer explained that, because he had a summer cottage on the beach, in the summer he reviewed establishments near the ocean (Leonard, 1985, p. 374n).

Despite this lack of effective or consistent enforcement, affirmative action has significantly improved the employment of women and nonwhite males in traditionally white male occupations. Leonard estimates that in the contractor sector, affirmative action has increased the demand for black males relative to white males by 6.5%, the demand for other minority males by 11.9%, and the demand for white women by 3.5%. The demand for black women increased 11.0% relative to the demand for white women (Leonard, 1984b, p. 459). A separate study by the Department of Labor also found employment increases in the contractor sector for women and nonwhite men and additionally found that significant numbers moved from service and low-skilled blue-collar to skilled production, craft, and white-collar jobs (Pear, 1983). This Department of Labor study was suppressed by the Reagan administration; the reported information was leaked to the press.

III. THE REAGAN ADMINISTRATION RESPONSE

In his first presidential campaign, Reagan stated his opposition to affirmative action goals and timetables, declaring them to be disguised quotas that resulted in reverse discrimination against white males. During his first year in office, in August 1981, Reagan proposed changes in the executive order that would have exempted many federal contractors from filing affirmative action plans and weakened the definition of "compliance" with affirmative action goals and timetables for the rest. This proposal appears to have been in the nature of a trial balloon. It met with a flurry of protests, from civil rights groups for imperiling affirmative action and from the Chamber of Commerce for not eliminating goals and timetables entirely. Although talk of reforming the executive order continued to surface periodically through Reagan's first term in office, neither the 1981 proposal nor any other was in fact carried out. Technically, the affirmative action guidelines remained as they had been since 1972, although the Reagan administration's Department of Labor was anything but vigorous in their enforcement.

No further attempts to alter the affirmative action executive order were made during Reagan's first term in office. The battle against the use of goals and timetables continued, however, as the Civil Rights Division of the Justice Department engaged in a number of court battles, unsuccessful to this point, to reverse consent decrees mandating affirmative action hiring goals (these consent decrees were negotiated by the Justice Department under previous administrations).

The Justice Department also supported the plaintiffs in four reverse discrimination cases before the Supreme Court in June and July 1986, and February 1987. Here the judicial strategy for disarming affirmative action met a considerable setback. Although the Supreme Court ruled that laying off white teachers in preference to black teachers with less seniority was illegal, it upheld the preferential hiring and promotion of members of minority groups in three cases (involving a local of the Sheet Metal Workers Union, promotion of state police, and municipal hiring of firefighters) in which there was evidence of past discrimination. The Supreme Court as presently constituted has sent out a clear message that it may restrict the use of affirmative action goals and timetables to some extent, but it will continue to uphold their use. It appears that, for the present at least, the Justice Department's strategy to dismantle affirmative action through the courts has not been effective, returning attention to revising the executive order. However, a negative January 1989 ruling on preferential awarding of city contracts may indicate a reversal in the Supreme Court's support for affirmative action.

In August 1985, early in Reagan's second term in office, the administration began its second direct offensive against the executive order. Attorney General Edwin Meese initiated a proposed revision that would revoke the use of goals and timetables and any other rules that "discriminate against or grant any preference to any individual or group" in recruitment, hiring, promotions, pay, and transfers (quoted in Trost, 1985). The proposal would also bar the use of statistical measures to infer discrimination in a company's hiring practices, making charges of discrimination nearly impossible to prove.

As in 1981, the 1985 proposal met with an immediate negative response from civil rights groups, but it was also vigorously opposed by a considerable segment of the business community and by members of the Reagan cabinet. In fact, the proposal resulted in a highly publicized fight within the Reagan administration, between what the media has labeled the administration *conservatives,* led by Attorney General Meese, and the *moderates,* led by Secretary of Labor William Brock, who continue to support the use of goals and timetables. As a result, the new executive order never reached Reagan's desk.

Within the business community, the dispute over goals and timetables breaks down roughly on the basis of size. The Chamber of Commerce, which represents small employers, often in retaining and service, strongly opposed the use of goals and timetables, as does the Associated General Contractors of America, representing 8,000 construction companies. In contrast, the National Association of Manufacturers, whose 13,600 members are medium-to-large-size manufacturing companies, lobbied vigorously against the Reagan proposal, stating that goals and timetables are an "integral part" of an effective affirmative action plan. In addition, the Business Roundtable, whose

membership consists of chief executive officers of 194 major U.S. corporations, has endorsed the use of federally established goals and timetables.
Many of the largest corporations have individually stated their support for
goals and timetables, including IBM, Schering-Plough, AT&T, Exxon, West-
inghouse, and Alcoa.

IV. WHY SUPPORT GOALS AND TIMETABLES?

This rallying of support for affirmative action on the part of segments of
capital is, on the face of it, rather surprising. After all, antidiscrimination
regulations interfere with the "free" market for labor, which is supposed to
achieve neoclassically optimal outcomes. In addition, affirmative action involves government scrutiny and regulation, which capital traditionally re-
sents. In political-economic terms, affirmative action goals and timetables
may interfere with the more flexible use of the labor force that is part of the
Reagan administration's economic restructuring agenda (Rosenberg, 1983).
What has transformed large corporations into zealous supporters of civil
rights against their own apparent self-interest?

The answer is, of course, that given the perceived realities of the 1980s,
large corporations have a number of reasons to believe that federally mandated affirmative action goals and timetables are, in fact, in their own best
interest. Although many resisted the civil rights reforms in the 1960s when
they were first imposed, two decades later they have adapted to the new
regulatory framework and adapted it in turn to their own uses. This is not to
say they would not like to see the executive order reformed: In particular,
they would like to see more "flexibility" in the enforcement of the goals and
timetables. But, as the National Association of Manufacturers has made clear,
a substantial segment of capital would emphatically *not* like to see federal
goals and timetables removed.

The reasons for capital's support of goals and timetables can be divided
into two categories: protective reasons and positive reasons. In brief, capital
fears the alternatives to the federal order would be worse for their interests,
but additionally, they may have found affirmative action a useful wedge
facilitating the weakening of their traditional accord with white male skilled
workers.

V. PROTECTIVE REASONS

Given the established reality of civil rights pressure, large capital may
find the federal government easier to negotiate with than other entities that
might fill the federal vacuum. Congress has threatened to respond to a weakening of the executive order by passing an affirmative action law, which could
be far more stringent and inflexible. In addition, if state and local governments believe the federal affirmative action program is inadequate, they are
likely to impose their own standards (this already occurs to some extent). Not

only would this lead to a proliferation of different standards, greatly complicating companies' affirmative action planning, but those standards would be likely to be stricter and more rigorously enforced than at the federal level, given the much greater presence of women and nonwhite men in government at the state and municipal levels. Capital also fears that the elimination of affirmative action enforcement on the federal level would spur civil rights organizations to scrutinize corporate hiring and promotion practices more closely and to target direct action (demonstrations, boycotts, etc.) against those companies perceived to be discriminators. In a word, capital would rather face pressure in the courts than in the streets.

Companies may also be concerned about the effects of resentment, if not overt hostility, on the part of their own female and nonwhite male employees, if they believe management commitment to affirmative action is waning. IBM, for example, has 60,000 more minority and female employees than it would have if these groups were represented in the same proportions as in the early 1960s (Robertson, 1985). Even though affirmative action was undoubtedly not the only reason for this increase, IBM can ill afford to create dissatisfaction in this group by appearing to endorse the Reagan administration position: It responded quickly to the Reagan proposal by issuing a report affirming its commitment to affirmative action (as did several other companies).

Corporations may also find the federal goals and timetables useful in fighting litigation, both in discrimination and reverse discrimination suits. In these situations, voluntary goals and timetables set by the company are not an adequate substitute, because they can still be argued to be discriminatory. Externally imposed goals and timetables allow companies to argue that they were merely following government guidelines.

Finally, goals and timetables can be a defense against further government intervention. It is in this sense that the introduction of goals and timetables was seen as a deregulatory move. Although the new regulations imposed more paperwork on the companies, this was not a major problem because large corporations use numerical goals to monitor many aspects of their operations. In exchange, capital got the assurance that numerical compliance would guarantee freedom from closer surveillance of hiring and promotion behavior, which had occasionally occurred prior to 1972.

VI. POSITIVE REASONS

Clearly, many of the reasons certain segments of capital support federally mandated goals and timetables are purely defensive. But corporations have found the federal rules more than simply protective. Although many originally resented and resisted affirmative action, it is apparent that the goals and timetables have proven useful to firms interested in restructuring their labor forces. Faced with demographic and social changes that mean that around 75% of the growth of the labor force between 1990 and 2000 will be women and nonwhite men (Robertson, 1985; see also Fullerton, 1985), capital is con-

cerned with breaking down barriers to employment of these groups in traditionally white male skilled blue-collar and managerial jobs. Although firms
could, of course, develop programs on their own to facilitate the entrance of
nontraditional groups into these occupations, having the force of federal regulations behind them is a great help in confrontations with resentful white
males. In this sense, affirmative action may be seen as a positive tool by
employers, at the same time that it is beneficial to women and minority males,
and to the unity of the labor movement as a whole.

The decline of craft and skilled blue-collar jobs, both numerically and in
terms of wages and benefits, may also provoke employer interest in affirmative action. That is, the process of degrading, mechanizing, and deskilling
traditionally well-paid and strongly unionized occupations may be facilitated
by the admission of previously excluded workers, as has been a pattern
throughout the history of U.S. industrial capitalism. Employers may see the
entrance of women and nonwhite men into these occupations as advan-
tageous because they increase the labor pool, providing a reserve army to
threaten attempts at worker resistance. Additionally, employers may reason
that women and nonwhite men will more docilely accept pay and benefit cuts
and reorganization of the labor process because even with the degraded conditions, they are better off than workers in traditionally female and nonwhite
male occupations. Somewhat the same reasoning may hold for lower and
middle-management positions, which grew rapidly and became very costly in
the 1970s and are currently in the midst of a major shakeout. In short, precisely because of its success (albeit limited) in moving women into traditionally white male occupations, affirmative action may serve to weaken the
barriers workers in these occupations have historically struggled to maintain
between themselves and the pressures of the reserve army of labor. In the
1980s, with capital's concerted campaign for greater labor "flexibility," affirmative action goals and timetables may be proving useful in ways corporations had not initially anticipated.

VII. OPPOSITION TO GOALS AND TIMETABLES

If affirmative action goals and timetables have clear protective and
positive advantages, why do substantial segments of capital oppose their use?
The New York Times, among others, has suggested that there is a split between
large and small capital on this issue (Noble, 1986); and although this division
is not rigidly maintained, there is evidence that it is generally the case. This
disagreement between small and large capital seems plausible because small
capital has less to gain, and more to lose, from affirmative action.

On the simplest level, economies of scale in performing the required
affirmative action paperwork mean that it is a relatively trivial task for large
corporations, possessed of affirmative action staffs well experienced in the
vagaries of government bureaucracy. By contrast, small firms may find the
paperwork costly and confusing. For example, a small company that was one

of only two firms ever barred by the Reagan Department of Labor from bidding on government contracts had failed to file any affirmative action plan at all, declaring itself "overwhelmed by the mechanisms" (Noble, 1986). Economies of scale in affirmative action planning and implementation may, in fact, give large firms an advantage in bidding on government contracts.

Construction contractors may have additional reasons for hostility to goals and timetables because the rules governing them, generally calling for hiring goals of 6.9% female and 24.9% minority for skilled craft jobs, have been more strictly enforced than for other industries. This is the case, according to civil rights lawyers, because of a history of discrimination by craft unions and because the work force in construction is highly unstable (Pear, 1986).

Finally, small firms other than construction contractors may derive little "positive" benefit from affirmative action goals and timetables because they are more likely to operate at the periphery of the economy, utilizing workers from, in labor market segmentation theory terminology, the secondary labor market (Gordon, Edwards, & Reich, 1982, pp. 190–192). In fact, because the secondary labor market is heavily nonwhite (Gordon, Edwards, & Reich, 1982, pp. 206–210), if anything affirmative action may *restrict* the supply of secondary workers, by providing access (however small) into more skilled jobs. This slight effect, however, would very likely be mitigated by Reagan administration policies that serve to increase the reserve army of labor (Power, 1984; Rosenberg, 1983).

VIII. CONCLUSION

Capitalist firms operate within a social, political, and economic framework; and although they do their utmost to affect that framework, they also adapt (with varying degrees of success) pragmatically to those aspects of the environment they cannot control. In doing so, they may even derive unanticipated benefits.

The most zealous ideologues of the Reagan administration were deeply committed to the elimination of affirmative action goals and timetables, which they find repugnant as interference with the free market and discrimination against white males. They were confronted by considerable opposition within the administration by "moderates," backed by vigorous lobbying by representatives of medium and large capital. Capital, which initially opposed affirmative action, has learned to adapt to it. In essence, there appears to be a pragmatic realization on the part of large capital that civil rights pressure is a permanent aspect of the regulatory framework; the strategy, then, is to accommodate the pressure in the least painful (to profits) manner. Federal goals and timetables serve this strategy and, in addition, may have proven beneficial in the continuing process of labor force restructuring.

That affirmative action may have been used in some cases for the nefarious purposes of deskilling and degrading does not imply that affirmative action has simply become a tool of the capitalist class, to be opposed by anyone whose sympathies lie with labor. The use of goals and timetables, however poorly enforced, has clearly improved the economic position of women and minority males, and the need for rigorously enforced affirmative action has by no means ended. If employers do use the goals and timetables as a means to restructure jobs, this practice must be exposed and combated by the labor movement as a whole. Whatever advantage employers may have culled from affirmative action, it is still most clearly in the interests of labor, as part of a strategy to promote a unified working class, with no inequality by race or sex.

IX. REFERENCES

Boyer, R. (1979). Wage formation in historical perspective: The French experience. *Cambridge Journal of Economics, 3,* 99–118.

Fullerton, H. N. Jr. (1985). The 1995 labor force: BLS' latest projections. *Monthly Labor Review, 108,* 17–25.

Goldstein, L. (1984). The historical case for goals and timetables. *New Perspectives* (U.S. Commission on Civil Rights), Summer, 20–26.

Gordon, D. M., Edwards, R., & Reich, M. (1982). *Segmented work, divided workers.* New York: Cambridge University Press.

Leonard, J. S. (1984b). The impact of affirmative action on employment. *Journal of Labor Economics, 2,* 439–463.

Leonard, J. S. (1985). Affirmative action as earnings redistribution: The targeting of compliance reviews. *Journal of Labor Economics, 3,* 363–384.

Milkman, R. (1983). Female factory labor and industrial structure: Control and conflict over "women's place" in auto and electrical manufacturing. *Politics and Society, 12,* 159–203.

Noble, K. B. (1986). Hiring Goals: A big-vs-small business split. *New York Times,* March 3.

Pear, R. (1983). Study says affirmative action rule expands hiring of minorities. *New York Times,* June 19.

Pear, R. (1986). Justice official says data show quotas for jobs. *New York Times,* March 29.

Power, M. (1984). Falling through the 'safety-net': Women, economic crisis, and Reaganomics. *Feminist Studies, 10,* 31–58.

Robertson, P. C. (1985). Why bosses like to be told to hire minorities. *Washington Post,* Nov. 10.

Rosenberg, S. (1983). Reagan social policy and labour force restructuring. *Cambridge Journal of Economics 1983, 7,* 179–196.

Rubery, J. (1978). Structured labour markets, worker organization and low pay. *Cambridge Journal of Economics, 2,* 17–36.

Trost, C. (1985). White House plans to review proposal to lift some affirmative action rules. *Wall St. Journal,* Aug. 16.

Wilkinson, F. (1983). Productive systems. *Cambridge Journal of Economics, 7,* 413–429.

United States Office of the Federal Register (1985). *Code of federal regulations, 41,* Chapter 6 (Affirmative Action Executive Order), revised as of July 1.

11

Work-Sharing Public Policy in France, 1981–1986

Annie Gauvin and François Michon

In the early 1980s, work sharing was a main topic of French debate on employment policy.[1] Rapid economic growth did not seem possible. Working-time reduction appeared to be the only means available for decreasing unemployment. Various ways were considered, including reducing the work week and lowering the retirement age.[2]

Macroeconomic studies and firm surveys reached different conclusions concerning the likely effects of work sharing. But the findings from both types of studies suggested that working-time reductions needed to be accompanied by changes in working-time organization if they were to significantly reduce unemployment. The Reduction and Reorganization of Working Time (RRWT) would have to be bargained over at the firm level (a very unusual occurrence in France) and not be imposed by the government.

From 1981 to 1986, RRWT was a main component of the employment policy of the socialist governments. Nevertheless, from the beginning, the hoped-for scenario did not emerge. Firm-level bargaining over work sharing did not occur. Law had to fill in for the failures of employers and unions.

Two approaches were used to encourage RRWT. First, there were legal

---

[1]With work sharing, the available work is distributed among more individuals. In effect, people who have work share it with those who do not. It refers to every form of individual working-time reduction undertaken to lower unemployment. For example, work sharing may involve reductions in working time through earlier retirement, shorter work weeks, longer vacations, and reduced overtime.

[2]Job sharing (the sharing of the same full-time job between two part-time employees) was not encouraged by the Socialist government.

Annie Gauvin and François Michon • Labor Economics Research Institute, University of Paris 1, 75634 Paris, Cedex 13, France.

means. In 1982, a law was passed reducing the legal workweek from 40 to 39 hours, lessening possibilities for overtime, lengthening annual paid vacations from 4 to 5 weeks, and lowering the normal retirement age from 65 to 60.

Supplementing the legal means were contractual means. Solidarity Contracts were in operation from 1982 to the beginning of 1985. They were agreements between a firm and the government or local authorities whereby the employer agreed to create or preserve jobs and reduce working time. For a Solidarity Contract to become operational, the unions representing a firm's workers must also be in agreement. Compensatory hirings were mainly reserved for younger workers. There were several types of solidarity contracts. The Solidarity Contracts for Working-Time Reductions (SCWTR) encouraged a shortening of the workweek. Firms involved in this arrangement were exempted from a portion of their social insurance contributions. The Solidarity Contracts for Early Retirement Resignations (SCERR) encouraged early retirement, whereas the Solidarity Contracts for Progressive Early Retirement (SCPER) fostered partial early retirement, by having the pension institutions rather than the employers provide the funds for the pensions. Some of these arrangements (or similar ones) were extended and were still operating at the end of 1986.[3]

This work sharing program was only partially successful. The policy of lowering the retirement age and forming a younger labor force was a success. The number of workers offering their services fell by 210,000 in 1982, and by more than 320,000 in 1983. The policy of shortening the workweek was a failure. In 1982, 50,000 to 60,000 jobs were created or protected by the introduction of the 39-hour workweek. But hardly 20,000 new hirings occurred during the 3 years in which the SCWTR was in effect.[4]

This chapter compares the initial debates over work sharing with the employment effects of work-sharing policies. The first section summarizes the work sharing debate in France in the early 1980s. The second discusses the findings from macroeconomic investigations of the RRWT programs. They are supplemented by information gained from firm surveys, presented in the third section, showing how firms responded to the measures implemented by the government.

I. THE WORK-SHARING DEBATE IN FRANCE IN THE EARLY 1980s

The simple mathematics of work sharing suggests that every decrease in the working time of an individual will result in additional hiring and less unemployment. But this approach to work sharing is unrealistic. Economic

[3]SCERR disappeared in the beginning of 1985. SCPER has been extended and still operates. SCWTR was modified many times from 1982 to 1985. In March 1985, it was replaced with the system called "Agreement for Working-Time Reorganization and Modernization" that gives up the direct work-sharing objective and only tries to encourage RRWT without any additional employment.

[4]Estimated data from Marioni and Ricau (1984), Levi (1984), and Commissariat Général au Plan (1985).

analysis points to three possible counterbalancing factors. First, the labor supply may expand. Second, productivity may increase. Third, the hourly wage rate may rise to maintain weekly earnings.

The problems involved in work sharing are not identical for lowering the retirement age and reducing the workweek. All things being equal, work sharing by reducing the retirement age substitutes younger employees for older ones and lowers unemployment by shrinking the labor force, not by creating jobs. Work sharing by workweek reduction may create jobs, or at least maintain jobs which would otherwise disappear.

The question of early retirement did not generate difficult discussions, compared with workweek reduction. Early retirement had been used by firms before 1981. This was mainly in order to cut the number of employees, rather than to really share work. In April 1983 when the normal retirement age was reduced to 60, 60% of the private sector employees over the age of 60 had already retired (through the system of "garantie de ressource").[5] In addition, 25% of those 50 to 59 years old were also receiving a guaranteed minimum income from specific early retirement schemes (two-thirds of them by means of solidarity contracts, in existence since 1982).[6]

At the microeconomic level of the firm, there are great differences in the impact of early retirement and workweek reduction. The clearest illustration of these differences concerns cost. When workweek reduction is combined with some income guarantee for employees, hourly wage costs rise. But the cost of substituting younger employees for older ones does not seem very high. Wage costs can even be reduced where wages sharply increase with seniority. The true cost of the policy appears only at the macroeconomic level in the form of expanded transfer payments. Thus employers accepted the early retirement policy, whereas they struggled against workweek reduction schemes.

In France, the debate over work sharing has emphasized the effects of workweek reduction. It has focused on the different findings from analyses based on macroeconomic models as compared to those derived from case studies of firms. Macroeconomic models, constructed for short-term predictions and medium-term planning, played the initial role in justifying the work sharing policy. They were clearly optimistic about the impact of work week reduction (including extending paid holidays) programs on employment and unemployment. For example, in 1978–1979, the METRIC and DMS models estimated that, in the best case, a 1-hour reduction in the average workweek would cause there to be 70,000 fewer unemployed in 3 years (Oudiz, Raoul, & Sterdiniak, 1979).[7]

Two key parameters are important for determining the success or failure

[5]The *garantie de ressource* is a benefit paid until the normal retirement age to employees over the age of 60, with more than 10 years of contribution to ASSEDIC, the agency providing unemployment insurance. ASSEDIC is managed by union and employer representatives.
[6]Calculated with data from Revoil (1983).
[7]With a model inspired by DMS and specially constructed for analyzing workweek reduction effects, Charpin and Mairesse (1978) have obtained similar results. There were 1,250,000 people officially unemployed in March 1979 and 1,540,000 officially unemployed in March 1981.

of work sharing with a workweek reduction. The first one is the possible loss of productive capacity. French models seem in agreement about the negative effects of possible declines in capacity. But their common optimism may be related to the same underestimate of this negative effect. All of them reduce the question of production capacity to whether shift work can be extended and the functioning time of equipment lengthened.[8]

The second key parameter is wage compensation and possible wage sharing. Does the hourly wage rate remain unchanged and thus individual weekly incomes fall, or do individual weekly incomes remain unchanged, and thus hourly wage rates rise? The models do not agree. Their disagreements flow from their assumptions.[9]

The findings from firm surveys are more critical of the job creation potential of a policy of shortening the workweek. Their results emphasize three points. First, there must be a substantial shortening of the workweek. Second, any increase in the hourly wage accompanying a reduction of the workweek must be less than any increase in productivity. Unit labor costs cannot rise. Third, the particular means of implementing such a policy will vary across firms and, thus, must be bargained over at the firm level (Barou, Rigaudiat, & Doyelle, 1982; Colin, 1981).[10]

These conditions are not easy to fulfill. In particular, firms tend to reduce the workweek more for productivity increases than for job creation. If there is a positive effect on employment, this tends to result from job preservation rather than from job creation.

Furthermore, firm surveys emphasize that the question of working time and wage costs are very complicated. The working time and wage aggregates used in macroeconomic models do not come close to giving an accurate account of this complexity.

The workweek itself has varied meanings at the level of the firm. Different work schedules may exist in the same workplace. Specific employee groups may work more or less hours than the average workweek. Individuals may be at work but may not be productive. The shortening of the workweek may occur in as many different concrete ways as there are firms, plants, workshops, jobs, and work force groups. Shift work may have to be reorganized.

---

[8]This simplification is largely improper. Firm surveys show that it results from the difficulties of estimating production capacity. For a discussion of this issue, see Barou, Peronnet, and Rocherlieux (1982).

[9]The METRIC model assumes that total individual incomes are maintained. This assumption reinforces the optimism of METRIC regarding the job creation effects of a workweek reduction. METRIC is Keynesian in orientation and accepts an income effect favorable to investment. The DMS model balances the positive effects on employment that result from maintaining incomes with the negative effects of increases in labor costs on investment. On this last point, see Passeron (1982). Van Ginneken (1984) emphasizes that the differences between the main European econometric models that he analyzes are largely due to the theoretical assumptions on which they are based.

[10]On the question of firm surveys, see Autrand (1982), Boisard (1982), Duval (1982), Jobert and Rozenblatt (1982), Pepin, Sardas, and Tonneau (1982), and Tahar (1981).

In addition, there are various ways to improve efficiency. Labor intensification can occur by quickening the pace of work, or by canceling breaks, or by reducing preparation time. The traditional systems of shift work can be supplemented by weekend shifts or part-time shifts to increase the use time of equipment.

Insofar as time is an essential dimension of a firm's organization of activities, it is the entire internal firm organization, its great variation from one firm to another, and its great internal heterogeneity and discontinuity that matters. Also, the matter of wage compensation is very complex, and it is a main component of bargaining between employers and unions.

II. THE QUANTITATIVE EVALUATION OF FRENCH WORK-SHARING PUBLIC POLICY, 1981–1986

A. The Macroeconomic Framework

Macroeconomic analyses argue that at the present time reasonably rapid economic growth would not reduce the level of unemployment. Levi (1984) finds that an annual growth rate of gross domestic product of 3% can stabilize the employment level, and a growth rate of 5% can stabilize the unemployment level. From 1985 to 1995, to provide a job for each new entrant to the labor market and to reduce the number of unemployed from 2,448,000 in March 1986 to the 1973 level of 575,000, it would be necessary to create 4 million new jobs. If discouraged and additional worker effects are taken into account, an additional 2,500,000 new positions would be needed.[11]

Several macroeconomic forecasts were undertaken to predict the employment effects of shortening the workweek. Their results for 1988 are presented in Table 1. The a scenario, the most optimistic one regarding employment and unemployment trends, was constructed by INSEE and CGP for the preparation of the ninth plan. It assumed that plant and equipment would be modernized in manufacturing and that active employment policy regarding working time would be implemented. This scenario is ambitious. It projects a very quick reduction of the average workweek in order to attain a 35-hour week in 1988 and a 30-hour week in 1994. This would result from various local and decentralized initiatives, especially regarding the creation of part-time jobs. An unemployment rate of 9.8% would be attained in 1990. These expectations seem overly optimistic given the events of the past few years.

Scenarios b and c assume a longer average workweek and a lower level of economic growth. They predict a decline in employment and an increase in unemployment.

[11]Thus, from 400,000 to 650,000 new jobs would need to be created annually. During the late 1960s and early 1970s, there was strong employment growth. But, even then, only 200,000 new jobs were created annually.

Table 1. Macroeconomic Forecasts for 1988

	a	b	c
Real gross domestic product (annual average rate of growth 1983–1988)	2.5	1.4	1.5
Workweek in 1988 (in hours)	35.0	36.5	36.5
Change in total employment, 1983–1988 (thousands)	280	−570	−650
Change in total unemployment, 1983–1988 (thousands)[a]	n.a.[b]	900	860

[a]Each percentage point of the unemployment rate constitutes approximately 220,000 people.
[b]The change in total unemployment is not available. The unemployment rate in 1990 is predicted to be 9.8%.
Note: a = "pivot" account E.Z., D.M.S. model, INSEE-CGP; b = medium-term plan INSEE-BIPE; and c = medium scenario, INSEE-Senat.
Source: Groupe Politique Economique (Délègation à l'Emploi) (1984).

B. Workweek Reduction: The Break in 1982

The interindustry collective agreement of July 1981 on working time and the agreements that followed, the January 1982 legislation on working time, and the solidarity contracts contributed to a clear break in average working time. The average length of the workweek sharply declined. The January 1982 act was immediately implemented. The 40-hour threshold was crossed in April 1982. This sharp reduction in the length of the workweek is in contrast

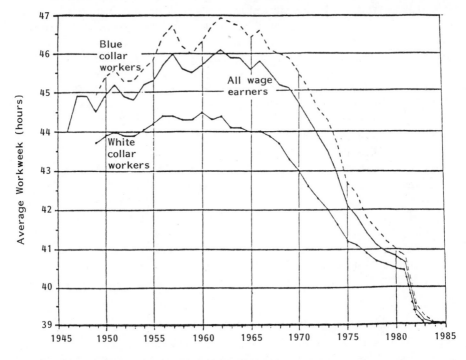

Figure 1. Evolution of the workweek, 1946 to 1985. The data are for plants with more than 10 employees. *Source:* Ministère du Travail and Ministère de l'Emploi.

to the smooth decline, from 1968 to 1974 (from the national interindustry collective agreement called the "Accord de Grenelle" to the first oil shock) and from 1974 to 1982 (see Figure 1).

A 39-hour workweek has been substituted for the 40-hour one. From 1984 to the first quarter of 1986 (the last quarter for which data are available), the average duration fluctuated around 39 hours. New work schedules have been developed. Blue-collar workers are now working approximately the same number of hours as white-collar workers, in contrast to previous years when they worked longer hours.

C. The Quantitative Impact of Work-Sharing Policy

The effects on unemployment of various employment policy measures are estimated in Table 2. France has been moving from an active policy of job creation (including public employment programs, reduction of legal working time, and assistance to the unemployed for creating new firms) that contributed to approximately 70% of avoided unemployment in 1982, to a social policy of unemployment management—human resources policy and other measures—(including reducing the labor force by early retirement and delay-

Table 2. Annual Evolution of Avoided Unemployment, 1981–1983[a]

	1981	1982	1983
Active employment policy			
Public employment	−26	−78	−46
Working time (public administration not included)	—	−25	0
Other economic policy measures: expansionary (1981–1982), devaluation (June 1982, March 1983), contractionary (1983)	−10	−40	−10
Induced effects of specific employment policy	−4	−5	−7
Aids to firm creation by the unemployed	−8	−13	−16
Measures for youth hirings	−27	−28	−23
Total	−75	−189	−102
Policy for Training (training periods for youth, Department of Education)	−15	+5	0
Human resources policy			
Guaranteed minimum revenue for those laid off and job leavers	−41	−46	−34
Early retirements (except solidarity contracts)	−10	−14	−18
Solidarity contracts	—	−8	−66
Retirement at 60 years at age	—	—	−7
Total	−51	−68	−125
Other measures			
Partial unemployment	−7	+5	−2
Long-term unemployed	—	−15	−45
Total incidence on unemployment	−148	−262	−274

[a]The figures represent the change in annual averages in thousands. The data are merely indicative. They do not represent a precise evaluation of the policies. The table is reproduced and translated from Colin, Elbaum, and Fonteneau (1984).

ing the entry of younger employees into the labor market, for example, the "Employment-Training" Contracts and all the measures for helping unskilled youth find employment) that contributed to close to 70% of avoided unemployment in 1983. These government policies reduced unemployment by 148,000 in 1981, 262,000 in 1982, and 274,000 in 1983. The contribution of specific work sharing measures is low. These policies caused total unemployment to decline by 33,000 in 1982 (lines 1-b and 3-c) and 73,000 in 1983 (lines 1-b, 3-c, and 3-d).

It is estimated that reducing the length of the legal workweek resulted in 70,000 avoided layoffs or new jobs created. Forty thousand of these workers were in manufacturing with the bulk of them retaining their jobs rather than being laid off. The rest were in nonmanufacturing where it is estimated that 20,000 to 30,000 new jobs were created, mainly part-time jobs. The employment effects of shortening the legal workweek are mainly felt in large plants where shift work is used.

Lowering the retirement age led to 52,000 additional persons retiring in 1983 and 75,000 additional in 1984. Even so, this policy led to only 7,000 fewer people being unemployed in 1983. Early retirements rarely led to the hiring of new workers except where solidarity contracts were in operation.

Data on the number of solidarity contracts and the number of people potentially affected by these arrangements from 1982 to 1985 are presented in Table 3. The success of SCERR is clear. Approximately 200,000 people, 60% of those eligible, took early retirement in 1982 and 1983 (Galland, Gaudin, & Vrain, 1984). In 95% of the cases, workers were hired to replace those who retired.[12] SCERR has been used more frequently by thriving firms—those paying relatively high wages, having relatively stable work forces, often utilizing professional training, rarely using fixed-term labor contracts, and experiencing net job creation from 1976 to 1981.

There were rather few SCPER contracts signed, and their employment effects were minimal in 1983 and 1984. The usage of SCPER accelerated in 1985. This type of solidarity contract is now one of the measures being used for expanding the number of part-time jobs (a more individualistic means of work sharing). Those who are partially retired are working part-time rather than full-time.

Firms have not found SCWTR very attractive. There were fewer than 18,000 new workers hired due to this contract. In addition, 9,000 jobs were preserved from 1982 to 1984. The signatory firms are large ones in both manufacturing and nonmanufacturing. In the majority of cases, workweek reductions are combined with some internal reorganization of the firm.

D. Forms of Reduction of Working Time after 1985

The measures used for RRWT in 1985–1986 do not refer to work sharing. They include SCPER and agreements concerning the reorganization of work-

---

[12]This information is taken from a survey quoted in Ministère des Affaires Sociales et de la Solidarité Nationale (1984). It included only national-level SCERR and SCPER—that is only those signed by multiplant firms.

Table 3. Contractual Agreements—SCERR, SCPER, SCWTR, and RRWT Agreements

Solidarity contracts	1982	1983	1984	1985	1/1–7/31, 1986
SCERR					
Number of contracts	28,362	4,319	—	—	—
Potentially concerned people	310,562	17,637	—	—	—
Number of beneficiaries	52,700	148,300	9,000	100	—
SCPER					
Number of contracts	1,173	254	241	751	529
Potentially concerned people	8,220	570	1,052	5,859	4,144
Number of beneficiaries	170	1,512	n.a.	1,400	—
SCWTR					
Number of contracts	736	277	174	142[a]	55[a]
Concerned people	214,027	84,976	28,713	14,800[a]	6,585[a]
Expected hirings	14,524	2,621	264	248[a]	125[a,b]
Potentially created or preserved jobs	n.a.	7,000	2,000	1,268[a]	n.a.

[a]RRWT and modernization agreements from 1985.
[b]From January 1 to May 31.
Source: Ministère du Travail, Service des Etudes et de la Statistique.

ing time and modernization of the plant. Their main purpose is to attempt to improve the ability of employers to vary their usage of labor in accordance with variations in product demand and changing conditions of production. In addition, they are aimed at lengthening the operating time of machinery. To the extent that the workweek is shortened, it is mainly as a result of factors such as shift work, seasonal declines in the use of labor, and a general decline in labor demand. It is not, any longer, through legislation mandating a shorter workweek.

The increased importance of part-time work has the effect of shortening the length of the average workweek. It compensates, to a degree, for the absence of social consensus and the failure of more collective attempts at working time reductions. Bargaining is occurring at the local level over expanding the use of part-time workers.

III. THE QUALITATIVE EVALUATION: THE REDUCTION OF WORKING TIME WITHIN THE FIRM

A. Negotiating Work Sharing[13]

All of the difficulties of RRWT bargaining within the firm can be summarized in the following way. "When work sharing seems the most necessary, the obstacles look the greatest" (Michon, 1985, p. 6). Work sharing seems the most necessary when the economy is in a crisis and there is no net job

[13]The studies summarized here were carried out with P. Bouillaguet Bernard, in a research project of the Séminaire d'Economie du Travail, on the general topic, "Work Sharing and Flexibility." This research was funded by the Commissariat Général du Plan. Its purpose was to

creation. At this time, there may be no other means for fighting unemployment. But it is exactly in this situation that the obstacles to work sharing seem the greatest. Prices cannot be increased, and there is excess capacity. Increased productivity is unlikely. The only offset to the increased hourly labor costs arising from work sharing is to cut the hourly wage. Yet the unions often find that alternative unsatisfactory. Finally, if only healthy firms are able to share work, this drastically reduces the efficiency of the policy in a period of crisis.[14]

Most French unions argue that hourly wages must increase if the workweek is shortened. Weekly wages must be maintained. If weekly wages were to fall, the unions would view this as a form of income and unemployment sharing rather than real work sharing. Although this is the official and traditional position of most interindustrial union federations, at the firm level, unions can tolerate some income sharing in order to limit the growth in hourly wage costs. This may occur when, for example, the possible beneficiaries of work sharing are close enough to the affected workers so that feelings of worker solidarity are activated. In addition, income sharing would also be accepted if the threat of job loss is real enough.

The Confédération Francaise Démocratique du Travail (CFDT) was the only major union federation to favor an income sharing corollary to work sharing, in the beginning of the socialist experience. The Confédération Générale du Travail (CGT) and Force Ouvrière (FO) opposed income sharing. Yet as time went on, the CFDT seemed to be less supportive of income sharing in particular and work sharing public policy in general.

Employers are willing to maintain the weekly wages of their employees while shortening the workweek only if labor productivity increases accordingly. The sense that "it does not have to cost the firm" seems widespread. Labor productivity often increases with working-time reduction because work reorganizations favorable to increased flexibility often occur at the same time.

In short, two issues are at the center of bargaining over sharing the work. Will income be shared or maintained? Will new means of work organization be allowed, thus improving labor productivity?

B. The Multidimensionality of Working-Time Reduction

Analysis of the practices and strategies of firms concerning RRWT shows how work sharing is a relatively minor consideration in firm calculations. These practices and strategies are more often driven by two other logics: one

---

highlight the relationships between work sharing public policy, firm strategies for greater flexibility, and ways of life of employees affected by the RRWT process. Nine case studies of manufacturing and nonmanufacturing plants belonging to three firms (three plants in each of three firms) were carried out as part of this project. See Barrére, Bouillaguet, Gauvin, Michon, and Outin (1985).

[14]Statistics on firms signing solidarity contracts very clearly indicate that these contracts have attracted large and prosperous manufacturing firms. See Galland, Gaudin, and Vrain (1984), and Barbezieux (1983).

of "human resources management," the other of "firm reorganization" (Gauvin & Michon, 1986). In other words, these practices and strategies separate clearly enough work sharing and RRWT. To distinguish these three logics does not mean that they are mutually exclusive. Each case study emphasizes how intertwined they are. The RRWT strategies and practices vary according to the relative influence of each of the three logics.

The logic of work sharing is a macroeconomic one. As such, it should have little or no effect on the hiring decisions of firms. Yet our own investigations (Barrere, Bouillaguet-Bernard, Gauvin, Michon, & Outin, 1985) lead us to believe that some employers are concerned with their public image, not merely with profit maximization. They are more likely to take work sharing considerations into account in their hiring practices. In addition, employers located in noncompetitive industries are more likely to pay greater attention to issues of work sharing than their counterparts in competitive industries.

Insofar as RRWT causes employee departures and/or hirings, the way is cleared for a renewal and reallocation of staff to different jobs. A human resources management logic seems to be one of the main bases of RRWT practices. It is a strong motivation for earlier retirements. It also concerns workweek reductions along with compensatory hiring and their possible impact on the average age of the staff.[15]

Along with a younger work force comes a regeneration of the internal labor market (Ferry, 1983). Internal mobility flows are reactivated. This appears to be particularly useful because the economic crisis has seriously held back external flows (Cezard & Rault, 1986). Reactivation of internal mobility flows increases the ability of the work force to adapt to new technologies. It makes it easier to modernize.

Human resource management is not only concerned with the age of employees. It also deals with managing industrial relations within the firm. With RRWT strategies and practices, there is an overall social game that can be very complex and that goes beyond the mere issue of RRWT. Strategies and practices are largely dependent on the social game within the firm. Meanwhile, and insofar as there is a changing staff, RRWT processes contribute in some cases to creating a "new deal" and to largely modifying the social game.

The effects of RRWT on productive organizations are complex processes.[16] Within-the-firm (or plant) organization is not easy to change. It is often a factor fostering rigidity.

The French debate (as has been shown in the case of large-scale macroeconomic models used for forecasting) emphasizes that RRWT must be accompanied by reorganizations such as extending the time of capital use (e.g., development of evening, night, or weekend shifts). Such changes will help to compensate for the costs of RRWT. The question of times of capital

---

[15]The compensatory hirings occurring under solidarity contracts mainly concern young people.

[16]Barbezieux (1983) emphasizes that, according to a survey taken of SCWTR signatory firms, two-thirds of the signatories said they had changed their organization of their work forces after signing the contracts.

use and shift work is often seen as a good proxy for the overall reorganization question.

But this is not a complete picture. It improperly generalizes an implicit model in which activity time and working time are largely constrained, mainly by technical factors, and changes in work organization are required by every reduction in working time. On the contrary, in nonmanufacturing, it is quite possible to perform the same activities in shorter periods of time. Also, manufacturing working-times are not more constrained than nonmanufacturing working-times. All cases exist.

Work reorganizations associated with RRWT practices are very varied. They can take the form of a reorganization of activities such as changes of job structures. They can also be (simultaneously as well as in a completely separate manner) reorganization of activity times and working times (e.g., hours and work schedules). Moreover, these associated reorganizations can be positive and deliberately sought out along with RRWT. However, they can also be negative; they can appear to be disorganization rather than reorganization.

IV. CONCLUSION

Since 1981, the French debate has changed considerably. More emphasis is now placed on human resource management and internal reorganization, and less attention is given to work sharing.

First, the relative failure of work sharing by reduction of the workweek has led to an emphasis on reorganization, as much if not more than on reduction of working time. This was the attitude taken by the Commissariat Général au Plan in 1984 (Commissariat Général au Plan, 1985). An arithmetical job creation effect compensating reductions in working time is no longer expected. The first consideration when reducing working time is reorganization in such a way as to overturn organizational rigidities that are an obstacle to job creation.

Secondly, increased efficiency, brought about by reorganization and greater work flexibility, is expected (Taddéi, 1985). Work flexibility has definitively overtaken work sharing as indicated by the new legislative measures adopted in February 1986 concerning working-time flexibility.

Legislative elections in March 1986 produced a conservative majority. This political change has been slow to be translated into new employment policies. It seems, nevertheless, that a policy for the development of "Formes Particulières d'Emploi," for example, temporary work and part-time jobs, is being substituted for a policy of RRWT for full-time employment.[17] The debate on public employment policies and their effects on firm strategies and practices will be largely renewed.

[17]See Michon (1981) for a discussion of common law work contracts and "Formes Particulières d'Emploi."

V. REFERENCES

Autrand, A. (1982). *La réduction de la duréee du travail dans les entreprises*, CRESTT, Université de Paris Sud.

Barbezieux, P. (1983). Le bilan des contrats de solidarité réduction de la durée du travail conclus en 1982. *Travail et Emploi*, No. 17, juillet–septembre, 9–21.

Barou, Y., Peronnet, F., & Rocherieux, F. (1982). Réduire la durée du travail. Analyse macroeconomique et enjeux sociaux. *Travail et Emploi*, No. 13, juillet–septembre, 5–20.

Barou, Y., Rigaudiat, J., & Doyelle, A. (1982). Réduction de la durée du travail et comportement des entreprises. Synthèse des études monographiques disponibles. *Travail et Emploi*, No. 13, juillet–septembre, 21–35.

Barrere, M. A., Bouillaguet-Bernard, P., Gauvin, A., Michon, F., & Outin, J. L. (1985). *Partage du travail et flexibilité, analyse des conditions économiques, techniques et sociales de la politique de partage du travail*, rapport définitif, Vol. 1, Séminaire d'Economie du Travail, CNRS-Université de Paris 1, 196 p. ronéo (avec la collaboration de M. L. Caspar, R. Silvera, & F. Streliski).

Boisard, P. (1982). La réduction des durées travaillées. Analyse micro économique de la réduction de la durée hebdomadaire du travail. *Cahier du Centre d'Etude de l'Emploi* (Presses Universitaires de France, Paris), 25, 5–90.

Cezard, M., & Rault, D. (1986). La crise a freiné la mobilité sectorielle. *Economie et Statistique*, No. 184, janvier, 41–62.

Charpin, J. M., & Mairesse, J. (1978). Réduction de la durée du travail et chômage: éléments de réflexion en forme de modèle. *Revue Economique*, 19, 189–206.

Colin, J. F. (1981). Temps de travail et emploi. Les enjeux d'une réduction de la durée du travail. *Futuribles*, No. 48, octobre, 3–18.

Colin, J. F., Elbaum, M., Fonteneau, A. (1984). Chômage et politique de l'emploi, 1981–1983. *Observations et Diagnostics Economiques*, No. 7, avril, 95–122.

Commissariat Général au Plan. (1985). *L'aménagement et la réduction du temps de travail*, La Documentation Française, Paris, janvier.

Duval, E. (1982). Réussir l'aménagement du temps dans l'entreprise. *Travail et Emploi*, No. 11, janvier–mars, 37–49.

Ferry, C. (1983). A propos des contrats de solidarité. *Revue Française des Affaires Sociales*, 37ème année, 3, juillet–sept., 69–76.

Galland, O., Gaudin, J., & Vrain, P. (1984). Contrats de solidarité de préretraite et stratégies des entreprises. *Travail et Emploi*, No. 22, décembre, 7–20.

Gauvin, A., & Michon, F. (1986). Work sharing, human resources management and flexibility of industrial organization (government employment policy and industrial organization), Séminaire d'Economie du Travail, CNRS—Université de Paris 1, 22 p. ronéo (paper for the 1986 conference of the International Working Party on labor Market Segmentation, Cambridge UK, 14–18 July).

Ginneken, W., van (1984). La réduction de la semaine de travail et l'emploi. Comparaison entre sept modèles macro économiques européens. *Revue Internationale du Travail*, 123, 37–56.

Groupe Politique Economique et Emploi (Délégation à l'Emploi). (1984). Politique économique et emploi. *Travail et Emploi*, No. 19, mars, 9–60.

Jobert, A., & Rozenblatt, P. (1982). *Réduction et aménagement du temps de travail*, CREDOC, Paris, ronéo.

Levi, M. (1984). Les politiques de l'emploi de la Gauche: bilan de trois années d'expérience. *Critiques de l'Economie Politique*, No. 28, (nouvelle série), septembre, 7–34.

Marioni, P., & Ricau, M. (1984). Préretraites et politiques de gestion du personnel. Approches sectorielles. *Dossiers Statistiques du Travail et de l'Emploi* (Ministère du Travail, service des études et de la statistique), No. 7, 7–28.

Michon, F. (1981). Dualism and the french labour market: Business strategy, non-standard job forms and secondary jobs. In F. Wilkinson, (Ed.), *The dynamics of labour market segmentation*. (pp. 81–98) London: Academic Press.

Michon, F. (1985). Succès et échecs d'un traitement social du chômage, L'expérience française d'une politique contractuelle de partage du travail. *Cahier du Séminaire d'Economie du Travail,* CNRS—Université de Paris 1, 135 p. ronéo.

Ministère des Affaires Sociales et de la Solidarité Nationale. (1984). Application des contrats de solidarité. *Dossiers Statistiques du Travail et de l'Emploi,* No. 1, 15–28.

Oudiz, G., Raoul, E., & Sterdiniak, M. (1979). Réduire la durée du travail, quelles consequences? *Economie et Statistique,* No. 111, mai, 3–17.

Passeron, H. (1982). Les utilisations de PROPAGE en variante. In INSEE, "PROPAGE: modèle de projections mutisectorielles annuelles glissantes," Collections de L'INSEE, série C, No. 103, juillet, 241–259.

Pepin, M., Sardas, J. C., & Tonneau, D. (1982). *Réduction des horaires et emploi, analyse organisationnelle d'une vingtaine d'entreprises,* Centre de Gestion Scientifique, Ecole des Mines de Paris.

Revoil, J. P. (1983). *Indemnisation du chômage et de la préretraite.* Note pour les rencontres annuelles franco-britanniques CNRS-SSRC, ronéo, Paris, avril.

Taddéi, D. (1986). *Des machines et des hommes. Pour l'emploi, par une miellente utilisation des equipements.* Rappri au 1 ministre, La Documentation Française.

Tahar, G. (1981). *Durée du travail, investissement et emploi.* CEJEE, Université des Sciences Sociales de Toulouse, ronéo.

12

Part-Time Employment
A Response to Economic Crisis?

Anne Marie Berg

I. INTRODUCTION

This chapter analyzes the grounds on which governments, capital, and labor accept and sometimes encourage part-time work. Part-time employment has increased in importance in many OECD countries during the late 1970s and early 1980s, a time of economic recession and rising unemployment. Is part-time work a response to economic crisis?

Of all the Organization for Economic Cooperation and Development (OECD) countries, Norway has the highest proportion of part-time workers among its working population. In Norway, as in other European countries, there is an ongoing debate concerning the microeconomic and macroeconomic effects of working time reforms. This chapter will not focus on these issues.[1] Rather, it will concentrate on the sociological and ideological effects of such reforms. It will investigate the potential conflicts between part-time work and other working time reforms.

The chapter is divided into three main sections. The first describes how European governments and various work life organizations have pushed part-time work and other working time reforms as a means for ameliorating the unemployment problem. The second investigates the development and nature of part-time work in OECD countries in general, and in Norway in particular. In light of these trends in part-time employment, the third analyzes part-time employment as a labor market policy. The possible contradictions between this policy and incomes policy and family policy are presented.

---

[1] For an investigation of the microeconomic and macroeconomic effects of working time reforms in France, see Chapter 11 by Gauvin and Michon in this volume.

Anne Marie Berg • Work Research Institute, Oslo 1, Norway.

II. UNEMPLOYMENT POLICY

A. Part-Time Work

During the last half of the 1970s, the European economies suffered a serious recession, and unemployment rose substantially in most countries. An increase in part-time work came to be seen as one way to restructure the labor market and reduce unemployment.

Part-time employment had been growing in relative importance in most OECD countries since the first oil shock in 1973.[2] In some countries, the number of people working full time, full year had even declined. In Europe, approximately one out of every two new jobs was a part-time job in the period 1973–1981 (OECD, 1983).

In June 1983, a recommendation was issued from the Steering Committee of the International Labour Organization encouraging governments to increase the use of part-time work as a means for increasing employment. The recommendation followed a report on unemployment in France, Germany, and the Netherlands.

The Socialist government in France issued a decree in 1982 which encouraged more extensive use of part-time work. Michel Rocard, Minister of the Planning Department at the time, states in a foreword to a book on part-time work in England, France, and Germany that the government views part-time work as a means for sharing work in order to combat unemployment (Jallade, 1982, p. 6). He also contends that part-time work is not contrary to the policy of a collective reduction of the workday, but complements it. He states that part-time work is a reversible phenomenon, which, in addition, does not increase the cost of labor for the employers.

The Norwegian government passed a supplement to the general Law on Work Environment in 1982, stating a conditional "right" of employees to demand part-time work. The conditions are linked to social and welfare grounds. In a statement to Parliament in 1983 on its employment and labor market agenda, the government presented part-time work as a policy for increasing labor market flexibility (St. m. nr. 85, [1982–1983], 1982, p. 87). Increased flexibility is seen as improving the ability of employers to vary their use of labor in accordance with variations in product demand and changing conditions of production.

B. Reduction of Working Time

A reduction of weekly working hours has also been put forward as a means for combatting unemployment. Several international work organiza-

---

[2]European countries measure the extent of part-time work in a variety of ways. However, for the purpose of this chapter, these variations are not important. Part-time work will be defined as working fewer hours for pay than the regular full-time employment of the standard work contract.

tions, trade unions, and governments support this policy, whereas employees generally oppose it.

Since 1977, the European Trade Union Institute has recommended reducing weekly working hours (The European Trade Union Institute, 1979, 1980). The Free International Labor Organization, in its congress in Oslo in 1983, adopted this as one of the methods for meeting the unemployment crisis. Labor organizations in Belgium, the Netherlands, France, and Germany have had the 35-hour workweek on their agenda for several years. The demand for working time reductions had ignited some of the severest labor conflicts in Europe during the 1980s.[3]

The Mitterrand government, soon after its election in 1981, launched an extensive program for working time reforms. This program included a general shortening of the workweek, a fifth vacation week, a general lowering of the retirement age, and voluntary contracts on a further shortening of the workweek, and preretirement schemes called solidarity contracts. The decree of 1982, to enhance more use of part-time work, was also part of this package of reforms.[4] Some working-time reductions have also occurred in Belgium and the Netherlands.

The situation in Scandinavia is somewhat different. The Scandinavian trade unions have been very reluctant to accept reductions of working time as employment policy. The debate, particularly in Norway, has been over different means of working time and labor reductions primarily in the context of social and welfare policy.

The increase in unemployment in Norway was less severe than in other European countries. Also, it occurred well after unemployment began rising in other countries. This was due to the fact that Norway, given its income from oil production, chose to utilize expansionary macroeconomic policy to forestall a recession. Yet by 1982–1984, the Norwegian unemployment rate reached levels not experienced since the depression years of the 1930s. In the early 1980s, working time reduction as a means of work sharing became a public issue.

But, in the Scandinavian countries, the shortening of the workday had already been raised by the women's movement in the early 1970s. It was seen as a means to enhance the equal participation of men and women in work and family life and partly as a countermeasure to the enormous expansion of part-time work taking place at the time. This may explain why the most radical of working time reform proposals emerged: the 6-hour workday. The 6-hour workday is still part of the ongoing debate on working time reform in Norway.[5]

---

[3]For a discussion of strikes over working time reductions in West Germany, see Chapter 5 by Bosch and Sengenberger in this volume.
[4]For a discussion of these French policies, see Chapter 11 by Gauvin and Michon in this volume.
[5]The 6-hour workday was discussed during the crisis of the 1920s and 1930s, but then mainly as a means to combat unemployment. Several local trade unions put the 6-hour workday on the agenda, and in 1932, even the Labor Party and the Federation of Trade Unions had a collective reduction of the workday as one of the items in their Joint Program to Combat the Crisis. With the upswing of the economy from the middle of the 1930s, this issue was quickly buried.

The Norwegian Federation of Trade Unions has not given priority to a general shortening of the workday. Rather, the federation has pushed for a fifth week of vacation and a reduction of the retirement age. These policies were adopted at the congresses of 1977 and 1981. Nevertheless, the question of a collective reduction of the workday has been hotly debated at the national congresses of the Federation, as the priorities of the federation have been strongly questioned by several of its member organizations. Several of the national unions have, since 1981, put the 6-hour workday on their political programs. They are unions representing municipal employees, government employees, employees in commerce and offices, food and allied workers, and employees in the graphic arts.

These are the main unions representing female labor and the main unions organizing in sectors with the highest concentration of part-time workers. They are most interested in a collective reduction of the workday as their members have experienced the bleaker aspects of part-time work. They also express the interests of women workers. The graphic arts union is the one exception. It has few female members. It is the only union that has a ban on part-time work and is also the only union with local agreements for 6-hour shifts and a 32-hour full-time workweek.

Although the Norwegian Federation of Trade Unions has not supported a general shortening of the workday, it did adopt in 1985 a program calling for a reduction of the workweek for groups of blue-collar workers in order to reach a standard week for both blue-collar and white-collar workers. This reform was negotiated between the employers and the unions in 1986 and implemented throughout 1987.

Collective reductions of the workday or workweek and part-time work are in many ways two opposing labor market policies with different social and political consequences. They may not be directly contradictory as Michel Rocard (tactically) assures us in his foreword to *L'Europe à Temps Partiel* (Jallade, 1982). But they have quite different effects within the labor market itself as well as different consequences in an income policy perspective and with respect to the politics of sex roles in general.

III. THE DEVELOPMENT AND NATURE OF PART-TIME WORK IN NORWAY

A. The Development of Part-Time Work

Denmark, Sweden, and Norway are the Western industrialized countries with the highest proportion of part-time workers among their working populations. Approximately 25% of the working populations are engaged in part-time work in these countries. In Central Europe, part-time workers comprise 19% of the labor force in the Netherlands, 15% in Great Britain, 10% in Germany, and 7% in France (OECD, 1983).

In all of these countries, women hold most of the part-time jobs. In 1981, the majority of working women in Norway worked part-time. Part-time work among women was already quite common by the latter half of the 1960s. But the development of part-time work as a main trait of the Norwegian labor market occurred later during the mid-1970s.

In order to understand these phenomena, Norwegian governmental policy during these years must be analyzed. The Norwegian economy became more service-oriented during the 1970s. Partly due to demographic changes, an increased demand for public services in fields like education, health care, and nursing occurred. In addition, throughout the latter part of the 1970s, public sector growth was greatly accelerated by expansionary macroeconomic policy.

During the period 1972–1978, community, social, and private services accounted for 94% of the total increase in employment. This sector also accounted for 31% of the person years worked in 1984, as compared with 29% in 1980 and 23% in 1970 (*National Accounts,* 1980, 1985).

The traditional labor market was tight, but there was a potential surplus of labor that could be activated. In 1970, the labor force participation rate among Norwegian women, and particularly married women, was low compared with other OECD countries. In order to activate this potential female labor force, the government took steps to encourage and facilitate the labor force participation of women. Statements to Parliament were given on childcare facilities and on family policies, and a law on equality between men and women particularly in the fields of work and education was passed during the 1970s.

The Norwegian labor market is strongly sex-segregated, and the demand for labor came in jobs and sectors traditionally dominated by female labor. Married women entering the labor market frequently desired part-time employment. In 1976, the state and municipal employers' organizations initiated a collective agreement with the respective trade unions of the sectors in order to facilitate but also regulate part-time work. There was a large increase in female employment in the mid-1970s. And the expansion of the female labor force came mainly in the form of part-time employment.

By 1981, the Norwegian government had instituted a more restrictive macroeconomic policy. Although the growth in overall employment slowed, the employment of women continued to increase. And between 1980 and 1981, a time when the economy slowed down, all of the increase in employment came in the form of part-time work. But by the mid-1980s, part-time employment began to decrease in the public and private sectors (*Labor Market Statistics,* 1985, 1986).

B. The Nature of Part-Time Work

There are certain characteristics attached to part-time work in Norway. In addition, these characteristics seem to hold fairly well for all national labor markets with a high proportion of part-time employment.

Part-time work is frequently based on individual work contracts or agreements differing from the standard collectively based work contracts.[6] It is not as heavily regulated as full-time work by the Norwegian government or the labor organizations. Thus, part-time work is more flexible than work under standard work contracts. The only governmental regulation of part-time work is proof of its intended flexibility. Part-time workers, if made redundant, are not eligible for unemployment benefits unless they declare themselves willing to take full-time work if that is what is available.

Part-time employment is profitable for capital. Hourly wage rates for part-time workers are often lower than for full-time workers. In addition, part-time workers are not usually entitled to the same range of fringe benefits as full-time workers, and sometimes are not covered by employment protection legislation. Temporary part-time employment permits employers more flexibility in meeting fluctuations in the demand for their firms' products or services.

Part-time work is a female labor market activity in Norway and in many other European countries (Foged, 1980; OECD, 1983; Peterson, 1981; Jallade, 1982). In Norway, 80% of the part-time employed are women. In Great Britain, France, and West Germany it is 80% to 90%. Less than 10% of the employed Norwegian men work part-time, whereas the majority of employed women do so. Many women work part-time in order to cope with family responsibilities. In Norway, 60% of the employed married women and 66% of the employed married women with children under the age of 16 work part-time, whereas only 28% of the employed single women hold such positions.

Part-time work is mainly found in the tertiary sector. In Norway, the community, social, and private service accounts for 41% of the part-time working population. Adding banks and finance, commerce and retail trade, and hotel and restaurant work, this sector amounts to 70% of the part-time working population. Approximately half of those employed in the service sector work part-time, whereas in manufacturing, only 14% of the employed work part-time.[7] The bulk of part-time employment is concentrated in the service sector in all OECD countries (OECD, 1983).

Not only are part-time jobs concentrated in the service sector, they are also most prevalent in female-dominated activities and jobs. Thus the expansion of part-time employment has reinforced the creation of two separate sex-segregated labor markets.

These are the characteristics of part-time work. In analyzing this phenomenon, it is also important to know to what extent people hold part-time jobs voluntarily or involuntarily. In addition, it is useful to determine to what extent part-time work has developed because of or as a response to the eco-

[6]The standard work contract is regulated partly by national labor laws and partly by collective agreements negotiated between unions and employers. The latter vary somewhat across industries. The labor laws apply in principle to part-time as well as full-time work. But part-timers are sometimes excluded from collective agreements. In addition, unionization is generally low in industries with a high proportion of part-time employment.

[7]The figures illustrating the Norwegian situation are from *Labor Market Statistics 1972, 1974, 1978, 1981, 1983, 1984, 1985* and from the Survey on Part-Time Work (*Deltidsundersokelsen*, 1978).

nomic crisis. There is a close relationship between the overall female labor participation rate and the evolution of part-time employment across countries (OECD, 1983, p. 48). It is possible that many women have been pushed into the labor force in order to protect the standards of living of their families. One wage earner per family may not have been adequate. Having entered the labor force, part-time work may have been the means of coping with both wage earning and family responsibilities. However, although this hypothesis is intuitively appealing, we do not have adequate data to determine its validity.

Also, the economic situation itself has led to an increased demand for part-time labor. Survey evidence from several countries (not including Norway) suggest that the share of involuntary part-time working in total part-time employment has risen over the past decade. This indicates that the unemployment situation has had some impact on the part-time labor market. Nevertheless, the vast majority of part-timers in these countries were "voluntary" (OECD, 1983, p. 45).

Thus it is difficult to establish to what extent part-time work has been a response to economic crisis. It has developed in countries with considerably different economic and labor market situations. There is evidently no simple explanation for the vast expansion of part-time employment across countries. The explanation is rather to be found in the relationship between several different factors. If we look at the characteristics of part-time employment listed before, some may be seen as causes and some as effects. The development of the service sector with the characteristics of these jobs, the great number of women seeking to resolve the double work load (household work and wage labor) with a job in this sector, employers seeing part-time work as increasing profitability, and the lack of intervention from the trade unions and governments are all factors explaining the expansion of part-time employment. In addition, at least for the Scandinavian countries, the impact of the women's movement in the 1970s on policy issues and on female labor force participation must not be underestimated.

IV. PART-TIME WORK AND EMPLOYMENT AND SOCIAL POLICY

A. Part-Time Work as Employment Policy

In Norway, neither the government nor the trade unions have admitted that the expansion of part-time work has kept the unemployment rate down. Paid work of 1 hour or more per week is registered as employment. And in Norway, approximately 5% of the employed population had an average workweek of less than 10 hours, and approximately 7.5% had an average workweek between 10 and 20 hours in 1984.

The hidden unemployment of married women has never been accepted as unemployment. Nevertheless, the tremendous growth in employment during the second half of the 1970s must be seen as an expression of a previously hidden unemployment. Employment rose by 8% for men and 33% for women between 1972–1983. The main part of the female increase was in part-time work.

There were hardly any official policy steps to encourage part-time work until the expansion of part-time work had been going on for several years. Thus part-time jobs have not developed as a result of labor market policy measures. But, an undeclared or declared policy of acceptance and nonintervention by the government and the trade unions made the development possible.

More recently, there have been official policy declarations encouraging part-time employment. This shows that part-time employment has come to be seen as having a positive effect on unemployment. What is uncommunicated or hidden in these policy declarations is that they are principally directed at women. It is doubtful that men will voluntarily engage in part-time work to a much greater extent than now without economic compensation. Thus proposing part-time work as a labor policy to reduce unemployment means offering less work for less income to women.

B. Part-Time Work in an Incomes Policy Perspective

There is a large gap between the average income of men and women in Norway. The difference in number of hours worked in paid employment accounts for the major part of this difference. But even when comparing only full-time workers, there is a considerable wage gap. Women's jobs are traditionally low paid, and most women hold low-paid jobs. Reducing the number of hours worked in a low-paid job (like the cleaning business where women constitute 90% of the workers and 73% of the workers work part-time) leads to a very low income level.

In 1978, only 24% of those working part-time had their own income from paid work as their main source of subsistence. A spouse's income was the main source of subsistence for 46% of the part-time workers. Of the part-time employed, 27% had an additional income from pensions and/or social security (*Deltidsundersokelsen*, Tables 35, 37, 1979).

Approximately 60% of the women working part-time had annual earnings of less than 20,500NK, the minimum pension in 1978. Their earnings are considered to be below the Norwegian poverty line. Approximately 40% of the women working part-time had annual earnings of less than 16,000NK. In a family with one income, or an additional income of less than 16,000NK, the breadwinner is entitled to a so-called provider tax deduction. Some men are not interested in having their wives earn more than what benefits their tax declaration. Still, the expansion of the part-time labor market throughout the 1970s has made the two-income family the rule rather than the exception. Yet, within the family, economic equality does not prevail. Men, generally, earn substantially more than do women. The majority of the part-time workers actually depend on either public economic transactions or on private economic support in addition to their wages.

C. Part-Time Work and Family Policy

The Norwegian government undertook several family policy measures during the 1970s to encourage the labor force participation of women. And the labor force participation of women increased. But the policies have not succeeded in creating the conditions for equal participation of men and women in work and family life.

Paid work for the wife has not led to important changes in the division of labor within the household. The number of hours husbands spend on housework and child care is much less than the time spent on these activities by the wives. This is the case regardless of whether or not there are children or the number of children in the household.[8] What has happened during the past 10 to 15 years is that the general division of labor between the sexes has changed. Until the 1970s, the general division of labor between the sexes implied that married women stayed at home and exclusively undertook the unpaid work of the household. The new division of labor between the sexes implies that married women participate to some extent in paid work and that they undertake the housework as well.

The part-time labor force participation of women, especially working mothers, is to a large extent regulated through the traditional concept of the sex roles on the one hand and the conditions of child-care facilities on the other. The regular work contract is too strict as to fixed hours and too long for the double workload. The dual-income family system has been created through the adjustments women have made between family and the labor market.

V. CONFLICTING INTERESTS

On what grounds do governments, employers, and trade unions eventually accept or encourage part-time work as a labor market phenomenon? To suggest some answers to this question, it is useful to elaborate on the contradictions that emerge over working time reforms serving as employment policy, incomes policy, and family policy. First, labor and capital have conflicts over labor market reforms. Second, men and women disagree over working time reforms. Third, men and women take different positions on incomes policy and family policy matters.

As a pattern of work, part-time work is beneficial to capital. As a suggested policy to reduce unemployment, the preference for such a reform is evident. It does not cost anything, and it does not imply difficult negotiations. It is thus both in the interests of most governments and employer organizations. Part-time work in itself is the ideal manifestation of the female population as a "reserve army of labor," even more flexible than in the traditional

---

[8]The literature on time budget surveys is extensive. For a discussion of the Norwegian data see Berg (1983), Bjoru and Skrede (1980), and Stromsheim (1982).

sense. In addition, part-time workers are less unionized, and those working few hours receive less social benefits than other employees.

The trade unions organizing in the sectors with the largest percentage of part-time workers and having the largest proportion of women as members pressure the Federation of Trade Unions toward a positive stand on the issue of a collective reduction of the workday. This indicates a conflict between unions of different sectors, but the main line of conflict must be drawn between men and women of the unions. The female-dominated unions have experienced the problematic sides of part-time work and conclude that a collective reduction of the workday is the best way to secure more employees on standard work contracts and thus a higher income level.

Men and women also disagree on other working time reforms. For example, public opinion polls in Norway show men expressing a preference for longer vacations and a lower retirement age, whereas women support a shorter workday and longer maternity leave.

Equal wages for men and women is one of those issues where sector or group interests usually supercede declarations of solidarity. Besides, the unequal access to money in the household is, in studies of power and influence within couples, held to be one of the main conditions for the power difference between the sexes.

Gaining increased leisure time is in the interest of men as well as women. But it is not necessarily in the interest of men to do so in a way that might in turn contribute to a reduction in their leisure time, as would be the case if they participated more in household work.

By working part-time, women contribute to the household economy, lessen the burden on the male as the sole provider, and increase the family standard of living, at the same time as they undertake the housework and the child care. It is understandable that men tend to prefer longer vacations and weekends to a shorter workday. It is also understandable that working mothers prefer a shorter workday to longer weekends and vacations.

VI. CONCLUSION

The logic of capital is to encourage labor market reforms that foster profitability. Encouraging a part-time sector of the labor market is such a reform. The rationale of men is to keep their privileges in the labor market as well as in the family. Because the labor movement in Norway is male dominated, there is a risk of an unholy alliance between labor and capital on certain working time reforms.

Working time reforms must be discussed not only in aggregate economic terms but also in light of incomes policy and family policy. In other words, working time reforms should be thought of in terms of what kind of future society they will contribute to.

VII. REFERENCES

Berg, A. M. (1983). Love and power: The household division of labour. In A. Leira (Ed.), *Work and womanhood, Norwegian studies*, Report 8/83: 215–234. Oslo: Institute for Social Research.

Bjoru, K., & Skrede, K. (1980). A decade of transition—changes in the labour force participation and family adjustments of Norwegian women in the seventies. Paper 80: 2. Oslo: Institute for Applied Social Science.

Deltidsundersokelsen. (1979). Report 79/4. Oslo: Central Bureau of Statistics.

Foged, B. (1980). *Deltid-Kvindetid.* Copenhagen: Modtrykk.

Jallade, J. P. (1982). *L'Europe à Temps Partiel.* Paris: Economica.

Labour Market Statistics, 1972, 1974, 1978, 1981, 1983, 1984, 1985. (1973, 1975, 1979, 1982, 1984, 1985, 1986). Oslo: Central Bureau of Statistics.

National Accounts, 1968–1979, 1975–1984 (1980, 1985). Oslo: Central Bureau of Statistics.

OECD. (1983). *Employment outlook.* Paris: OECD.

Petterson, M. (1981). *Deltidsarbete i Sverige.* Stockholm: Arbetslivscentum.

St. m. nr. 85 (1982–1983). *Om sysselsettingen og arbeidsmarkedspolitikken.* Oslo: Statenstrykksak-sekspedisjon.

Stromsheim, G. (1982). The organization of time and the question of equality—On the distribution of working hours in paid employment between the parents in Norwegian families. Oslo: Institute for Social Research.

The European Trade Union Institute. (1979, 1980). *Reduction of Working time in Europe,* Parts I and II, Günter Köpke, ETUI, Bruxelles.

IV
Conclusion

13

The State and the Labor Market
An Evaluation

Samuel Rosenberg

Over the past two decades, labor market conditions in the United States and many European countries have dramatically changed. Low unemployment rates have been followed by high unemployment rates. Taking their cue from neoclassical economics, many economists, politicians, and employers see rigidities in the labor market as being one of the chief causes of the high unemployment. These rigidities, due primarily to past actions of labor unions and governments, need to be eliminated if market forces are to be liberated. Freeing-up market forces will lead to a more well-functioning, flexible labor market. This, in turn, will have beneficial effects on employment and productivity. On the whole, workers, employers, and the entire society will be better off.

Thus, much has been promised for labor market flexibility. But a prior issue remains. What constitutes a flexible labor market? This question lies at the center of the policy debate over flexibility. Not surprisingly, agreement is lacking on this matter. There are many different forms of labor market flexibilities and, thus, many different paths for achieving such flexibility.

In policy discussions, two types of flexibilities have been emphasized— wage flexibility and numerical, or employment, flexibility. Questions of functional flexibility and working time flexibility have remained somewhat in the background.

The chapters in this book demonstrate that many governments have implemented policies with the goal of increasing labor market flexibility— particularly wage flexibility and numerical flexibility. They have done this either through deregulating the labor market and thus, in effect, increasing the relative autonomy of employers in wage setting and hiring and firing, or through bargaining between employers, unions, and the state.

Yet have the postulated beneficial effects of more flexible labor markets

Samuel Rosenberg • Department of Economics, Roosevelt University, Chicago, Illinois 60605.

emerged? Although the authors of the chapters in this book do not speak in one voice, they are generally skeptical of this policy direction. They do not believe the unemployment crisis has its roots in labor market rigidities. Many of them do not see increased wage and numerical flexibility as part of the solution to the unemployment problem. Rather, they generally see a dark side to these forms of labor market flexibilities—increased income inequality and a resegmentation of the labor market. Thus an alternate policy approach is required to increase economic growth, foster worker security, and lower unemployment.

This chapter is divided into four main sections. The first will summarize the policies undertaken by governments in the United States and such European countries as the United Kingdom, the Federal Republic of Germany, Spain, and Italy to foster labor market flexibility. The second will investigate whether increased wage and numerical flexibility should be expected to increase employment and decrease unemployment. The third will analyze the dark side of labor market flexibility. The fourth will discuss some questions for further research regarding the implications of the push for labor market flexibility.

I. STATE POLICIES FOR LABOR MARKET FLEXIBILITY

Rubery, Wilkinson, and Tarling (Chapter 2, this volume), Rosenberg (Chapter 4, this volume), and Bosch and Sengenberger (Chapter 5, this volume) analyze the deregulatory approach to labor market flexibility taken by governments in the United Kingdom, the United States, and the Federal Republic of Germany, respectively. These governments have abandoned any responsibility for even minimal job creation. Rather, macroeconomic policies, particularly monetary policy, are used to keep inflation in check. Microeconomic policies are designed to influence the functioning of the labor market and thus, indirectly, to affect employment opportunities.

In the face of a substantial number of unemployed workers, this particular policy approach attributes the unemployment to a poorly functioning labor market, not to a shortage of jobs. Improve the operation of the labor market, and employment gains will follow.

At the heart of this policy perspective lies the notion of the "natural rate of unemployment." The structure of the labor market and the behavior and expectations of employers, unions, and workers affect the level of the natural rate of unemployment. Whatever prevents markets from operating perfectly serves to raise the natural rate of unemployment. For the United States, the factors often pointed to as causing the natural rate of unemployment to increase are overly generous unemployment insurance, minimum wage regulations, and union strength. Employment protection regulations are added to these elements in explaining the high natural rate of unemployment for many European countries.

The policy prescriptions are clear—reduce unemployment compensation, lower minimum wages or eliminate them entirely, weaken unions, and weaken or eliminate employment protection regulations. Wage flexibility will be enhanced; the competitive forces of supply and demand will play a more important role in wage determination.

The floor of the wage structure will decline if minimum wages are lowered or eliminated. Wage determination will become more decentralized if unions are weakened. Unemployed workers will be less able to turn down jobs at the market wage if unemployment benefits are reduced. Numerical flexibility will be enhanced if restrictions on dismissals, fixed-term contracts, temporary workers, and part-time work are weakened.

Both the British and German governments have made it more difficult to qualify for unemployment compensation, strengthened the availability for work criteria, and decreased the amount of the payments. In the United States, taxes were increased on unemployment insurance recipients, and benefits beyond the standard 26 weeks were made more difficult to attain. In all three countries, a smaller percentage of the officially unemployed were collecting unemployment insurance during the depressed economic conditions of the 1980s than in similar periods in the 1970s.

Minimum wages are set in different ways in each country. The United States has a statutory minimum wage, whereas the United Kingdom and the Federal Republic of Germany do not. Thus the strategies of lowering the effective minimum wage vary across countries.

In the United States, the approach was relatively straightforward. The federal minimum wage has remained unchanged since 1981. Inflation has eroded the real value of the minimum wage.

A multifaceted program was instituted in the United Kingdom. The power of the wages councils, the bodies setting minimum rates of pay and other conditions in the retail, hotel and catering, hairdressing, and clothing manufacturing industries has been reduced. Now, they are only able to set a minimum single hourly rate. They are no longer able to regulate hours of work, overtime and weekend premium time payments, and holiday pay and other fringe benefits (Brosnan & Wilkinson, 1988, pp. 13–14; Wilkinson, 1988, p. 13).

Young people, under the age of 21, have been removed from the scope of the wages council. In addition, as Ryan (Chapter 9, this volume) shows, the relative pay of youth has been lowered even further by various youth employment programs. The government subsidizes employers who hire youth at specified low rates of pay. These pay rates are significantly lower than union rates.

Although these youth employment programs have had only minimal negative impact on British unions, minimum union pay scales have been threatened in other ways. The Fair Wages Resolution, requiring government contractors to observe customary—usually union—negotiated minimum terms and conditions for their industry or locality, has been abolished. Schedule 11 of the 1976 Employment Act, allowing weakly organized workers to ask industrial tribunals to require their employers to meet minimum terms and conditions of work for their trade—generally union rates—has been repealed (Wilkinson, 1988, p. 12).

In the Federal Republic of Germany, legally enforced contract rates affecting all employers in an industry set minimum pay floors in nearly all parts of the economy. There has been some erosion in collective pay standards as some firms have been paying less than the prevailing rates. The government has not created policies directly lowering the minimum pay floors, but it has done so indirectly by attempting to lessen union strength. The government has ended the eligibility of workers indirectly affected by strikes or lockouts for unemployment compensation.

More direct governmental attacks on union strength have occurred in the United States and the United Kingdom. Piore (Chapter 3, this volume) argues these antiunion policies are one of the factors that have caused the partial erosion of previous wage bargaining patterns in the United States. As pattern bargaining has declined in importance, wage determination has become more decentralized. The rulings of the National Labor Relations Board have made it more difficult for union organizing drives to succeed, less difficult for employers to move union jobs to nonunion locations, and more difficult for unions to wage effective strikes.

In the United Kingdom, legislation has been enacted that is designed to reduce union power. The right not to belong to a union has been strengthened, whereas the right to belong to a union has been weakened. The insertion of union-labor-only clauses in subcontracts has been prohibited. Employers can now fire strikers without notice. Legal immunities have been withdrawn for strikes deemed to be sympathy, interunion, or political. The nature of allowable picketing has been curtailed. The closed shop is now more difficult to attain.

Employment protection regulations have been weakened in the United Kingdom and the Federal Republic of Germany, though not in the United States. Workers in the United States generally do not have these rights to begin with. In the United Kingdom, eligibility under the unfair dismissal laws now require 2 years of employment with the same employer instead of 6 months. In addition, the length of short-term contracts for which these statutory job rights can be waived has been reduced from 2 years to 1 year.

In the Federal Republic of Germany, the Employment Promotion Act of 1985 has been an important vehicle for deregulating the labor market. This piece of legislation allows for the greater use of fixed-term contracts and personnel leasing, makes part-time work more attractive, grants special relief for small firms from existing employment protection legislation, and increases the freedom of employers to lay off workers without consulting the works council.

Although in the United Kingdom, the United States, and the Federal Republic of Germany wage flexibility and numerical flexibility have been handled by the government taking a deregulatory approach to the labor market, such matters have been dealt with through centralized bargaining in Spain and Italy. Fina, Meixide, and Toharia (Chapter 6, this volume) show that in the aftermath of Franco's death, a wage–price spiral occurred in Spain with the rate of inflation reaching 30% in 1977. At the same time, interindustry wage differentials strongly narrowed as workers in traditionally low-paid industries took advantage of the new environment and organized to press their demands. Thus the two central matters regarding wage flexibility were wage restraint to slow down the wage–price spiral and changes in wage payment systems to slow or stop the narrowing of interindustry wage differentials.

The centralized agreements between employers and unions had three basic features. First, wage guidelines were established in terms of the expected rate of inflation rather than the past rate of inflation. Second, ex-post cost of living adjustment clauses were also provided. Third, proportional wage increases were generally granted rather than lump-sum increases.

The wage–price spiral decelerated, and interindustry wage differentials were stabilized. Fina, Meixide, and Toharia argue that these results were mainly due to the centralized agreements.

Regarding numerical flexibility, the Spanish government created new grounds for the use of part-time, temporary, and limited duration labor contracts and provided incentives for hiring young people on a temporary basis. Also, the legal grounds for dismissal were enlarged, and the costs were reduced.

Centralized bargaining was the primary mechanism for handling questions of labor market flexibility in Italy in the late 1970s and early 1980s. As in Spain, the primary issues regarding wage flexibility were the pace of wage increases and the compression of the wage structure. The rate of inflation was high; a wage–price spiral was occurring. The system of wage indexation helped to fuel the rise in wages and served to compress the wage structure. All covered workers received the same absolute increase in wages for each 1% rise in the cost of living. As time went on and the rate of inflation remained high, the cost-of-living component of wages took on a larger share of the total wage payments, and wage differentials continued to narrow.

Brusco and Villa (Chapter 7, this volume) investigate how the process of centralized bargaining between union confederations, employers' associations, and the government was utilized to slow down the rate of increase in wages and widen wage differentials. In the late 1970s, the unions moderated their wage demands and did not strongly object to laws placing some restrictions on the wage indexation system. In return, the unions gained an expansion of the right to strike and better layoff payments.

Economic problems still remained in the early 1980s. A trilateral agreement was signed in 1983 restraining wage increases, reducing the cost-of-living allowance, and shortening annual working hours by 40. The government agreed to reduce the tax burden for workers and introduce legislation concerning employment, pensions, layoff payments, and the national health system. The legal changes in the wage indexation system together with the lowering of the rate of inflation led to a widening of the wage structure.

Brusco and Villa believe the changes that have occurred in the area of employment protection will have long-term implications for the labor market. Laws were passed making it easier to institute fixed-term and part-time contracts. In addition, a special type of temporary contract for youth was introduced.

II. THE EMPLOYMENT EFFECTS OF LABOR MARKET FLEXIBILITY

The advocates of more competition in the labor market assert it will lead to less unemployment and improved labor productivity. However, these claims are open to question. Soskice (1987, p. 99) argues that European countries most successful in maintaining relatively low rates of unemployment, such as Norway and Sweden, were also the countries that retained the type of "rigidities" laissez-faire proponents of labor market flexibility felt must be eliminated.

Although the empirical findings are not unambiguous, a strong case can be made that increasing wage flexibility will not necessarily relieve the unemployment problem. The claim is made that overly generous unemployment compensation programs have caused unemployment to rise. They raise the unemployed's "reservation wage" thereby creating "voluntary unemployment." Burtless (1987) investigates the effect of unemployment insurance on unemployment in the United Kingdom, France, the Federal Republic of Germany, Sweden, and the United States. Although more generous unemployment compensation is provided in Europe than in the United States, this does not explain the relatively higher unemployment rates in Europe than in the United States. The same situation regarding relative levels of unemployment compensation existed in the 1960s, a time when the unemployment rate in the United States was well above those of many European countries. In addition, across European countries there is no correlation between changes in the liberality of benefits and changes in unemployment. Finally, although jobless benefits in the United Kingdom, France, and the Federal Republic of Germany may have slowed the reemployment of the unemployed in those countries, the effect is minimal relative to the "large rise in unemployment durations in Europe or the enormous rise of unemployment levels in Britain, France, and Germany compared with those in Sweden and the United States" (Burtless, 1987, p. 155).

When job openings are plentiful relative to job seekers, overly generous unemployment benefits may raise the unemployment rate by increasing the average duration of unemployment. But when job vacancies are well less than the number of job seekers, the situation in the United States and in most European countries in the 1980s, unemployment compensation will affect the composition of the unemployed rather than the level of unemployment. If unemployment insurance increases the duration of unemployment of recipients, it will provide those ineligible for such benefits a better chance to find employment, thus decreasing their duration of unemployment.

In addition to raising the "reservation wage" of the unemployed, there is a second way unemployment compensation is said to raise unemployment.

The assertion is made that overly generous unemployment payments, by increasing the bargaining power of labor, reduces wage flexibility, particularly downward flexibility. Inflexible wages are said to be one of the causes of high unemployment.

The wage inflexibility argument has two components to it. First, wage differentials are too small and too inflexible. Thus, they cannot effectively influence labor mobility and do not provide effective incentives to workers to develop the requisite skills for success in the labor market. Those advancing this argument equate greater wage dispersion with enhanced labor market flexibility. Countries with greater wage dispersion would be expected to have better employment growth than those with less dispersion.

Freeman (1988) does not see these beneficial effects of greater wage dispersion. Rather he finds that OECD member countries with very high or very low wage dispersion did better in terms of employment since 1970 than those with intermediate degrees of wage dispersion. Thus all countries should not strive to develop the same set of labor market institutions. They should not necessarily try to emulate the U.S. model.[1]

Second, wage levels are said to be too high and inflexible. Thus workers are priced out of employment. The negative relationship between real wages and employment levels is based on the neoclassical analysis of the demand for labor under conditions of perfect competition. In support of this argument, Freeman (1988) finds, for a given output performance, a significant real wage–employment trade-off across countries and across industries within countries.

Though Freeman's results may be robust, it must be noted the "econometric estimates of wage equations are among the most fragile to be found in applied macroeconomics" (Boyer, 1987, p. 125). More importantly, however, the underlying theoretical framework of Freeman's work—the neoclassical analysis of labor demand—is open to question. Bowles and Boyer (1988) develop a macroeconomic model that takes account of the influence of the wage on both aggregate demand and the endogenous determination of output per labor hour. They determine that the level of employment may respond either positively or negatively to particular changes in the wage rate. Thus there is not necessarily a negative relationship between real wages and employment levels.

Furthermore, empirical work on the behavior of real wages over the business cycle does not support the neoclassical theory of labor demand. Michie (1987) investigates the cyclical movements in real wages over the 1950–1982 period for the United States, Canada, Japan, France, the Federal Republic of Germany, and the United Kingdom. His work demonstrates that there is no necessary cyclical wage behavior common to these six economies.[2]

In addition to wage flexibility, employment, or numerical, flexibility has

[1]In a related study, Bell and Freeman (1985) argue that for the 1970s the flexibility of the industry wage structure in the United States did not contribute to employment growth. Rather, they believe it had negative effects on employment.
[2]This discussion of Michie's work is based on Sawyer (1987).

been at the center of discussions over labor market flexibility. The claim is made that restrictions on dismissals, fixed-term contracts, temporary work, and part-time work have caused employers to hold back on their hiring. Less hiring leads to a higher level of unemployment. Lessening or ending these rigidities would, it is claimed, result in increased job creation and a lower level of unemployment.

As in the case of wage flexibility, the empirical findings are not unambiguous. But, a strong case can be made that increasing employment flexibility will not necessarily solve the unemployment problem. In practice, European dismissal regulations are less rigid than critics have asserted. In fact, during the 1970s and early 1980s, the percentage of unemployment arising from dismissal was only slightly less in such European countries as France, the Federal Republic of Germany, and the United Kingdom, than in the United States, where such laws are virtually nonexistent (Flanagan, 1987, p. 196).

Furthermore, even had these dismissal regulations been rigid in practice, it still would not necessarily be the case that they would increase unemployment. For increased unemployment to result from these employment protection rules, their negative impact on the outflow from unemployment to employment would have to exceed their positive effect on the outflow from employment to unemployment. There are few empirical studies of this issue. The work that has been done by Nickell on British legislation on dismissal is inconclusive. In a 1979 study, he concluded these regulations increased unemployment, whereas in a 1982 study, he found these same regulations decreased unemployment (Boyer, 1987; Nickell, 1979, 1982).[3]

Flanagan (1987) speculates that although the dismissal restrictions may not affect the level of unemployment, they may influence the composition of the unemployed. Protected workers may have more security, whereas those looking for work may have longer durations of unemployment or repeated spells of unemployment associated with temporary work.

In addition, these regulations may serve to increase the incentives to employers to shift their hiring patterns toward more part-time, temporary, and fixed-term workers, not covered by employment protection legislation, and away from full-time, long-term workers. In fact, governments in the Federal Republic of Germany, Spain, and Italy have made it easier for em-

---

[3]Soskice (1987, pp. 97–98) is more critical of the impact of European employment security measures. In the face of uncertainty, the cost to a company of employment security depends on the extent to which a company can increase product innovation, capture additional markets, and continue to employ workers it would have otherwise fired. The ease of adjustment is fostered by the availability of financing based on the long-term needs of a company, effective retraining programs, consensus-based systems of industrial relations, and government aid in restructuring and research and development. He finds these complementary elements existing in Austria, the Federal Republic of Germany, Norway, and Sweden. But, in the United Kingdom, much of France, and in some Italian industry they are lacking. In these instances, employment security is very costly to a firm, implying excessive levels of employment and an increased likelihood of bankruptcy.

ployers to do so (Bosch and Sengenberger, Chapter 5, this volume; Fina, Meixide, and Toharia, Chapter 6, this volume; Brusco and Villa, Chapter 7, this volume). But France is an important exception to this direction in government policy. The socialist governments of France in the 1980s have not made the increased use of temporary workers on fixed-term contracts a central aspect of their employment policy. In 1982, a law was passed restricting the use of such contracts.[4] However, Gauvin and Michon (Chapter 11, this volume) speculate that French employment policy may come to emphasize more the expansion of part-time and temporary jobs.

It is difficult to determine the impact of governmental policies easing restrictions on the use of temporary, part-time, and fixed-term labor on the level of unemployment and the unemployment rate. There are two crucial issues. First, is additional employment being created, or are people working under these arrangements merely being substituted for full-time, long-term workers? Second, are the officially unemployed taking new part-time or temporary jobs or are the jobs being filled by new entrants into the labor force?

The authors in this volume provide differing views on the effects of these policies. Although they do not investigate the question of substitution, Fina, Meixide, and Toharia (Chapter 6, this volume) find a sharp increase in hiring after Spanish employers were provided more freedom in using part-time, temporary, and fixed-term workers. But Bosch and Sengenberger (Chapter 5, this volume) cite studies done by German unions showing that substitution is a very serious problem. Full-time jobs have been replaced by part-time jobs and normal unlimited work contracts by fixed-term contracts. There has been no significant addition to employment.[5]

Marshall (1988) feels the growth of part-time employment has had minimal impact on the level of unemployment. Rather, she argues that part-time work appeals to a labor force—mainly adult women—who, had these jobs not been available, would have likely stayed out of the labor force. Thus the growth of part-time employment may have lowered the unemployment rate but not the level of unemployment. She does not see temporary work growing in relative terms in the 1980s. As a result, it has likely had limited impact on the level of unemployment.

Neither increased wage flexibility nor increased employment flexibility seems to have had a positive impact on unemployment. Unemployment has remained high. The high rates of unemployment along with cutbacks in employment protection legislation and unemployment payments have increased worker insecurity. Worker insecurity improves the relative bargaining power of employers, potentially giving them a freer hand in reorganizing the work

[4]See Gallie (1986) for a discussion of this law. However, a 1986 law relaxed the rules for hiring fixed-term and temporary workers (Marshall, 1988, p. 33).
[5]The Employment Promotion Act of 1985 did not begin the trend to temporary employment. Dombois (1986) shows that the proportion of temporary hiring in relation to total job vacancies had increased before the law had been enacted. He views the law as legitimizing the practice of temporary employment rather than being the primary factor behind the spread of temporary employment.

process in order to increase efficiency and raise the rate of profit. Advocates of a deregulatory approach to the labor market generally call for freeing-up the hands of employers. They also support improving functional flexibility. And although they do not say so explicitly, employer unilateralism seems to be their way to gain improved functional flexibility.

Yet, will increased worker insecurity lead to increased labor productivity and more workplace innovations? Weisskopf (1987) investigates this issue for the manufacturing sectors of the United Kingdom, France, the Federal Republic of Germany, Italy, Sweden, Japan, Canada, and the United States. He finds that higher rates of unemployment augment the level and rate of growth of productivity in the United States. In this country, there is the lowest degree of worker security, and labor–management relations are relatively antagonistic. Although Italy and the United Kingdom also showed some evidence of the level of productivity being positively related to the level of unemployment, in no country besides the United States was the rate of growth of productivity positively related to the level of unemployment. In fact, sustained high employment was found to be favorable to productivity growth in countries such as the Federal Republic of Germany and Sweden, where there is a relatively high degree of labor–management cooperation and worker security. Thus, outside of the United States, the deregulatory approach to improved functional flexibility seems misguided.

III. THE DARK SIDE OF LABOR MARKET FLEXIBILITY

The deregulatory policies have not solved the unemployment problem. Substantial numbers of people remain without work. Moreover, there is a dark side to this approach to labor market flexibility. It primarily removes protection from the weaker groups in the economy rather than exposing all groups to competition.

This raises the likelihood of increased income inequality. The United States is advanced as a model of labor market flexibility. Freeing-up the labor market has been a primary goal of the Thatcher government in Great Britain. Though labor market policies are not the only factor in this development, in both countries inequality is increasing.

Harrison and Bluestone (1987) have investigated trends in wage and salary levels in the United States from 1963 to 1985. Adjusting for the business cycle, annual wage and salary income became more unequally distributed from 1975 to 1984. That reversed a trend toward greater equality beginning in the early 1960s. In addition, after improving steadily since the 1950s, the real weekly wage of the average American worker peaked in 1973 and has fallen or stagnated since. Thus, "the wage distribution is shifting 'downhill' and becoming more skewed" (Harrison & Bluestone, 1987, pp. 5–6).[6] These

---

[6]Harrison and Bluestone (1987) use data on individuals. Bell and Freeman (1987) find that industrial wage dispersion in the United States has also increased from 1970 to 1985.

trends coincide with the implementation of governmental and employer policies designed to increase the amount of wage and employment flexibility in the economy.

The story in the United Kingdom is somewhat different. Real wages have not been falling. But the dispersion of wage settlements in the private sector has been increasing (Rubery, Wilkinson, & Tarling, Chapter 2, this volume). It appears as if relative employment growth has been occurring at both the top and bottom of the occupation structure, whereas jobs in the middle have been disappearing (Wilkinson, 1988).

An additional component of the dark side of labor market flexibility derives from policies enabling more part-time and temporary jobs to be created. Although the situation varies across countries, temporary workers and those working part-time generally do not have the same basic rights or access to the same social benefits as full-time, long-term workers. In such European countries as the United Kingdom, France, and the Federal Republic of Germany, temporary workers legally have the same rights as more permanent workers. But in practice they do not. Workers often need to work a specified continuous length of time with a single employer before qualifying for various forms of employment protections and a variety of social benefits. Not surprisingly, temporary workers are less likely to gain the requisite work experience.

With part-time workers, the problem is somewhat different. The crucial issues are generally the weekly hours of work and weekly or monthly pay. Countries differ in the threshold levels used for excluding part-time workers from various governmental programs. For example, in the United Kingdom, nearly 30% of those working part-time are unable to qualify for the National Insurance Scheme. Part-timers have more access to transfer payments in the Federal Republic of Germany. But here, as well, 11% of part-time workers are not covered by the social security system (Marshall, 1988; Schoer, 1987).

The problems raised by an employment policy emphasizing part-time work go beyond the lack of rights or benefits. Using Norway as her case study, Berg (Chapter 12, this volume) argues that encouraging part-time work rather than shortening the standard workweek, in the interest of increasing employment, allows men to keep their privileges in the labor market and in the home. Women are more likely than men to work part-time. Given their responsibilities in the home, married women have difficulty holding jobs with a standard work contract. Shortening the length of the standard workweek would enable both men and women to hold full-time jobs and participate equally in running the household. But Norwegian unionists, unlike unionists in countries such as the Federal Republic of Germany, have generally not pushed for a shorter workweek.

Labor market flexibility through deregulation raises the specter of increased inequality along a variety of dimensions, including wage payments, job security, and social benefits. Thus, rather than eliminating labor market segmentation as its proponents assert, deregulation policies may merely lead to a reshuffling of the boundaries of segmentation and perhaps even a hardening of the lines of segmentation. Those whose earnings are relatively high and whose jobs are relatively secure may struggle harder to protect their positions if they feel threatened by those bearing the brunt of the flexibilization process. Many of the authors of chapters in this volume predict that the institutional changes taking place in the labor markets in their respective countries will lead to a resegmentation of the labor market along new and perhaps more complex lines.[7]

IV. THE STATE AND LABOR MARKET FLEXIBILITY: SOME ISSUES FOR THE FUTURE

The long-term implications of the push for more wage and employment flexibility concern the contributors to this volume. They speculate that governmental policies in some European countries and in the United States are causing the patterns of labor market segmentation to change. Changes in the nature of labor market segmentation need not necessarily have negative implications for vast numbers of workers. But many of the authors fear that the labor market restructuring being induced by current policy initiatives will, over the long term, hurt many workers.

In this regard, several questions need to be addressed. Will core and periphery work forces emerge with core workers providing functional flexibility and periphery workers providing numerical flexibility? Will temporary work be linked with continued employment instability, or will temporary positions be one step along the road to more permanent employment? To what degree will the pay and job security of more protected workers be threatened by the existence of a large unprotected labor force?

Although the long-term implications of the deregulatory policies need to be analyzed, the future of this policy direction must also be addressed. In some countries, the thrust for deregulation of the labor market may be losing steam. In the United States, the supposed paragon of flexible labor markets, strong opposition to further deregulation has appeared. Power (Chapter 10, this volume) shows that many large employers, who would be expected to favor a freer hand in personnel decisions, successfully opposed the Reagan administration's attempts to weaken the federal government's affirmative action policy against racial and sexual discrimination. In addition, in August 1988, a law was passed in the United States requiring employers to provide workers with 60-days' notice of a plant closing or a major layoff. And, although Ryan (Chapter 9, this volume) does not claim the Thatcher administration's attempt to free up the labor market is running its course, he does make the point that the government's emphasis on youth training programs reflects a countercurrent to deregulation.

In some capitalist societies, deregulation policies may be reaching their limits. But, in some socialist countries such as the Soviet Union and China,

---

[7]Atkinson (1987, p. 102) also argues that governmental policies and employer initiatives in the United Kingdom will lead to a more highly stratified work force.

these policies are in their infancy. Galasi and Sziráczki (Chapter 8, this volume) describe the tensions between centralization and decentralization policies in Hungary. They show how the expansions and contractions of the "second" economy provide a measure of flexibility for the state sector. However, they also point out the incompatibilities between the state sector and the "second" economy. They question whether an efficient and flexible system of production can be created in Hungary without radical institutional changes. Though they do not speak to this issue, their analysis raises the following question. What lessons can the Hungarian experience provide policymakers in the Soviet Union and China?

If policies aimed at decentralizing the terms and conditions of employment are reaching their political limit, at least in some capitalist societies, what should be the new policy direction? Recent attempts at freeing-up the labor market have not significantly raised employment or lowered unemployment. Thus new forms of deregulation should not be on the policy agenda. Rather, policies for further regulation of the labor market merit some consideration.

The appropriate initiatives will vary across countries given national differences in institutional structures for regulating the labor market. With this caveat in mind, the Swedish approach to employment policy provides a promising direction. Under the Swedish scenario, macroeconomic policy is utilized to generate high levels of employment, though not at the cost of high rates of inflation. Thus full employment cannot be achieved with macroeconomic policies alone.

Complementing monetary and fiscal policies are the solidaristic wage policies of unions and the active labor market programs of the government. With solidaristic wage policies, both high-productivity and high-profitability firms and low-productivity and low-profitability firms pay the same wages for the same types of work. Differences in job content not in the demand for labor underlie wage differentials. Low-productivity firms are forced to innovate, rationalize, or close. To the extent these policies are successful, labor will be utilized more efficiently.

But unemployment may emerge in weak industries due to the solidaristic wage policies or throughout the economy due to the antiinflationary constraints on macroeconomic policy. Active manpower policies, for example, retraining programs and relocation allowances, together with increased public sector hiring, will then come into play (Fraser, 1987; Rehn, 1985).

Governmental policies have a major role to play in expanding employment opportunities. But they alone are not adequate for attaining full employment. The Swedish attempts to achieve full employment reflect a prior commitment on the part of the government and the society to that goal.[8] Thus it is crucially important to build a strong political movement calling for full

[8]In fact, Therborn (1986, p. 23) argues that the existence or nonexistence of an institutionalized commitment to full employment is the primary explanation for the divergence of unemployment rates across most advanced capitalist countries in the 1980s.

employment in countries experiencing persistently high rates of unemployment.

The contributors to this volume speculate that the drive for labor market flexibility in the 1980s in many European countries and in the United States will change the nature of labor market segmentation in these societies. If they are correct, an additional question remains. Will the new patterns of labor market segmentation help or hinder the building of movements for full employment? Only time will tell.

V. REFERENCES

Atkinson, J. (1987). Flexibility or fragmentation? The United Kingdom labor market in the eighties. *Labor and Society, 12*(1, January), 87–105.

Bell, L. A., & Freeman, R. B. (1985). Does a flexible industry wage structure increase employment?: The U.S. experience. NBER Working Paper No. 1604, Cambridge, MA, National Bureau of Economic Research.

Bell, L. A., & Freeman, R. B. (1987). The facts about rising industrial wage dispersion in the U.S. In *Proceedings of the Thirty-Ninth Annual Meeting* (pp. 331–337). Madison, WI: Industrial Relations Research Association.

Bowles, S., & Boyer, R. (1988). Labor discipline and aggregate demand: A macroeconomic model. *American Economic Review, 78*(2, May), 395–400.

Boyer, R. (1987). Labor flexibilities: Many forms, uncertain effects. *Labor and Society, 12*(1, January), 107–129.

Brosnan, P., & Wilkinson, F. (1988). A national statutory minimum wage and economic efficiency. *Contributions to Political Economy, 7*(March), pp. 1–48.

Burtless, G. (1987). Jobless pay and high European unemployment. In R. Z. Lawrence & C. L. Schultze (Eds.), *Barriers to European growth: A transatlantic view* (pp. 105–162). Washington, DC: The Brookings Institution.

Dombois, R. (1986). *Flexibility by law? The Employment Promotion Act and the practice of temporary employment on a local labor market.* Paper presented at the 8th Conference of the International Working Party on Labor Market Segmentation, Cambridge, UK, July 14–18.

Flanagan, R. J. (1987). Labor market behavior and European economic growth. In R. Z. Lawrence & C. L. Schultze (Eds.), *Barriers to European growth: A transatlantic view* (pp. 175–211). Washington, DC: The Brookings Institution.

Fraser, N. (1987). Economic policy in Sweden: Are there lessons from the Swedish model? *International Review of Applied Economics, 1*(2, June), 209–224.

Freeman, R. B. (1988). Labor markets. *Economic Policy,* (6, April), 63–80.

Gallie, D. (1986). *Labor market reform and the crisis of French trade unionism.* Paper presented at the 8th Conference of the International Working Party on Labor Market Segmentation, Cambridge, UK, July 14–18.

Harrison, B., & Bluestone, B. (1987). The dark side of labor market "flexibility": Falling wages and growing income inequality in America. Working Paper No. 17, World Employment Program, Geneva, International Labor Organization.

Marshall, A. (1988). The sequel of unemployment: The changing role of part-time and temporary employment in Western Europe. Discussion Paper No. 10, Geneva, International Institute for Labor Studies.

Michie, J. (1987). *Wages in the business cycle.* London: Frances Pinter.

Nickell, S. (1979). Unemployment and the structure of labor costs. In K. Brunner & A. Meltzer (Eds.), *Policies for Employment, Prices, and Exchange Rates* (pp. 187–222). Carnegie-Rochester Series on Public Policy, Vol. 11. Amsterdam: North-Holland.

Nickell, S. (1982). The determinants of equilibrium unemployment in Britain. *Economic Journal, 92* (September), 555–575.

Rehn, G. (1985). Swedish active labor market policy: Retrospect and prospect. *Industrial Relations*, *24* (1, Winter), 62–89.

Sawyer, M. C. (1987). Review of J. Michie, *Wages in the Business Cycle. International Review of Applied Economics*, *1* (2, June), 247–250.

Schoer, K. (1987). Part-time employment: Britain and West Germany. *Cambridge Journal of Economics*, *11* (1, March), 83–94.

Soskice, D. (1987). Flexibility and unemployment: The view from Western Europe. In *Proceedings of the Thirty-Ninth Annual Meeting* (pp. 93–100). Madison, WI: Industrial Relations Research Association.

Therborn, G. (1986). *Why some peoples are more unemployed than others: The strange paradox of growth and unemployment*. London: Verso.

Weisskopf, T. E. (1987). The effect of unemployment on labor productivity: An international comparative analysis. *International Review of Applied Economics*, *1* (2, June), 127–151.

Wilkinson, F. (1988). *Government policy and the structure of the labor market, 1979–1986*. Paper presented at the Conference on Economic Development and Segmentation: An International Comparison, Notre Dame University, Notre Dame, IN, April 18–21.

Index